General editor: Andrew S. Thompson
Founding editor: John M. MacKenzie

When the 'Studies in Imperialism' series was founded more than twenty-five years ago, emphasis was laid upon the conviction that 'imperialism as a cultural phenomenon had as significant an effect on the dominant as on the subordinate societies'. With well over a hundred titles now published, this remains the prime concern of the series. Cross-disciplinary work has indeed appeared covering the full spectrum of cultural phenomena, as well as examining aspects of gender and sex, frontiers and law, science and the environment, language and literature, migration and patriotic societies, and much else. Moreover, the series has always wished to present comparative work on European and American imperialism, and particularly welcomes the submission of books in these areas. The fascination with imperialism, in all its aspects, shows no sign of abating, and this series will continue to lead the way in encouraging the widest possible range of studies in the field. 'Studies in Imperialism' is fully organic in its development, always seeking to be at the cutting edge, responding to the latest interests of scholars and the needs of this ever-expanding area of scholarship.

Britain and the formation of the Gulf States

Manchester University Press

SELECTED TITLES AVAILABLE IN THE SERIES

WRITING IMPERIAL HISTORIES
ed. Andrew S. Thompson

MUSEUMS AND EMPIRE
Natural history, human cultures and colonial identities
John M. MacKenzie

MISSIONARY FAMILIES
Race, gender and generation on the spiritual frontier
Emily J. Manktelow

THE COLONISATION OF TIME
Ritual, routine and resistance in the British Empire
Giordano Nanni

BRITISH CULTURE AND THE END OF EMPIRE
ed. Stuart Ward

SCIENCE, RACE RELATIONS AND RESISTANCE
Britain, 1870–1914
Douglas A. Lorimer

GENTEEL WOMEN
Empire and domestic material culture, 1840–1910
Dianne Lawrence

EUROPEAN EMPIRES AND THE PEOPLE
Popular responses to imperialism in France, Britain, the Netherlands, Belgium, Germany and Italy
ed. John M. MacKenzie

SCIENCE AND SOCIETY IN SOUTHERN AFRICA
ed. Saul Dubow

Britain and the formation of the Gulf States

EMBERS OF EMPIRE

Shohei Sato

MANCHESTER
UNIVERSITY PRESS

Copyright © Shohei Sato 2016

The right of Shohei Sato to be identified as the author of this work has been asserted by him in accordance with the Copyright, Designs and Patents Act 1988.

Published by MANCHESTER UNIVERSITY PRESS
ALTRINCHAM STREET, MANCHESTER M1 7JA
www.manchesteruniversitypress.co.uk

British Library Cataloguing-in-Publication Data
A catalogue record for this book is available from the British Library

Library of Congress Cataloging-in-Publication Data applied for

ISBN   978 0 7190 9968 7   hardback

First published 2016

The publisher has no responsibility for the persistence or accuracy of URLs for any external or third-party internet websites referred to in this book, and does not guarantee that any content on such websites is, or will remain, accurate or appropriate.

Typeset by
Servis Filmsetting Ltd, Stockport, Cheshire
Printed by Lightning Source

THE UNIVERSITY OF MANCHESTER LIBRARY

CONTENTS

List of maps and figures—*page* vi
Acknowledgements—vii
Maps—viii

Introduction	1
1 'Pirates' turned sovereign states, 1819–1964	5
2 Labour's clinging on to the Gulf, 1964–67	29
3 Jenkins and the withdrawal decision, 1968	51
4 Dilemmas and delay, 1968–70	67
5 The 'secret' agreement, July 1971	95
6 Formal sovereignty and continuing collaboration, 1972	121
Conclusion	140

Bibliography—147
Index—159

LIST OF MAPS AND FIGURES

Maps

1 The current Persian Gulf and surrounding areas   *page* viii
2 Trucial States based on Walker's research, 1962–63   ix

Figures

1 'Majority of five' in the secret agreement   107
2 Duality of Britain's informal empire in the Persian Gulf   144
3 Multiple channels of diplomacy   144

ACKNOWLEDGEMENTS

This book would not have been possible, first and foremost, without the guidance I received from Avi Shlaim. A large part of the research was conducted when I was pursuing my master's and doctoral degrees at the University of Oxford, where he provided me with essential advice, support and encouragement.

St Antony's College and the Department of Politics and International Relations at Oxford gave me the institutional and social basis for my studies and research. The later stages of this research were supported by the Organization for Islamic Area Studies, Waseda University (Japan), as well as the Center for International and Regional Studies, Georgetown University (Qatar), the University of Tokyo (Japan), Kanazawa University (Japan) and the National Archives (United Arab Emirates).

I am also grateful to the late Tsugitaka Sato, Eiji Nagasawa, Yuzo Shitomi, Warwick Knowles, Roger Goodman, Rosemary Foot and James Piscatori for inspiring me to embark on a long-term project. Comments from John Darwin and Wm. Roger Louis as examiners of my doctoral degree gave me the encouragement to carry on, and editorial support from Emma Brennan and James Disley as well as the comments from the referees of Manchester University Press enabled me to finalise it.

Various stages of this research were financially supported by the Swire Educational Trust, the Royal Historical Society, the Japan Society for the Promotion of Science (Asia–Africa Science Platform Program; KAKENHI grant numbers 23720311, 13J09266, 26760003), the Kajima Foundation and the Mitsubishi Foundation. In addition, Oashi Kyohei helped me with the visual materials. Kai Hebel, Iason Gabriel, Lee Jones, Noriko Kanahara, Joydeep Sen, Daisuke Ikemoto, Alex Buck, Thomas Williams and Hiro Katsumata went through my manuscript at various stages of my research. Comments from Roham Alvandi, Suzi Mirgani, Laurent Lambert, Reo Matsuzaki, Toshi Higuchi, Roland Popp, Hiromi Mizokami, Retzu Hashizume, Jin Noda, Kazuaki Sawai, Takenori Yoshimura, Mayumi Abe, Noriyuki Osada, Osamu Otsuka, Osamu Kobayashi, Takumi Miyazaki, Hiro Katsumata, Tatsuya Koizumi, Hisao Ueda, Monica Malik, El Mehdi Chatouaki, Mariam Sultan Al Mazrouei, Maitha Salman Al Zaabi, Shareena Said Al Qubaisi and Aisha Bilkhair Abdulla all provided insights to the project.

Finally, I would like to thank all my friends and family, particularly my mother and father, for helping me give meaning to this book and to my life.

MAPS

1 The current Persian Gulf and surrounding areas

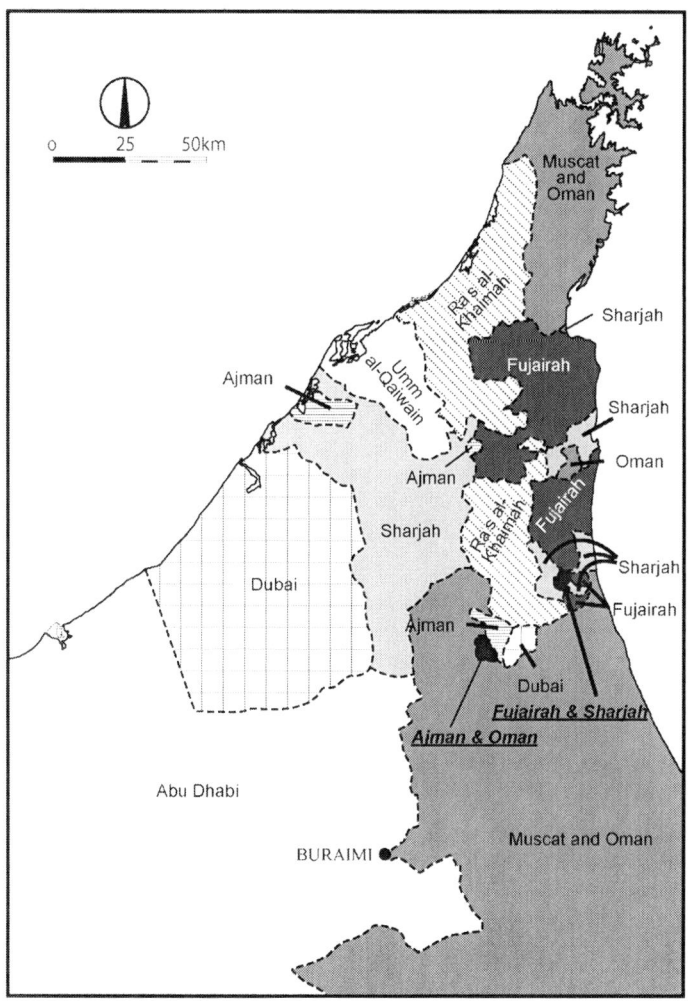

2 Trucial States based on Walker's research, 1962–63[1]

[1] The above map is based on three maps that were issued in slightly different formats and at slightly different times: 'Boundaries of the Trucial States, prepared and drawn from sketch maps and information provided by Julian Walker, map no. 1 (north)', Foreign Office Research Department, February 1962; 'Boundaries of the Trucial States, map no. 2 (south)', Foreign Office Research Department, February 1963; 'Boundaries of the Trucial States, map no. 3 (covering the Southern Abu Dhabi–Oman boundary)', unpublished, Foreign Office Research Department, May 1963. The original copies of the first two are accessible as HAW/Map 2–3, Donald Hawley Papers, available at Palace Green Library, Durham University, Durham. All three are also compiled in Julian F. Walker (ed.), *The UAE: Internal Boundaries and the Boundary with Oman*, 8 vols (Archive Editions, 1994), p. 8, maps pp. 26–28. The map presented was reproduced by Chie Akashi based on the Archive Editions version.

INTRODUCTION

The Persian Gulf region is often associated with upheavals and conflicts. Since the 1970s, it has experienced oil shocks, wars and challenges from its own citizens; however, the basic entities of the Gulf States have remained largely in place. How did this resilient system come about for such seemingly unstable societies? In particular, the eventual emergence of the smaller but prosperous members such as Qatar, Bahrain and the United Arab Emirates (UAE) was not at all evident until 1971. Before then, nine separate entities had stood in parallel to each other as, in British terms, its 'Protected States'. At various points, plans were discussed to amalgamate the nine into one, two, three or even four separate entities. What, then, drove the formation of the three states we see today? Was it the local call for self-rule against a century and a half of British presence? Or was it Britain's carefully designed strategy to serve its economic interest and the 'special relationship' with the US in order to survive the Cold War? Why was the process so delayed? And who made crucial decisions in the final reckoning?

These questions are not only pertinent to the current Middle East but they are also deeply related to the transformation of the modern world more broadly. The majority of peoples in the world today have experienced these challenges at some point in their histories. I myself am no exception. I was born in northern Japan. My mother used to recall with much affection how her blind grandmother sewed *kimono*. She was an *Ainu*, an ethnic minority, which imperial Japan once deemed barbaric subjects needing its 'protection', and it eventually divided *Ainu* territories with Russia. On my father's side, my late grandmother described in her Tokyo accent how she had returned with her family from the Korean Peninsula to Japan at the end of the Second World War. I was curious to know in what capacity they had lived in Korea, but she never provided much detail. Today I happen to hold a Japanese passport, but that does not convince me that either the state or the nation of Japan has always been what a lot of its people would like to believe today. Self-determination versus 'better together' is an almost universal dilemma accompanying the rise of modern states and in some cases the concurrent decline of empires.

This book will explore these fundamental dilemmas of the modern world by looking into the end of the British Empire in the Middle East. It will shed light on the last moment of the Empire, which, in its hasty retreat from the 'East of Suez' in 1971, midwifed the birth of Bahrain, Qatar and the UAE. The event was a crucial watershed in terms of both British decline and the rise of the new Persian Gulf States, and one which has naturally captured the attention of many authors. Given its profundity, it is unsurprising that some scholars have looked for comparably substantial causes, such as the worldwide 'wind of change' calling for decolonisation.[1] Others have also looked to the major drivers of the post-war era like the long-term decline of the British economy and the related change in domestic opinion.[2] Either way, the unspoken agenda has so far been to explain the big event with reference to big causes.

When I first started to study the subject as a postgraduate student, I was hoping to make some modest modifications to the already established grand narratives. The picture I formed after eight years in the archives in both Britain and the Gulf, however, led me to explore a different dimension of the story. As emphasised by the existing literature, British economic retrenchment and, to a lesser extent, local self-determination no doubt played their part. However, the most consistent thread to the entire story was the absence of a central agent.

For example, my research located a secret agreement signed between Abu Dhabi and Dubai, which led to the independence of the UAE, in a somewhat unexpected place – the British National Archives. I enquired in the National Archives in the UAE but they did not seem to hold a copy. Why is such a crucial document of state-building not in the hands of its original party but in the safe of a former imperial metropole? As implied by this episode, neither Britain nor the new states drove the whole process with a central will or a fully thought-out plan. It was a series of ad hoc decisions and actions that often emerged through the negotiations between British diplomats and the Gulf rulers, such as Shaikh Zayid of Abu Dhabi, that unwittingly caused the region to take its current shape, yet even the protagonists at the time could not fully conceive of the implications of their own actions.[3] Examination of primary sources – some newly discovered – offers new insight into how the relationships with the Gulf rulers nurtured at the height of the British Empire affected the structure of international society that remains in place today. It is this element of spontaneity and collaboration with unexpected consequences that I aim to explore here.

This book will build upon three groups of studies: the literature on the Gulf region, the history of the British Empire, and the larger scholarship on decolonisation. It does not purport to exhaustively document all of the details of the British withdrawal, but rather aims to illustrate the dynamism of the profound change that took place. In particular, it will ask the following questions: Why was Britain able to leave the

INTRODUCTION

region in relative peace? Why was this departure accompanied by the orderly emergence of Bahrain, Qatar and the UAE? And what does the whole story tell us about the larger dynamics of decolonisation? In a strict legal sense the region was never a British colony, but the relevance of the idea to the argument will soon become clear. On the whole, the book will advance John Darwin's argument on 'the fallacy of believing that the decolonisation process was the intended consequence of the actions of British policy makers or colonial politicians'.[4]

This is an empirical study mainly based on documented evidence. I have examined papers available in archives and libraries in Britain, the US and the Gulf region. Wherever possible, I have conducted interviews as complementary sources of information. The largest bulk of paper documents was collected at the National Archives in London, but the time I spent in the National Archives of the UAE was equally valuable if not as easy to reference. All sources were read critically and compared with each other wherever appropriate.

The discussion of the book will proceed in the following order. Chapter 1 will lay out the antecedents that preceded the eventual British withdrawal. In the early nineteenth century, Britain sent military expeditions to the southern coast of the Gulf in order to combat what they called 'pirates'. Thanks to its subsequent military victory, London coerced the local forces into entering a series of treaties. The primary aim of these unequal treaties was to establish a peace in the region that was favourable to British commerce and communication, yet the very act of signing these treaties implied that Britain had acknowledged the legal status of its counterparts. Consequently, the territories concerned were given the standing of sovereign states, a dubious status reflected in their British name 'Protected States'.

Chapters 2 and 3 will examine the decision-making process that led to the withdrawal announcement in January 1968. Commonly known as the 'East of Suez' decision, it was taken in the context of the British Empire's long-term economic retrenchment and military retreat. Yet the actual process through which the Labour government reached the final decision was significantly affected at the last minute by domestic negotiations. In particular, the need to justify social cuts in the wake of the devaluation of the pound pushed the Labour government towards making an explicit Cabinet decision, setting a rigid timeframe that otherwise appeared unnecessary and even publicly announcing it.

Chapters 4 and 5 will move on to the implementation of the withdrawal decision. The Gulf rulers responded quickly, albeit unsuccessfully, in deciding how they would become independent, if at all. In Britain, the Conservatives took over the government but their initial attempt to reverse Labour's plan did not help. It was only after the

BRITAIN AND THE FORMATION OF THE GULF STATES

British diplomats on the ground and the Gulf rulers made feasible compromises to come together very late in the day that the nine Protected States became independent in the form of three sovereign states: as Bahrain, Qatar and the UAE. Investigation of some newly discovered sources reveals that a secret agreement, signed between Abu Dhabi and Dubai and then handed over to Britain, marked a crucial turning point in deciding the fate of the three states.

Chapter 6 will look into the consequences of the British withdrawal and challenge the assumption that the overall process was led by the local call for self-determination. In one episode, Britain and the US rejected a plea for sovereign status from Ra's al-Khaimah, one of the smaller Protected States. On the one hand, the independence of Bahrain, Qatar and the UAE meant that the new states possessed legal personalities equal to those of the former imperial metropole and superpowers. On the other hand, it also enabled both Britain and the US to maintain an international order favourable to the West by means of consensus and collaboration, whilst minimising direct involvement and the use of coercive measures. In the end, the whole process did not alter the collaborative relationship that had developed during the period of Britain's informal empire, instead only entailing the rearrangement thereof.

Notes

1. See, especially, Helene von Bismarck, *British Policy in the Persian Gulf, 1961–1968: Conceptions of Informal Empire* (Basingstoke: Palgrave Macmillan, 2013). See also Simon C. Smith, *Britain's Revival and Fall in the Gulf: Kuwait, Bahrain, Qatar, and the Trucial States, 1950–71* (London: RoutledgeCurzon, 2004); Jayanti Maitra, *Zayed: From Challenges to Union* (Abu Dhabi: Center for Documentation and Research, 2007); Abdullah Omran Taryam, *The Establishment of the United Arab Emirates, 1950–85* (London: Croom Helm, 1987); Frauke Heard-Bey, *From Trucial States to United Arab Emirates: A Society in Transition*, new edition (London: Longman, 1996).
2. See, especially, Jeffrey Pickering, *Britain's Withdrawal from East of Suez: The Politics of Retrenchment* (Basingstoke: Macmillan, 1998). See also Wm. Roger Louis, *Ends of British Imperialism: The Scramble for Empire, Suez and Decolonization* (London: I.B. Tauris, 2006).
3. This book follows the system of transliteration of Arab names and words used by Heard-Bey in *From Trucial States to United Arab Emirates*. Where Arab names or words have a common British English form that differs from this system of transliteration, I prefer the common form. For the convenience of readers I have avoided using diacritics.
4. John Darwin, *Britain and Decolonisation: The Retreat from Empire in the Post-war World* (Basingstoke: Macmillan, 1988), p. viii.

CHAPTER ONE

'Pirates' turned sovereign states, 1819–1964

Although tacit 'influence' over another state is a part of international politics today, the sovereignty of a state must, formally, be exclusive, not hierarchical or multiple, and it must be unambiguous.[1]

This quote may sound like a statement of the obvious and, indeed, it does summarise the way in which the norm of sovereignty operates in international society today. However, this was not the case when Britain originally entered the Gulf.

Britain's arrival in the Gulf

Four hundred years ago, the earth appeared to be much larger than it does today. Only a century after some European sailors thought they had discovered a new world, European colonies in the Americas were still expanding. Back in Europe, the Holy Roman Empire was going into irreversible decline, though it was yet to witness the final blow of the Thirty Years' War. In contrast, in its neighbourhood were the Ottomans, who boasted a larger empire covering south-eastern Europe, much of North Africa, Anatolia and Mesopotamia. Further east were their rivals, the Safavids, the great power of Persia. And beyond that were a number of prospering dynasties, such as the empires of the Mughal in north India and the Ming in China. Multiple civilisations seemed to coexist. And this was no different in the case of the theatre of our story – the Persian Gulf.

At the turn of the seventeenth century, two English brothers arrived on the northern coast of the Gulf. Their aim was to see the King of Persia, commonly known as Shah Abbas I of the Safavid Empire, and ask for permission to open up trade. Having come from a remote and minor state in Europe, their attitude was humble and their aims limited. After several exchanges, the elder brother was given an accord, or a *firman*, as follows:

Our absolute Commaundment, will, and pleasure is, that our countries and dominions shall be, from this day open to all Christian People, and to their religion ... I do giue this Pattent for all Christian Marchants, to repaire and trafique, in, and through our Dominions, without disturbances or molestations ...[2]

With this accord in place, the English East India Company opened its first establishment in the Gulf. No less important was the style of the *firman*. Unlike the format of other treaties that later became the standard, it was not presented as an agreement between states or sovereigns of comparable status. Instead, the Persian King was addressing all Christian people and merchants about their rights in his territories. It was not set upon the basis of perceived institutional symmetry between the parties involved. This is a crucial point. In order to fully appreciate it, one needs to have some understanding of the political situation of the region prior to British entry.

In ancient times, the Persian Gulf was among the most prosperous of all civilisations. The southern coast was known as the Land of Paradise. It was fertile with abundant water, thanks to one of the earliest examples of irrigation.[3] Over sea and land mingled the people who later came to be known as Persians and Arabs.[4] By the turn of the seventeenth century, however, the coastal areas were lagging behind their richer neighbours. The harsh environment and the intense heat had constrained economic activities to transit trade, exportation of dates and pearls, and ship-building.[5] Land for agriculture was limited, and many people led a nomadic life. Travelling along the southern coast from the east, we would first have found a desert with salt marshes, a few oases and temporary camps of pearl fishers, then several valleys ending in small bays with towns and villages. We would have met peasants and fishermen, the better-off living in houses and fortresses made of stone, the poorer in palm-frond huts or mud fortresses.[6]

These people living on the coastal line were organised in tribes.[7] The tribal system was a multilayered structure of authority organised around kinship, with larger groups controlling and protecting smaller groupings. The degree of control varied and the relationship between different groups could also shift over time. On the southern littoral were three main tribal groupings: Banu Khalid in the east, Banu Yas in the middle and the Omani tribes in the west.[8] They were not comparable in scale to their neighbours and, at around the turn of the seventeenth century, three major powers were looking over the region. To the west was the Ottoman Empire, to the north the Persian Empire of the Safavids, and to the east the Portuguese controlling the Kingdom of Hormuz, an islet located at the exit to the Indian Ocean.[9] Amongst them, the Persians gained the upper hand over the course of the seven-

'PIRATES' TURNED SOVEREIGN STATES, 1819-1964

teenth century, expelling the Portuguese and crushing the trade routes of the Ottomans.[10]

Supposing these to be the main actors in the Gulf at the point of British entry, how did they divide or share authority over the territories and population concerned? The aforementioned *firman* seems to suggest that the nature of international relations in the region at that time was quite different from today's standards, where authority over land and people is by and large permanently fixed and divided in a mutually exclusive manner between sovereign states with equal legal status. This book does not purport to conduct a full empirical investigation; however, the following studies suggest that, prior to the British entry, the nature of authority was more fluid than stable, and more multilayered than mutually exclusive.

James Onley points out, in his extensive research of the political traditions in the Gulf, that 'Fierce competition between and within ruling families for control of the limited economic resources in the Gulf created an atmosphere of uncertainty and insecurity.' As a result of this, 'the need for protection dominated and shaped regional politics more than any other factor'.[11] And in order to secure protection, the leaders of the weaker groups paid to the more powerful a tribute named *khuwah* (a brotherhood fee), *guwayzah* (a fee of free passage), *sufah* (general tax) or even *zakat* (Islamic alms).[12] Once the latter received the tribute, he assumed responsibility for protecting the former. Hence, when weaker tribes perceived a threat, they tended to resort to the protection of their less hostile and more powerful neighbours. In reverse, the payment of a tribute was contingent on the perceived likelihood of attack from a third actor, and the protégé would shift between different protectors or even choose to go without one, depending on the circumstances. Additionally, a protector of one protégé might ask for the protection of a leader of a yet stronger group if he saw the need for this. This is partly because protégés enjoyed varying degrees of autonomy, even when under the control of a protector. Thus the protector–protégé relationship was generally fluid, flexible and multilayered,[13] which meant that the political geography of the Gulf was characterised by 'the lack of firm borders in an area where tribes and conglomerates of population were separated by empty stretches of sea and desert.'[14] M.H. Mendelson succinctly summarises this point:

> Whereas in modern international law the basis of allegiance is ... essentially (albeit indirectly) territorial, traditionally much of the Arab world was not like that. Your primary affiliation was to your tribe; and any allegiance of that tribe to some other leader ... was temporary and contingent.[15]

BRITAIN AND THE FORMATION OF THE GULF STATES

At the same time, underneath this political fluidity, religion provided another dimension of identity. The traders in the Gulf had various faiths, but the majority of the inhabitants in the coastal areas were Muslim. Irrespective of the sectarian divisions, the most notable being the one between Sunni and Shi'ah, they shared a certain sense of unity from living in the Islamic community, or *umma*.[16] In short, when the Persian Gulf opened its doors to the English merchants, as well as the Dutch and later the French, authority in the region was fluid, shared and competed for at multiple levels by different tribes and polities. This is why the accord of the Shah was issued as an agreement between groups that did not seem to be on par with each other.

Having established the state of affairs in the Gulf prior to British entry, we must now explore why Britain came to this region, and how its presence evolved over time. During the sixteenth century, the British had attempted to penetrate the profitable trade with the East, initially trying the northern route via Russia and the Caspian Sea. Having met with little success, Britain went south and tried the passage via the Mediterranean to Mesopotamia, and approached the Persian Shah.[17] The Shah accorded freedom of passage and commercial activity to Christian merchants in 1600 as we have just seen, and consequently the English East India Company was incorporated under Royal Charter in London.[18] After establishing a foothold in India, the East India Company went to the Gulf in 1616 and opened an agency in Jask, a town on the Persian coast.[19] By the same token, the Dutch East India Company was founded in 1602 and eventually came to the Gulf. Yet, as B.J. Slot summarises, during the seventeenth and eighteenth centuries the English and Dutch East India Companies had to play a 'humble part in an area where only trade and diplomacy, not colonial expansion, was their goal'.[20] Moreover, their activities were largely limited to the northern side of the Gulf. In contrast, most of the southern coast 'remained unknown territory to the Europeans' during this period.[21] Thus, Britain entered the Gulf in the seventeenth century mainly for the purpose of trade, but kept a low profile for two hundred years and was rarely present on the southern shore.

Towards the end of the eighteenth century, British trade in the Gulf had declined significantly and its commercial interests had dwindled to next to nothing. Yet what followed was further penetration.[22] During the late eighteenth and early nineteenth centuries, Britain perceived two strategic reasons to increase and consolidate its foothold in the Gulf. Firstly, Arab maritime raiders had caused great concern to British ships between 1797 and 1819.[23] Britain referred to these people as 'pirates' and considered it necessary to control what it perceived as their illegitimate military activities. The response from the local

[8]

'PIRATES' TURNED SOVEREIGN STATES, 1819-1964

seamen is unclear, but one source notes that they called the British 'infidels'.[24]

Whether or not Britain's condemnation was fair, the point here is that, at least from the British perspective, it was a strategic imperative to contain the activities of the 'pirates'. Secondly, on top of the regional crisis, the Gulf began to have a global significance for Britain during the Napoleonic Wars. Having witnessed France sending an expedition to Egypt between 1798 and 1801, Britain formed a military alliance with the Shah of Persia between 1807 and 1809. In order to insulate India from French influence, Britain quickly decided to secure buffer states in the Gulf. Persia and Oman were the obvious candidates, but the southern coast also came under increased attention.[25] Since Britain's economic interests in the Gulf had diminished considerably by this point, J.B. Kelly argues that it was the global threat of France that forced Britain to remain.[26]

Therefore, for these strategic reasons, in the winter of 1819/20 British India dispatched gunboats to the Gulf and scored a decisive victory over the dominant local power, al-Qawasim. Following this triumph, Britain signed a series of treaties throughout the nineteenth and early twentieth centuries. Kelly has produced a detailed study of the developments during this period, and the following paragraphs largely rest upon his work.[27]

Britain's informal empire in the Gulf has its roots in the signing of a General Treaty for the Cessation of Plunder and Piracy in the early months of 1820. British involvement increased further with the first Maritime Truce signed on 21 May 1835 between the acting Resident, Lieutenant Samuel Hennell, and the rulers of Abu Dhabi, Dubai, 'Ajman and the al-Qawasim. It imposed 'a cessation of hostilities at sea' until 21 November 1835.[28] James Onley emphasises that the idea of the truce was not unilaterally imposed upon the local people but emerged out of the negotiations between Hennell and the aforementioned groups.[29] Indeed the Maritime Truce not only prohibited the local parties from engaging in military activities but also stipulated that if 'an act of aggression by sea' was reported, the Political Resident at Bushire (Bandar Bushehr of Abu Shehr) would 'take the necessary steps for obtaining reparation for the injury inflicted'.[30] To that extent it obligated the British side to be responsible for the maintenance of order in the region.

The 1835 Maritime Truce only covered the pearling season of that year, but it was deemed a great success and was extended to cover the next year. It was succeeded by a series of annual truces before a ten-year Maritime Truce was signed in 1843 and, after its completion, a Perpetual Maritime Truce signed in 1853. Under these treaties, military activities were banned, residencies and agencies were established, and Britain gradually increased its involvement in local affairs. At any given time, only a handful of British officers worked in the British establishments; however, by and large, the Gulf was kept peaceful thanks to locally employed multinational agents.[31] In order to support the political mission, Britain assigned a naval unit, known as the Gulf Squadron, to patrol the waters of the Gulf.[32]

While Britain persisted in its efforts to tighten its grip on the Gulf with minimum work on the ground, the strategic significance of the region continued to increase. In 1865, Britain established two telegraph lines throughout the Gulf, linking India and Britain. Now the sea became an indispensable route for the communication of the British Empire. In 1868, Russia captured Samarqand, and in 1885 it obtained a common border with Persia. While the Russian threat was coming from the north, the opening of the Suez Canal in 1869 further increased the importance of the surrounding areas. Throughout 1871 and 1872, the Ottoman Empire expanded within the Arabian Peninsula and occupied the Al-Hasa region and Qatar.[33] All of these changes increased Britain's impetus to secure the Gulf. As Onley points out, Britain's primary motive for consolidating and increasing its presence in the Gulf during this period was a strategic one: 'to establish a *cordon sanitaire* to protect British India'.[34] Thus, throughout the course of the nineteenth century, Britain significantly increased its presence and established itself as the sole external power in the Persian Gulf. The informal empire of British India was constructed upon three pillars:

(1) Cooperative local elites, including the native agents who enabled Britain to minimise its involvement in the internal affairs of the region;
(2) The military presence of the Gulf Squadron, which ensured compliance; and
(3) Treaties with the local rulers that justified the British presence.[35]

The next section will look into the third pillar more closely.

Curzon and the law

Military coercion is decisive, but never conclusive. Unless the defeated party is given some place in the new order, it will constantly challenge the status quo and, history shows, it will eventually expel the victor. A sophisticated conqueror would attempt to assuage the frustration of the defeated side, knowing that inequality can be created by coercion but needs to be sustained by co-option. One of the common strategies on the part of the victor is to explain why the military expedition was necessary in the first place, thereby getting the leaders of the losing side to persuade their people to come to terms with the new status quo. This section examines how Britain justified and legitimised its presence after the military expeditions in the early nineteenth century, and what the implications were.

As laid out in the previous section, Britain defeated the local rivals in the early nineteenth century. Such a forceful intrusion and violent challenge to the status quo by a foreign power will typically end in failure unless some justification is provided, and Britain justified its actions by calling the local counterparts 'pirates'. It condemned the local maritime military activities, mainly undertaken by al-Qawasim, as illegitimate and hence a threat to the peace and stability of the Gulf. However, to what extent the divisive discourse of 'pirates' conformed to the reality is highly debatable and controversial – not least because the primary sources available were written by Europeans – and also raises the question of the legitimacy of both the local society and the British presence. At one end of the spectrum, Wilson agrees with the then British official view:

> Arab rule in the Gulf was for long periods synonymous with piracy, and very early in the evolution of the English power in Asia the obligation to control and suppress that evil forced itself upon the agents of the East India Company. By their tardy and unwilling intervention three results of capital importance to humanity were eventually achieved – the suppression of piracy; the cessation of war between the chiefs of the various petty states; and the extinction of the slave trade.[36]

At the other end of the spectrum, however, Sultan al-Qasimi criticises Wilson and others for being mere apologists for British imperialism. He claims that the English East India Company 'had no intention of protecting anybody's trade' and that its 'obvious intention, in face of increasing competition, was to use "protection" as an excuse to employ the force ... to squash the competitors'. He continues, 'Instead of peaceful trade, it became gun-boat trade.'[37]

Between these two opinions, Zahlan points out that the term 'piracy' is relative and 'seems to have been used by English and Dutch traders who were angered when the Qawasim established a trading station on the island of Kishm off the Persian coast in the eighteenth century'.[38] Charles E. Davies also hesitates to call them pirates even though he remarks that 'some of what they did was piracy'.[39] Onley further advances the literature by reminding us that it was common practice at that time in the Gulf for powerful tribal leaders to ask for tribute from the leaders of the weaker tribes. In many cases, this was a deal that benefited not just the protector but also the protégé. The protector received tribute, but in return offered free passage and assumed responsibility for protecting the protégé in a crisis. On his side, the protégé occasionally refused to pay the tribute if an attack from a third actor was thought to be unlikely. It was usually in these instances that the stronger tribes launched raids.[40] One can perhaps only reach a confident conclusion about such a hotly contested debate after conducting original empirical research into primary sources.[41] However, at the bottom line the scholarship agrees that Britain did indeed call the local people engaged in military activities 'pirates'. This in itself is highly significant for our discussion, because it highlights the function of the notion of law and state. When one group or individual ('X') calls another ('Y') 'pirates', the whole rhetoric rests upon at least three sets of assumptions:

(1) That the sea concerned has been, and should remain, regulated by some law;
(2) That X is complying with that law while Y is not; and
(3) That Y is a private actor.

Here, the third assumption is particularly important, because it is buttressed by another two sets of assumptions:

(1) Either that a state does not exist on the side of Y; or
(2) That a state exists on Y's part but Y is not authorised to launch military actions on its behalf.

Here, one can detect the implicit notion that law and state should exist universally. In the Gulf, Britain justified its military expedition by calling the local forces 'pirates'. After victory, it signed a series of treaties with the local leaders but, ironically, by signing these treaties Britain effectively upgraded the status of those people whom hitherto it had called 'pirates', and eventually acknowledged some degree of statehood on their part.

The paradox stems from the philosophical foundation for European treaties. The format of a treaty typically assumes an agreement between parties who are comparable in terms of status, if not in terms of capabilities. Even if the content of the treaty itself was designed to bring about unequal consequences, the format usually required some mutual acknowledgement of the personalities of the parties involved, at least at the time of its signing. Therefore, as Edward Keene points out in his perceptive study of treaties between European and non-European states during the nineteenth century, treaties, particularly cession treaties, tended to grant 'legal personality, competence or rights' to both parties, and 'typically endorsed the sovereignty of non-European rulers'.[42]

In the case of the Persian Gulf, things were not so clear-cut, but the overall picture supports Keene's observation. When Britain imposed the General Treaty for the cessation of plunder and piracy in 1820, the local counterparts were only mentioned as leaders of the groups surrendering to the British General.[43] However, the Maritime Truce signed in 1835 gave cognisance to the fact that each 'chief' was controlling his 'subjects' and 'dependants'. Bahrain was not part of the Maritime Truce, but became incorporated into the arrangement with a Friendly Convention signed in 1861.[44] The Convention was entered into by the 'independent ruler of Bahrain, on the part of himself and his successors' and the Captain of 'Her Majesty's Indian Navy, Political Resident of Her Britannic Majesty in the Gulf of Persia, on the part of the British Government'. Tracing the Anglo-Bahraini relations further, in 1880 they reached an agreement in which 'the Government of Bahrein [sic]' was recognised as the counterpart of 'the British Government' and would not enter into negotiations with any other foreign governments without the consent of Britain.[45] Bahrain is the most illuminating case, but other territories on the southern coast followed a largely similar path and Qatar joined this system in the early twentieth century.[46]

The paradox of signing treaties with those hitherto labelled 'pirates', and thereby acknowledging their legal status, had two important implications. Firstly it set up a mutually dependent relationship between Britain, as an imperial metropole, and the local rulers in the Gulf. Although resting upon Britain's military supremacy, the series of treaties brought benefits to both sides. On the one hand, it enabled Britain to wield almost exclusive influence over the region without the cost of establishing formal control, meaning Britain secured cooperation from the local elites by embracing their legitimacy. For their part, by signing the treaties the local leaders ensured not only their own survival but also military and political support from a global empire. In many cases, they suggested that Britain should increase its involvement on the ground. They sought British protection against external enemies, such as the Saudi Wahhabi political movement, the Persians, the Ottomans, the Omanis and other powers in the Arabian Peninsula such as the amirs of the inner region of Najd and the coastal area of Al-Hasa.[47] In fact, Britain was initially hesitant to get caught up in the region, partly out of its lack of understanding of the local culture of protection-seeking.[48]

This relates to the second point, which is that the treaties imposed a façade of external sovereignty over the region, where the local traditions were at worst in conflict with and at best simply differed from the European concept of sovereignty. This was a by-product of British informal rule; means rather than ends. It derived from the synergy between the wording of the treaties and the actual relationship between Britain and the local rulers. The rhetoric employed in the treaties helped Britain consolidate and institutionalise a new regional order designed in favour of Britain. No longer was Britain a mere outsider; now it had a stake in the preservation of the status quo. The system of sovereign states is resistant to change and creates a certain barrier to new players. As a result, the rulers were accorded 'a status higher than the traditional way of life had allowed them'.[49]

This line of argument might be taken by some as disrespectful to the origins and legitimacy of the present states in the Gulf. However, legal discontinuity is not necessarily mutually exclusive of social continuity. Slot states that, by the end of the eighteenth century, Kuwait, Qatar, Bahrain, the UAE and Oman existed in more or less their present form.[50] In contrast, Mendelson remarks from a legal standpoint that 'the idea of sovereignty and of the State itself was rather alien' in the region until the twentieth century.[51] From this point of view, it was British protection that 'bestowed a legal status on the concept of sheikhdom'.[52]

Although these states were given sovereignty as a consequence of the series of treaties, their effective statehood remained dubious in practice. For a start, they were called 'Protected States', which were supposed to have a higher degree of autonomy than 'protectorates', although the reality did not necessarily conform to the constitutional jargon.[53] They were also given a collective name of the 'Trucial States' or the 'Trucial Coast', although Bahrain and Qatar were usually not included in these two usages. In any case, while they were referred to as sovereign states, in practice Britain supervised their external affairs and also exercised significant influence over their internal affairs.

Seen in this way then, sovereignty was more rhetorical than substantial. Nonetheless, this mattered. Keene puts forward a framework that helps us explore this point. He demonstrates that nineteenth-century international society was multilayered and not based on a clear distinction between European and non-European societies. Nor was the world divided between fully sovereign states and territories with inferior status; instead, it consisted of a more heterogeneous arrangement with multiple political stratifications.[54] In the case of the Gulf States, the façade of sovereignty bestowed upon them was in itself important, because it gave them an official personality in this multilayered system of states and also because that status was an inferior and nominal one. If, at some point in the future, the system of states as a whole were to be transformed into a more homogeneous arrangement wherein actors were either states or not, the Protected States would need to be pushed out of this grey zone, either losing their status or becoming fully sovereign states.

On 21 November 1903, Lord Curzon, the Viceroy of India, during his visit to the Persian Gulf, declared to the rulers of the southern coast:

> We were here before any other Power, in modern times, had shown its face in these waters. We found strife and we have created order. It was our commerce as well as your security that was threatened and called for protection ... The great Empire of India, which it is our duty to defend, lies almost at your gates ... We have not seized or held your territory. We have not destroyed your independence but have preserved it ... The peace of these waters must still be maintained; your independence will continue to be upheld; and the influence of the British Government must remain supreme.[55]

The British flag was flying high over the Gulf, projecting its own vision of the past and the present.

However, even if this was a diplomatic fiefdom of the Government of India, one may question how much difference it made. On the other hand, there was little change on the surface, since the whole point of the system was to preserve the status quo. It served the purpose of excluding British rivals, but it was not the most important region for the British Raj nor was it among the top priorities in London. Neither did it bring considerable changes to the everyday life on the ground along the southern coast of the Gulf until after the mid-twentieth century.

On the other hand, Britain's willingness to exclude rival influence at military and diplomatic levels gradually tempted it to expand its policy into other areas. During the Second World War, discussions took place on setting up in Bahrain 'a recreation ground on which matches, football, cricket, etc., can be arranged and the occasion utilised for inviting the younger Arabs and Persians to come either as spectators or players'. Opening a cinema and making propaganda films were also on the agenda. The motive behind these cultural policies was the fear that the local population were spending 'their leisure time in reading clubs imbibing wrong ideas from outside literature'.[56] Britain had to increase its soft power.

On the whole, this informal empire of Britain laid the structural foundation for the international society of the region. An invisible, yet fundamental, difference was made to the *rules* rather than the immediate outcomes of the game. The European idea of sovereignty provided the template for the new system, and the local tradition of protection gave the substance. Moreover, as will be demonstrated in later chapters, this hybrid international system would have a profound impact on the way in which the British Empire was to retreat from the region and how the Protected States emerged into international society in later years.[57]

Walker's jigsaw puzzle

As we have seen then, the legal foundations of Britain's informal empire in the Gulf had been laid by the early twentieth century, but a number of important changes would follow over the course of the subsequent years. For a start, the centre of Britain's establishment in the Gulf moved southwards. The headquarters of the Political Residency had been located in Bushire in southern Persia (or Iran under the Pahlavi dynasty after 1925), but were moved to Bahrain in 1946.[58]

The institutional transition also witnessed a more substantial transformation. Oil came into play. In 1909, the Anglo-Persian Oil Company, which later became the Anglo-Iranian Oil Company (AIOC) and then British Petroleum (BP), was founded to exploit the oil deposits that were discovered in south-west Persia.[59] Even though oil had not yet been discovered in the territories of the Protected States at this point, its discovery elsewhere was beginning to change the fate of the Gulf dramatically. Amongst the various developments of oil politics in the Gulf, the most important was the nationalisation of the AIOC by Mohammad Mosaddeq in 1951.[60] By this point, the southern Gulf had also come to be associated with oil. In 1932, oil was discovered in Bahrain, followed by Qatar in 1940.[61] In Abu Dhabi, the exploration for oil started in 1948, the first indication of hydrocarbons was discovered in 1953/54, and exports of oil began in 1963.[62] The commencement of commercial drilling not only helped the local economy when the pearling industry was hit hard by Japanese rivals but also promoted the region to a position of global significance. In the 1950s, when Iran was going through a crisis following the nationalisation of the AIOC, Abu Dhabi and Muscat also clashed with Saudi Arabia over an anticipated oil reserve, as will be discussed later. In any case, by the mid-1960s the Persian Gulf and its surrounding lands had grown to provide half the oil supply used in the Western world outside North America. Although the Protected States accounted for less than 10% of the oil produced in the Gulf, and Britain by itself was not dependent on Gulf oil, maintaining the stability of the overall region was vital in order to secure the oil supply for the Western world as a whole.[63]

Equally importantly, the increasing significance of oil during the mid-twentieth century also accompanied some unintended changes both in ideas and in practice. On 31 August 1952, some 40 to 50 men arrived with the former Saudi governor of Ras Tanura in an oasis called Buraimi in the south-east of the Arabian Peninsula.[64] Today, the area of Buraimi straddles the boundary between the UAE and Oman. However, at this point the territories were not as clearly defined. Saudi Arabia believed it to be under its sovereignty, while Abu Dhabi, yet to form a part of the UAE at that point of course, together with Oman, argued that it was their territory. Thus the Saudi occupation of the oasis prompted a border dispute between Saudi Arabia, Abu Dhabi and Oman. With a growing expectation of oil reserves being present, Saudi Arabia was supported by the US, whereas Abu Dhabi and Oman were under the informal empire of Britain.

The case was brought to an international arbitration tribunal in Geneva and became known as the Buraimi Oasis dispute.[65] In the end, Britain unilaterally and forcefully closed the case in 1955, which became a source of tension between the actors involved until Saudi Arabia and the UAE came to a settlement in 1974.

Just which side had the better case had it not been for the forceful closure is still disputed. Either way, reading of the earlier documents suggests that both sides of the conflict were projecting their own idea of territory. In fact, the local way of living was resistant to the assumption that the region belonged exclusively to one side. Before the Saudi forces entered Buraimi, Britain had been detecting the expansion of Saudi Arabia and the Arabian American Oil Company while observing that the local tribes were shifting their nominal allegiance or even retained ties with both sides for economic and political calculations.[66]

The Buraimi dispute had two major impacts on the region. The first effect was that it laid the territorial foundation, or the conception thereof, which later became the basis for the formation of the UAE. Secondly, the practical necessities of life encouraged the rulers to cooperate across their borders.

While Britain and Saudi Arabia were arguing over Buraimi in the early 1950s, a young Arabist British diplomat was asked to tour and map the Protected States. Julian Fortay Walker was born in 1929 into a middle-class family in Marylebone, London.[67] After military service in the navy, he went to Gonville and Caius College, Cambridge, to read history. His graduation from university coincided with the onset of the Cold War, and he entered the diplomatic service with the hope of becoming a Soviet or European expert. However, by a twist of fate, the Foreign Office decided to train him in Arabic. He studied Arabic first at the School of Oriental and African Studies in London, and then at the Middle East Centre for Arab Studies (MECAS) in Shemlan, Lebanon. Having gone through an orthodox Arabist training, at the age of 24 he started his career as Third Secretary in the Political Residency of Bahrain in 1953. It was the middle of the Buraimi Oasis dispute, and one of his first tasks was to produce a map of the Protected States clarifying their boundaries.[68] Using the back of the nib of his fountain pen, he dotted in detail the information gathered from the local people, with the aid of a compass and the milometer of his Land Rover.[69] The locals tend to refer to the past as *ams* (an Arabic word that stands for both yesterday and the past in general), which was confusing when he was interviewing them. Carefully examining the local customs, he drew boundaries based upon the difference in the types of wells, and the oral history of 'tribal clashes and alliances, camel raids and other incidents in the desert'.[70] Although Walker is not as well known as some of his seniors such as Donald Hawley or William Luce, and he modestly calls himself a 'tyro on the Trucial Coast', his efforts to examine the complexities on the ground with rigour deserve greater attention.

After the tour, he produced a map that was too close to reality for his seniors' liking; they decided to temporarily discard it for fear that it would be inconvenient for Britain's stance in the Buraimi Oasis dispute against Saudi Arabia.[71]

In 1963 the Foreign Office finally felt able to issue a map drawing on the evidence presented by Walker, which is reproduced here (p. ix). The first point to be noted is that it does not contain Saudi Arabia, reiterating the British position that Buraimi is divided between Abu Dhabi and Oman. What is more surprising, however, is the fact that it contains a number of enclaves and areas of joint jurisdiction. Dubai, Sharjah, 'Ajman, Ra's al-Khaimah, Fujairah and Oman have multiple enclaves between each other. And within the sea of enclaves, Fujairah and Sharjah share jurisdiction over one area, with 'Ajman and Oman sharing another. The map was so perplexing that it later became named 'Mr. Walker's jigsaw puzzle'.[72] More pertinently, there seemed to be a fundamental tension between the idea of sovereign territoriality, characterised by exclusivity, and the way in which the local societies, where migration was an integral part of life, had been organised. And yet, as it later turned out, it was this 'jigsaw puzzle' that laid the territorial foundations of the region. The Buraimi dispute had a major impact on the international relations of the region by generating tentative borders that complicated as well as contributed to the later formation of the UAE.

In addition, it also created a major change in the domestic and everyday lives of the people living in the region. One may entertain the impression that oil has always been one of the most important concerns in the Gulf shore of the Arabian Peninsula. Although this would conform to our current image of the region, during the 1950s and early 1960s the impact of oil was limited compared to later years. For most of the locals, there was something more vital to their lives than oil – water. Traditionally, water was scarce and in many cases brackish. Water was a source of living, cooperation and conflict. Developing infrastructure to increase the supply of fresh water was of utmost importance, something that Shaikh Zayid, later first president of the UAE, well understood. Improving the water supply was the first major project that he initiated when the wealth of oil, or the hope thereof, reached his territory.

With the heightening of the Buraimi dispute, in December 1953 William Crawford from the Middle East Development Division at the British Embassy in Beirut, Lebanon, came to the region to inspect the water resources. After a week of touring the traditional irrigation systems (*falaj*, or *aflaj* in plural), he concluded that it might be worth it for Britain – 'both from a political and economic point of view' – to provide assistance to the local rulers to develop their water management facilities. Most important of all was to increase the supply of drinking water and then the irrigation systems needed to foster agricultural land for growing vegetables.[73] Following the recommendation of Crawford, Britain allocated £13,000 to well-drilling and £4,000 to the restoration of *aflaj* in Buraimi. These water-related projects amounted to 68% of the total budget for 1954/55.[74]

Britain was starting to provide a significant amount of technical and financial support to the restoration of irrigation systems and the drilling of new freshwater sources. The next year, the Foreign Office increased the budget by projecting £30,000 in total for 1955/56. However, the Treasury was reluctant to take on the financial burden of water-resource development, stating that the Chancellor had only agreed to the last budget 'because of the frontier problems and on the understanding that we should not be committed to giving further financial assistance for drilling in later years'.[75]

So, Britain was being strategic as usual. It perceived the need to keep the allegiance of Shaikh Zayid and other local leaders in order to counter the Saudi influence in the region. If water was the utmost concern to the local population, why not help? An internal letter in the Foreign Office outlined the expectation that 'the siting of a successful well there [in Fujairah] would help to bolster the loyalty of the Ruler, for whom we have done nothing'.[76] Water development was deemed to be 'one of our most useful and eye-catching schemes', countering 'the Arab League's policy of trying to monopolise the most important and popular projects'.[77] Water was the key to keeping external threats such as Arab nationalism and Saudi influence under control. But the Treasury clearly did not wish to make such a commitment a permanent one. It saw the assistance as a temporary measure to boost Britain's position in the Buraimi dispute.

Eventually, the budgetary concerns grew. In 1960, Britain concluded that it could not on its own continue to foot the bill for the development of water-related infrastructure and asked the United Nations (UN) for support.[78] In response, the Food and Agriculture Organization of the UN agreed to sponsor a prominent hydrologist to conduct an examination of the region.[79] After a preliminary inspection he concluded that more research was required to attain a fuller understanding of the underground freshwater resources.[80] A private company – Sir William Halcrow and Partners – was chosen to conduct the survey, and asked for photographs from the Ministry of Defence (MOD).[81] These surveys were estimated in 1965 to have cost as much as £126,000 over four financial years, more than seven times the budget allocated to water development projects in 1954/55.[82] A series of reports containing detailed mapping of water sources followed.[83] And securing fresh water for consumption and agriculture would remain an important social concern in the region even after the eventual independence.[84] More importantly, during these projects it became increasingly clear that the Protected States needed to cooperate in water management, working across their borders.

On the whole, during the mid-twentieth century, the territoriality of the region went through a silent yet fundamental transformation. This came from two different directions. On the one hand, expectations in regard to oil reserves unwittingly brought the notion of sovereign territoriality to the region and laid the foundation for more rigidly defined boundaries between the Protected States. On the other hand, the practical necessities of life, in the form of water development, encouraged the rulers to cooperate across those borders.

Cold War and informal empire

Naturally, the two world wars had a lasting impact on Britain's informal empire. The cripplingly overstretched former world empire now thought that its best remaining option was to strengthen its alliance with the US. Already in 1944, the British Foreign Office was considering the following: 'Instead of trying to use Commonwealth as an instrument which will give us the power to outface the United States, we must use the power of the United States to preserve the Commonwealth and Empire, and the pacification of Europe.'[85] From Washington's point of view, Britain's imperial influence appeared to be a convenient shield against Soviet expansion. Consequently, after 1947, as Wm. Roger Louis and Ronald Robinson maintain, 'the Americans subsidized the imperial system generously in one way or another to defend the United States', although neither 'side cared to publish the fact, the one to avoid the taint of imperialism, the other to keep the prestige of Empire untarnished.'[86] Under the Anglo-American alliance, a relatively small scale of commitment would suffice to win the allegiance of imperial proxies to the extent that the Western powers could 'keep out of the limelight' and 'pull the strings whenever necessary'.[87] Britain's realisation of its standing in the world was to then prompt disengagement in the Middle East as a whole.[88]

That said, the story in the southern Gulf was slightly different. Here, British disengagement was more nominal than substantial. The independence of India in 1947 meant that the Gulf was no longer part of the informal empire of British India, but this did not prompt Britain to leave the Gulf. It coped with the situation by simply transferring supervision of the Protected States from the Government of India to the British Foreign Office. This was partly due to the strategic value of oil, and also partly because of the importance of the Gulf as a transportation route. On the seas, the Gulf had been incorporated into the lane of the British India Steam Navigation Company (BI Line, 1862–1972) after 1860. As to the air, Imperial Airways (1924–39) opened airfields in Bahrain and Sharjah.[89] The company later became the British Overseas Airways Corporation (BOAC) and eventually British Airways from 1974 to the present, but a British diplomat recalls that the BOAC was locally known as 'Better On A Camel'.[90] In any case, despite the independence of India, the Gulf was still an important route for Britain towards its east.

This is not to say that the region was insulated from the various changes that took place in the mid-twentieth century. For example, the Suez Crisis in 1956 did not bring immediate change to British policy towards the region, but the influence of Arab nationalism was widely felt. In Dubai, many of the schoolteachers came from Egypt, Iraq, Syria, Lebanon and Yemen. These expatriate teachers greatly influenced the rise of Arab nationalism in the 1950s. In the summer of 1958, a Pakistani doctor working from the British Agency in Dubai was shot at. The same year, a Union Jack was stolen from the agency and thrown into the creek of Dubai, being discovered there the next morning.[91] In 1960, the Political Agent in Dubai wrote in a personal letter to his parents regarding a tour of the local school about someone shouting about the Arab cause in relation to the Arab–Israeli conflict, stating that he found it depressing that Arab nationalism was influencing the local youngsters.[92]

At the same time, the Arab League made a series of attempts to establish a presence in the Protected States. It was partly in response to this that the Political Resident set up the Trucial States Council in 1952.[93] In 1956, the council established a police and military force called the Trucial Oman Scouts.[94] Christopher M. Davidson notes that, 'in an effort to provide the rulers with some experience of foreign relations, Britain also began to allow the Council members to develop contacts and make visits outside of the British network, thereby ending the 1882 treaties of exclusivity'.[95] Although it is debatable whether Britain was indeed 'ending the exclusivity', his observation captures the duality of the international system in operation during this period.

In addition, Kuwait achieved independence in June 1961. Nonetheless, the following month Britain launched a military intervention in order to protect Kuwait from the perceived threat of Iraqi invasion. Somewhat ironically, the episode convinced Britain of the importance of preserving the informal empire.[96]

Thus, partly through ideological inertia, but largely owing to the Anglo-American Cold War interests in keeping the Soviets out and securing oil for the West, in the early 1960s Britain maintained its position in the Gulf. The territories of 'Ajman, Fujairah, Ra's al-Khaimah, Sharjah, Umm al-Qaiwain, Abu Dhabi, Dubai, Qatar and Bahrain were all in treaty relationships with Britain. Moreover, just as in the past, British policy was underpinned by military presence. Britain had an army garrison of one battalion with supporting arms and services, as well as a Royal Air Force (RAF) station, in Sharjah. In Bahrain, it maintained an army garrison of one battalion, an RAF station and a small naval station. Britain also financed and effectively controlled the Trucial Oman Scouts, and supervised the locally financed Abu Dhabi Defence Force. In the surrounding areas, Britain had RAF staging posts on the islands of Masirah and Salalah, a liaison team and a small RAF stockpile in Kuwait, and RAF units for use in Kuwait or Cyprus.[97]

On top of the military protection, the relationship with the local elites was the key to Britain's informal empire in the Gulf. On the one hand, Britain needed the cooperation of the local elites in order to ensure that the region remained sympathetic to it. It rarely interfered in their internal affairs, even though it always had the potential power to replace the local rulers by resorting to force, or indeed by merely giving tacit support to local oppositional movements. One of the few cases where Britain proactively interfered in the domestic affairs of the Gulf societies on an issue that was not directly related to Britain's strategic positioning was the abolition of slavery. A British diplomat proudly recalls that the freed slaves 'demanded certificates, which I gave them with solemnity'.[98] Nonetheless, Britain's general policy was to avoid paying the cost of getting involved in internal matters as long as things were kept quiet, and with that purpose in mind it was willing to maintain a friendly relationship with the local rulers.[99] Further to this point, Balfour-Paul remarks that Britain did not propagate democracy but helped the rulers to preserve their relationship with their society, since 'it was seen as more accommodating to Britain's own interests than any alternative mode of government that might have been encouraged'.[100]

On the other hand, the local leaders were able to exercise influence by selecting what information they gave to the British agents, but the military protection given from Britain was certainly indispensable. Because their relationship with Britain weakened their legitimacy within their own society, they could not afford to lose British protection. Local cooperation was the essential device of the informal empire, which enabled Britain to yield maximum benefits to the dying British Empire with minimum economic, military and administrative costs.

It has also been pointed out that there were some indigenous movements towards unity in the region that later became the UAE.[101] However, these local attempts towards unity did not materialise at this point, nor was Britain considering helping in the near future. In 1951, a British internal document noted that 'anything in the nature of a formal federation may well be a long way ahead'.[102]

Thus, six decades after Lord Curzon's self-serving speech, British imperial spirit remained intact but the environment had changed dramatically. In 1957, a correspondent from *The Times* called the British presence in the Persian Gulf the 'white man's burden',[103] but the continuing presence of Britain was not merely a function of imperialistic ideology. The British informal empire in the Gulf had survived by flexibly adapting itself to the drastically changing climate.

The aim of this chapter was to identify the antecedent factors behind the British withdrawal. It has established that the essence of the British presence in the Persian Gulf up to the 1960s can be comprehended as an informal empire – the holding of indirect control over the region, achieved by means of cooperation with the local elites, enabled by a legal façade of sovereignty on the receiving end.

After Britain scored a one-sided military victory in the early nineteenth century, it chose to sign a series of treaties with the hitherto so-called 'pirates'. The primary aim of these unequal treaties was to establish a peace in the region favourable to British commerce and communication by subjugating the local societies and establishing Britain as the single external power. However, the very act of signing these treaties implied that Britain had acknowledged the legal status of its counterparts, as what Edward Keene calls 'petty states'.[104] Upon these bases, by the early 1960s the Persian Gulf had become one of the most enduring, albeit informal, corners of the British Empire.

Notes

1. Tongchai Winichakul, *Siam Mapped: A History of the Geo-Body of a Nation* (Honolulu: University of Hawaii Press, 1994), p. 88.
2. Anthony Shierlie, *A True Report of Sir Anthony Shierlies Iourney Ouerland to Venice, Frõ Thence by Sea to Antioch, Aleppo, and Bablion, and Soe to Casbine in Persia: His Entertainment There by the Great Sophie* (London: 1600), p. 8.
3. Rosemary Said Zahlan, *The Making of the Modern Gulf States: Kuwait, Bahrain, Qatar, the United Arab Emirates and Oman*, Revised and updated edition (Reading: Ithaca Press, 1998), p. 7.
4. Thomas R. Mattair, *The Three Occupied UAE Islands: The Tunbs and Abu Musa* (Abu Dhabi: Emirates Center for Strategic Studies and Research, 2005), p. 29; B.J. Slot, *The Arabs of the Gulf, 1602–1784: An Alternative Approach to the Early History of the Arab Gulf States and the Arab Peoples of the Gulf, Mainly Based on Sources of the Dutch East India Company* (Leidschendam: B.J. Slot, 1993), p. 7; Zahlan, *The Making of the Modern Gulf States*, p. 8.
5. James Onley, 'The Politics of Protection in the Gulf: The Arab Rulers and the British Resident in the Nineteenth Century', *New Arabian Studies*, 6 (2004), 34.
6. Slot, *The Arabs of the Gulf*, p. 7.
7. For a classical study of the tribes in this region, see Fuad I. Khuri, *Tribe and State in Bahrain: The Transformation of Social and Political Authority in an Arab State* (Chicago: University of Chicago Press, 1980).
8. Slot, *The Arabs of the Gulf*, pp. 61–65.
9. Regarding the Kingdom of Hormuz, see: Slot, *The Arabs of the Gulf*, pp. 54–57; and L. Lockhart, 'Hormuz', in *Encyclopaedia of Islam*, second edition, accessed through www.brillonline.nl on 25 March 2009.
10. Slot, *The Arabs of the Gulf*, pp. 53–88.
11. Onley, 'The Politics of Protection in the Gulf', pp. 33–34.
12. Onley, 'The Politics of Protection in the Gulf', pp. 36–37, 42–43.
13. Onley, 'The Politics of Protection in the Gulf', pp. 36–37, 42–71.
14. Slot, *The Arabs of the Gulf*, p. xiii.
15. M.H. Mendelson, 'The Application of International Legal Concepts of Sovereignty in the Arabian Context', *Geopolitics*, 3:2 (1998), 134.
16. For example, see Aquil A. Kazim, *The United Arab Emirates, A.D. 600 to the Present: A Socio-discursive Transformation in the Arabian Gulf* (Dubai: Gulf Book Centre, 2000), p. 81.
17. Abudul Amir Amin, *British Interests in the Persian Gulf* (Leiden: E.J. Brill, 1967), pp. 2–3.
18. Arnold T. Wilson, *The Persian Gulf: An Historical Sketch from the Earliest Times to the Beginning of the Twentieth Century* (Oxford: Clarendon Press, 1928), p. 133.
19. James Onley, 'Britain's Informal Empire in the Gulf, 1820–1971', *Journal of Social Affairs*, 22:87 (2005), 36; James Onley, *The Arabian Frontier of the British Raj: Merchants, Rulers, and the British in the Nineteenth-Century Gulf* (Oxford: Oxford University Press, 2007), p. 18; Wilson, *The Persian Gulf*, pp. 136–137.
20. Slot, *The Arabs of the Gulf*, p. xi.
21. Slot, *The Arabs of the Gulf*, p. 29.
22. Amin, *British Interests in the Persian Gulf*, pp. 108–116, pp. 133–141.
23. Onley, 'The Politics of Protection in the Gulf', p. 39.
24. Graeme H. Wilson, *Zayed: Man Who Built a Nation* (Abu Dhabi: National Center for Documentation and Research, 2013), p. 31.
25. Onley, 'The Politics of Protection in the Gulf', p. 40.
26. J.B. Kelly, *Britain and the Persian Gulf, 1795–1880* (Oxford: Clarendon Press, 1968), p. 61.
27. Kelly, *Britain and the Persian Gulf*, pp. 139–166. Also, see Donald Hawley, *The Trucial States* (New York: Twayne Publishers, 1970).
28. Kelly, *Britain and the Persian Gulf*, pp. 165–166, 840–841.

'PIRATES' TURNED SOVEREIGN STATES, 1819–1964

29 James Onley, *Britain and the Gulf Shaikhdoms, 1820–1971: The Politics of Protection* (Doha: Center for International and Regional Studies, School of Foreign Service in Qatar, Georgetown University, 2009), p. 7.
30 Kelly, *Britain and the Persian Gulf*, p. 840.
31 For a detailed study of the native agents, see Onley, *The Arabian Frontier of the British Raj*.
32 Onley, 'Britain's Informal Empire in the Gulf', pp. 44–54.
33 Onley, 'Britain's Informal Empire in the Gulf', pp. 40–41.
34 Onley, 'Britain's Informal Empire in the Gulf', p. 42.
35 Onley, *The Arabian Frontier of the British Raj*, pp. 57–58.
36 Wilson, *The Persian Gulf*, p. 11.
37 Sultan ibn Muhammad al-Qasimi, *The Myth of Arab Piracy in the Gulf*, second edition (London: Routledge, 1988), p. 28.
38 Zahlan, *The Making of the Modern Gulf States*, p. 13.
39 Charles E. Davies, *The Blood-Red Arab Flag: An Investigation into Qasimi Piracy, 1797–1820* (Exeter: University of Exeter Press, 1997), p. 276.
40 Onley, 'The Politics of Protection in the Gulf', pp. 36–37, 42–43.
41 For a study of the history and traditions of maritime trade in the Persian Gulf, see George Fadlo Hourani, *Arab Seafaring in the Indian Ocean in Ancient and Early Medieval Times* (Beirut: Khayats, 1963).
42 Edward Keene, 'International Law and Diplomacy in the European and Extra-European Worlds during the early Nineteenth Century' (unpublished article, 2008), pp. 12, 14.
43 C.U. Aitchison, *A Collection of Treaties, Engagements and Sanads Relating to India and the Neighbouring Countries*, vol. 11 (Delhi: Government of India, 1933), pp. 245–249.
44 Kelly, *Britain and the Persian Gulf*, pp. 525–527, 840–841.
45 Aitchison, *A Collection of Treaties, Engagements and Sanads Relating to India and the Neighbouring Countries*, pp. 234, 237.
46 Habibur Rahman, *The Emergence of Qatar: The Turbulent Years, 1627–1916* (London: Kegan Paul, 2005), p. xxv.
47 Onley, 'The Politics of Protection in the Gulf', pp. 44–57.
48 We can take the case of Bahrain. The General Treaty of 1820 provided no protection to Bahrain. After 1839, Britain started to provide protection, but only unofficially, until 1861 – when it agreed to become the permanent protector. Following this institutionalisation of military protection, in 1880 Britain assumed responsibility for the foreign affairs of Bahrain. To this extent, the treaties functioned as a deal between Britain and the local rulers, an instrument for power-sharing, legitimising both parties while excluding other potential players. Onley, 'The Politics of Protection in the Gulf', pp. 71–75.
49 Peter Lienhardt, *Shaikhdoms of Eastern Arabia*, ed. Ahmed Al-Shahi (Basingstoke: Palgrave Macmillan, 2001), p. 15.
50 Slot, *The Arabs of the Gulf*, p. 399.
51 Mendelson, 'The Application of International Legal Concepts of Sovereignty in the Arabian Context', p. 135.
52 Peterson quoted in Onley, 'The Politics of Protection in the Gulf', p. 66.
53 The British government officially acknowledged the usage of the term 'Protected States' only in 1949. Onley, *The Arabian Frontier of the British Raj*, pp. 25–29; Glen Balfour-Paul, *The End of Empire in the Middle East: Britain's Relinquishment of Power in Her Last Three Arab Dependencies* (Cambridge: Cambridge University Press, 1991).
54 Keene, 'International Law and Diplomacy in the European and Extra-European Worlds during the early Nineteenth Century'.
55 John Gordon Lorimer, *Gazetteer of the Persian Gulf, 'Oman, and Central Arabia*, vol. 1 (Calcutta, 1915), pp. 2638–2639.
56 British Library, London, UK (BL), India Record Office (IRO), D.O. No. c/965, R/15/2/927, Letter to Prior, signed by 'L', 14 December 1940.

57 As a parallel example, Martin H. Geyer points out that 'the decision to introduce the metric system was fundamentally a political one', exemplifying the contingent nature of the process through which rules are standardised. Martin H. Geyer, 'One Language for the World: The Metric System, International Coinage, Gold Standard, and the Rise of Internationalism, 1850–1900', in Martin H. Geyer and Johannes Paulman (eds), *The Mechanism of Internationalism: Culture, Society, and Politics from the 1840s to the First World War* (Oxford: Oxford University Press, 2001), p. 66.
58 For details of the organisational structure of the Political Residency and its development over time, see Onley, *The Arabian Frontier of the British Raj*, pp. 225–259.
59 Onley, *Britain and the Gulf Shaikhdoms*, p. 14.
60 For a detailed account of the nationalisation of the AIOC and the Anglo-American response, see Wm. Roger Louis, *The British Empire in the Middle East, 1945–1951: Arab Nationalism, the United States, and Postwar Imperialism* (Oxford: Clarendon Press, 1984), pp. 632–689.
61 Onley, *The Arabian Frontier of the British Raj*, pp. 35, 217–218.
62 The National Archives, Kew, UK (TNA), Foreign and Commonwealth Office (FCO) 1016/842, 'Oil on the Mainland of Abu Dhabi', attached to 'Abu Dhabi Oil', issued in July 1965.
63 TNA, Cabinet Office (CAB) 148/80, 'Long-term Policy in the Persian Gulf', a note by the Secretaries, Defence and Oversea Policy (Official) Committee, 7 June 1967.
64 Abdulrahman Rashid Al-Shamlan, 'The Evolution of National Boundaries in the Southeastern Arabian Peninsula: 1934–1955' (unpublished PhD dissertation, University of Michigan, 1987), p. 267.
65 For classical accounts that are representative of the British perspective on the Buraimi Oasis dispute, see Bernard Burrows, *Footnotes in the Sand: The Gulf in Transition, 1953–1958* (Wilton: Michael Russell, 1990); P.S. Allfree, *Warlords of Oman* (South Brunswick: A.S. Barnes, 1967).
66 BL, IRO, R/15/6/251, Hay to Furlonge, 28 September 1951; Wilson to Pelly, 28 June 1951; Furlonge to Hay, 2 April 1951.
67 Born on 7 May 1929. *The Diplomatic Service List, 1972* (London: Her Majesty's Stationery Office, 1972), p. 463.
68 Julian Walker, *Tyro on the Trucial Coast* (Durham: The Memoir Club, 1999), pp. 109–121.
69 Telephone interviews with Julian Walker, 19, 21, 28 October 2009; Walker, *Tyro on the Trucial Coast*, pp. 39–40.
70 Telephone interviews with Walker, 19, 21 October 2009.
71 '[T]hey decided that much of the evidence I had used for my decisions was dangerously similar to that which the Saudis had put forward'. Walker, *Tyro on the Trucial Coast*, p. 121.
72 TNA, FCO 8/1509, 'Dubai and the Northern Trucial States Review of the Year 1969', Bullard to Crawford, 30 December 1970.
73 TNA, Foreign Office (FO) 957/169, 'Report on water supplies of part of the Trucial Coast', attached to a letter from Bahrain to Foreign Office, 23 December 1953.
74 TNA, FO 371/109893, 'Trucial States Development: 1954–55 Allocation', by Laver, c. 1954.
75 TNA, FO 371/114698, Russell to Minshull, 14 January 1955.
76 TNA, FO 371/109892, Foreign Office to Bahrain, 3 February 1954.
77 TNA, FO 1016/840, Tait to Phillips, 28 August 1965.
78 TNA, FO 371/149078, 'Application by the Government of the United Kingdom for the provision of a Soil Conservation and Water Supply Consultant to carry out a survey in the Trucial States under the United Nations Expanded Programme of Technical Assistance', enclosed to a letter from Melhuish to Warburton, 28 June 1960; Melhuish to Warburton, 1 July 1960; Owen to Warburton, 1 July 1960.
79 TNA, FO 371/149078, Olsen to Morris, 3 October 1960.
80 TNA, FCO 371/149078, Eyre to Marshall, 11 November 1960.
81 TNA, FO 1016/840, Goulding to Rich, 8 January 1965.

'PIRATES' TURNED SOVEREIGN STATES, 1819-1964

82 TNA, FCO 1016/840, Howell to Balfour-Paul, 9 April 1965.
83 H.M. Political Agent, Dubai, Arabian Gulf, *Trucial States Hydrological and Groundwater Survey: Interim Report, 1965* (London: Sir William Halcrow and Partners, 1965); H.M. Political Agent, Dubai, *Trucial States Hydrological and Groundwater Survey* (London: Sir William Halcrow and Partners, 1965), compiled in FO 1016/840. See also Trucial States Council, *Hydrological Year Book 1965/66* (London: Sir William Halcrow and Partners, 1967); Trucial States Council, *Hydrological Year Book 1966/67* (London: Sir William Halcrow and Partners, 1968), accessible at the National Center for Documentation and Research, Abu Dhabi.
84 For example, see articles in *al-Ittihad* (11 October 1972), p. 3; 22 August 1973, p. 3; 26 August 1973, p. 3; 27 August 1973, p. 3; 28 August 1973, p. 4; 13 September 1973, p. 3. Similar concerns were also reported in Bahrain. See 'Clamp-Down to Wells to Beat Water Crisis', *Gulf Weekly Mirror* (14 February 1971), p. 12.
85 TNA, FO 371/38523, 'The Essentials of an American Foreign Policy', 21 March 1944. Also compare with: 'From Balfour to Mason', 11 January 1945, compiled in Roger Bullen and M.E. Pelly (eds), *Documents on British Policy Overseas, Series 1, Vol. 4: Britain and America: Negotiations of the United States Loan, 3 August – 7 December 1975* (London: Her Majesty's Stationery Office, 1987), p. 39.
86 Wm. Roger Louis and Ronald Robinson, 'The Imperialism of Decolonization', *Journal of Imperial and Commonwealth History*, 22:3 (1994), 468–469.
87 Louis and Robinson, 'The Imperialism of Decolonization', p. 472.
88 For a detailed study of British disengagement in the Middle East following the Second World War, see Louis, *The British Empire in the Middle East*.
89 Onley, *The Arabian Frontier of the British Raj*, pp. xxvi, 34–218.
90 Paul Tempest, 'Qatar: A Strong New Bridge, 1967–2007', in Paul Tempest (ed.), *Envoys to the Arab World: MECAS Memoirs, 1944–2009*, vol. II (London: Stacey International, 2009), p. 133.
91 Christopher M. Davidson, *Dubai: The Vulnerability of Success* (London: Hurst, 2008), pp. 41, 48.
92 Donald Hawley Papers, available at Palace Green Library, Durham University, Durham, HAW 10/1/27, Donald Hawley to his parents, 6 May 1960.
93 Kristi N. Barnwell, 'Formation and Function: British Institutions and Antecedents to a Federation of Arab Emirates', conference paper presented at the 2010 annual British Scholar Conference at the University of Texas, Austin, 2010.
94 Davidson, *Dubai*, pp. 55–57.
95 Davidson, *Dubai*, pp. 56–57.
96 Helene von Bismarck, 'The Kuwait Crisis of 1961 and Its Consequences for Great Britain's Persian Gulf Policy', *British Scholar*, 2 (2009), 75–96. For details concerning discussions on defence arrangements for the protection of Kuwait in the early 1960s, see various documents in TNA, CAB 21/5578.
97 TNA, CAB 148/80, 'Long-Term Policy in the Persian Gulf', a note by the Secretaries, Defence and Oversea Policy (Official) Committee, 7 June 1967.
98 Anthony Parsons, *They Say the Lion: Britain's Legacy to the Arabs: A Personal Memoir* (London: Jonathan Cape, 1986), p. 112.
99 Sir James Craig, Political Agent in Dubai between 1961 and 1964, recalls an episode involving the Ruler of Fujairah, Shaikh Muhammad bin Hamad, in which he refused to tell Craig the name of a mountain, which later turned out to be *zibb al a'zab*. Shaikh Muhammad told Craig that he did not want the name, which meant 'bachelor's penis', to be reported to the Queen. See James Craig, 'Dubai and the other Trucial States', in Tempest (ed.), *Envoys to the Arab World: MECAS Memoirs, 1944–2009*, vol. II, p. 169.
100 Balfour-Paul, *The End of Empire in the Middle East*, p. 173.
101 Abdullah El Reyes and Jayanti Maitra, 'Federation in the Making: Exploring the Historical Roots, Role of Leadership and the Voice of the People', conference paper presented at the World Congress for Middle Eastern Studies, Ankara, 21 August 2014.

102 BL, IRO, R/15/R/6/251, Furlonge to Hay, 2 April 1951.
103 'No British Withdrawal from Persian Gulf', *The Times* (24 August 1957), p. 5. For accounts of the British officials deployed in the Gulf during this period, see Parsons, *They Say the Lion*.
104 Keene, 'International Law and Diplomacy in the European and Extra-European Worlds During the Early Nineteenth Century'.

CHAPTER TWO

Labour's clinging on to the Gulf, 1964–67

On 16 December 1964, the new Prime Minister of Britain Harold Wilson proudly proclaimed in the House of Commons:

> I want to make it clear that whatever we may do in the field of cost effectiveness, value for money, and a stringent review of expenditure, we cannot afford to relinquish our world rôle [sic], our rôle which, for shorthand purposes, is sometimes called our 'East of Suez' rôle ...[1]

At the beginning of his premiership, Wilson was openly sanguine about Britain's commitment to 'East of Suez'. Wilson's commitment to Britain's 'East of Suez role' was once portrayed by Philip Darby as 'a clash between Wilson the economist and the pragmatist and Wilson the romantic conservative'.[2] Wilson certainly had various faces. First of all, he was one of the brightest politicians of his generation. After completing his Bachelor's degree at the University of Oxford with exceptionally high grades, he had soon become one of the youngest economics dons at that university. At the same time he was from the Labour left, although he was also known to be a pragmatist. He also appeared committed to Britain's traditional role in the world, having once even proclaimed that 'Britain's frontiers are on the Himalayas'.[3]

During the ensuing years, however, his Labour government would change its position regarding Britain's commitment overseas and, in January 1968, it would announce its intention to leave the Persian Gulf. The next two chapters will address the question of why Britain ultimately decided to withdraw from the Gulf. This chapter will focus on the first three years of Wilson's premiership, critically re-examining the traditional explanations for the withdrawal, while the next chapter will put forward a different explanation, drawing on original archival research.

Our concern here corresponds directly to some of the central questions about the end of empire: Why, when and how does an empire end? John Darwin categorises the various explanations into three groups, according to their emphasis on metropolitan, peripheral or international factors.[4] This framework can be further advanced by dividing the three groups according to their analytical perspectives, depending on whether they give precedence to economic, political and military, or social and cultural factors. Of course, the nine factors are interconnected, but the division provides a helpful starting point for a concrete analysis. In particular, when looking at the reasons behind the Labour government's decision to withdraw from the Gulf, there are five plausible factors: the economic retrenchment of Britain; political and ideological changes in the international environment; ideological pressure at home; local opposition, either from the rulers or from their societies; and domestic political considerations. The existing literature is divided as to which factors were the more important. The prevailing view pivots around economic retrenchment, in the sense that the long-term relative economic decline had convinced the government by July 1967 that it should leave the 'East of Suez', including Aden, Malaysia, Singapore and the Persian Gulf. This view rests upon three ideas:

(1) That the withdrawal from the Gulf was decided upon as part of the retreat from a larger area 'East of Suez';
(2) That the decision had been taken by July 1967; and
(3) That economic pressure was the main driver behind the whole process.

The next two chapters will take issue with each of these components, and demonstrate that the decision-making process was far more contingent, contested and fraught.

In particular, this chapter will look at the first three years of Wilson's premiership and critically re-examine point (1) above by interrogating the extent to which the Labour government's policy towards the Gulf was crafted as part of the 'East of Suez' policy, and whether the withdrawal from the Gulf really had been decided by July 1967. The first section will set out the Wilson government's initial stance towards the Persian Gulf and look into the background behind it. The second section will take up the question concerning (1), and the third section will examine the significance of (2). Furthermore, this chapter will examine the international environment, whether there was significant ideological pressure pushing Britain out of the region, and whether any local considerations that moved Britain to leave the Gulf were emerging.

Wilson's Labour government and Anglo-American relations

On 16 October 1964, after 13 years in opposition, the Labour Party returned to power in Britain. It was a moment of exuberance for Labour but it was not the easiest time to take over government; the Permanent Secretary of the Treasury welcomed the new Prime Minister with a briefing about the 'serious problem' of the British economy. The export sector was performing poorly, while demand, especially in imports and private consumption, was only slowing down slightly.[5] Economic pressures were mounting, and the balance-of-payments deficit was equivalent to 1.1% of the national income.[6] In order to tackle this latter problem, on 13 November the government's economic departments suggested that defence expenditure in 1969/70, which had been projected to expand to £2.4 billion, should in fact be reduced to £2 billion.[7]

The connection between trade deficits and expenditure cuts is not a straightforward one. In general terms, cutting expenditure is only one of multiple options available for the purpose of improving the balance of payments. Yet the economic departments' assessment was that it was *'prima facie* unreasonable' to keep the defence budget so high if Britain were to economically compete with countries of similar productivity.[8] The figure of £2 billion 'gradually changed from a provisional target to an absolute ceiling' in the following months.[9]

Theoretically, there was an alternative option. Devaluation of the pound was another obvious measure for improving the balance of payments, but it was quickly ruled out. However, four years later, the Labour government would be forced to move to take that course. At that point, the 1964 decision was criticised retrospectively. In response, the Political Office of 10 Downing Street would state that the devaluation option had been rejected in 1964 because: (a) it would have caused marked inflation since there was no space to produce immediate additional exports, and (b) devaluation could have been seen by other countries as a writing-off of British debts.[10] In any case, in 1964 expenditure cuts became one of the pillars of the policies of the Labour government.

After confidently ruling out the option of devaluing the pound, Wilson also stipulated that expenditure cuts would not be accompanied by any major military retreat. In theory, the government could choose between three options in order to pursue cutbacks in defence and overseas spending: reduce military capabilities, reduce the level or scope of overseas commitments, or do both. At this stage, it went for the first option, and attempted to tackle the relative decline of economic capacity by reducing capabilities whilst nonetheless maintaining the same level of commitment. Thus, Wilson had made up his mind before Christmas that, despite 'a stringent review of expenditure', Britain 'cannot afford to relinquish ... our "East of Suez" rôle'.[11]

Together with Wilson, a number of cabinet ministers also championed Britain's role overseas. Denis Healey, the Defence Secretary, once opined at a meeting with his American counterparts that Britain should give the highest priority to the 'world-wide deployment outside the NATO area' since 'fighting was most likely to take place outside Europe'.[12] Other sympathisers included James Callaghan (the Chancellor), Patrick Gordon Walker (the Foreign Secretary), Michael Stewart (who would shortly replace Gordon Walker) and George Brown (the Secretary of State for Economic Affairs).

At first glance, it could appear counterintuitive that a non-Conservative British government should be so committed to a foreign policy with an imperial taste, particularly in the era of decolonisation. The Labour government's commitment to the 'East of Suez' role can be partly explained by ministers' personal beliefs. In fact, John Darwin points out that Wilson inherited the 'East of Suez' policy from the Conservatives.[13] However, this cannot be understood fully without looking at the Anglo-American relations underlying these beliefs. For example, in November 1964 Wilson told the American ambassador that 'the most important role for Britain for the future would be in the defence of western interests east of Suez'. The ambassador agreed that the President would be of the same opinion.[14]

Britain and the US had a longstanding partnership, which some called the 'special relationship', and which could be traced back to the Second World War or even earlier.[15] Although there was debate on both sides of the Atlantic regarding how the friendship should be understood, with Wilson preferring to call it a 'close relationship', the point is that Britain's continuing presence in the Gulf was much influenced by its calculations concerning the Anglo-American alliance.[16]

Amidst the climate of the Cold War, Britain and the US shared a considerable stake in the preservation of the status quo. For a start, a stable supply of oil was deemed vital. By 1968 British companies controlled 30% of oil production in the Gulf, British investment in the region totalled £900 million, and the annual foreign exchange income was calculated at £200 million per annum.[17] However, at this point the importance of oil was not felt as acutely as it would be after the first oil shock in 1973: neither the UK nor the US was as dependent on oil from the Gulf as Japan and some of their allies in Europe were. Moreover, British and American oil companies occasionally competed for concessions on the ground. Nonetheless, maintaining the stability of the region was believed to be crucial to securing the supply of oil to the Western world as a whole.[18]

At the same time, Britain and the US each saw the need to protect the Persian Gulf from the influence of communism. To the Americans, the British presence in the Gulf appeared, naturally, to be one of the 'remnants of colonialism', which could provide 'a peg for anticolonialism propaganda'. However, the Soviets were 'likely to preserve a discreet distance from the sponsorship of concrete solutions, while offering pious but generalised backing to the cause of "national liberation"'. Thus, while the threat of communism was differently assessed, or sometimes deliberately exaggerated, it did play an important part in convincing policy-makers that the Gulf had to be defended for the sake of the Western world.[19] Pertaining to the Soviet threat, Sir William Luce, one of the most perceptive Arabists regarding the British policy towards the Gulf, commented soon after Wilson's announcement that 'even limited Russian penetration seems to me to introduce a new hazard in a highly sensitive area, and to imply some change in the international balance of power to the disadvantage of the Western powers'. That said, he also noted that it was 'extremely unlikely that she will ever achieve the position of paramount influence which we have enjoyed for so long'.[20]

Furthermore, the US was having enough trouble in Vietnam, and wanted Britain to keep its troops in the region around the Indian Ocean. Even though the US liked to appear critical of Britain's imperial commitments, securing moral support from its primary ally in relation to the war in Vietnam was higher on the US agenda. By and large, Washington took a hands-off approach to the Gulf. In some documents, the US government even misunderstood the constitutional status of the Gulf Protected States, referring to them by the incorrect term 'British protectorates'.[21] The US position was well summarised in a report issued in March 1967:

> There is no discernible positive direct role USG [United States Government] can play in lower Gulf except by supporting UK. British position, even if we wanted it, is in all probability not transferable for more than a very short period. We should therefore support British and encourage them [to] stay, using whatever means [of] persuasion are needed.[22]

In contrast with later decades, when the US became willing to take on direct military engagements in the region, during the 1960s the maintenance of the security of the Persian Gulf was basically subcontracted to Britain.[23] In return, the US provided economic assistance to Britain, which was suffering from a series of economic crises and trying its best to maintain the Sterling Area. At the same time, however, this is not to deny that the transatlantic partnership was somewhat clumsily handled by the political leadership in both countries. Indeed, John Dumbrell characterises the Anglo-American relationship during the Wilson–Johnson era as a 'complex combination of respect and irritation, of occasional British sycophancy and American temper, of subtle acceptance of the unequal power relationship'.[24] However, there was also a considerable level of coordination, which linked US economic assistance with Britain's military and political commitment overseas. It is debatable whether any explicit agreement as to this quid pro quo between the Wilson government and the Johnson administration existed; however, there is no doubt that there was at least an implicit understanding.[25]

In addition, Britain's treaty relations with the Protected States meant that it had legal obligations to protect them, by military means if need be. Britain also perceived the Arab nationalist movements as a threat to its influence, as well as to other friendly regimes in the region. Another crucial point was the importance of the Gulf States to the Sterling Area. Kuwait was the single largest investor in Britain, and Britain had remained responsible for its military protection after its independence in 1961.

On top of these factors at the economic and international levels, there was also a domestic constraint imposed on the Labour government at this stage. The first Wilson government of 1964–66 had only a wafer-thin majority of four seats. It could not risk losing parliamentary support by adopting a controversial foreign policy, and its main focus for change was thus confined to domestic social policies. Indeed, there were domestic voices against a British presence in the Gulf, from both the left wing of the Labour Party, and also from the right. The shadow Defence Secretary made a proposal for withdrawal from 'East of Suez', but the opposition was not felt acutely at this stage.[26] Given all these considerations, the Labour government's initial approach was to maintain its involvement in the Persian Gulf, as well as in other areas 'East of Suez' – including Aden, Malaysia and Singapore.

It seems plain then that, at the beginning of his premiership, Wilson and his government had no plans to withdraw from the Gulf. Yet some authors contend that this was not the case. For example, Tore T. Petersen claims that the government was ideologically committed to withdrawal from the outset, even if the policy was not announced until 1968. Currently available sources can be said to support this claim as far as the retreat from Aden or South-East Asia is concerned – but not as regards the withdrawal from the Persian Gulf.[27] To give one example, in June 1965 Healey was even discussing the possibility of increasing the forces in the Gulf, in a secret document circulated within the MOD.[28] The complication arises from the rhetoric of 'East of Suez'. The next section will examine this rhetoric, and how it converged with or differed from British policy towards the Persian Gulf.

'East of Suez' and the Persian Gulf

The phrase 'East of Suez' was famously used in Rudyard Kipling's poem *Mandalay* in 1892. Winston Churchill's notion of the 'three circles' gave a strategic twist to it, and eventually the term became associated with Britain's self-appointed role beyond Europe and the transatlantic relationship. It coloured Britain's continuing imperial presence with a romantic nostalgia, but the problem was its substance.

A strictly logical interpretation of the phrase 'East of Suez' could encompass the whole hemisphere east of the Suez Canal. Yet, as in Kipling's verse, 'Ship me somewheres east of Suez', it was commonly associated with the sea lane from the Persian Gulf to the Indian Ocean, connecting the naval bases in the Gulf, Aden, Singapore and Hong Kong, leading to the west coast of Australia. Aggregating such geographically distant regions had its own merit in terms of naval strategy. As a military term, 'East of Suez' referred to the Indian Ocean and the surrounding areas where Britain continued to exercise imperial control, underpinned by its naval presence. And this naval presence was supported by bases and aircraft carriers.[29]

However, the phrase was particularly nebulous when used in connection with Britain's foreign or imperial policy towards the area concerned. In 1962, in response to the 'winds of change' heralding decolonisation, a Conservative Member of Parliament (MP) outlined a proposal for 'a fundamental change' in overseas policy, whereby British forces would no longer be 'dispersed round the world in small pockets' but rather concentrated in three main bases of 'Britain, Aden and Singapore'. In this context, the Conservative governments between 1962 and 1964 established that Britain should provide military assistance to the new states 'East of Suez'.[30]

John Darwin points out three considerations underlying the 'East of Suez' policy. Firstly, Britain assumed that it would 'not be faced with hostility from a first-class military power, so that the logistical burden would be comparatively modest and the risk of defeat minimal'. Secondly, it appeared unlikely that the commitment would grow substantially. Thirdly, 'the plans for South Arabia and South-East Asia were to some extent interdependent since the supply and reinforcement of Singapore required a Middle Eastern staging post, while Aden in turn was to be in certain respects a strategic dependency of the larger and more sophisticated base at Singapore'. This was also conceptualised as a 'three base strategy'. In 1962, the Minister of Defence remarked that it was indeed no longer a concept of British forces dispersed around the world but a concentration on the three main bases of Britain, Aden and Singapore.[31] Even so, it should be noted that the 'three base strategy' did not feature the Gulf.

Further to these points, David M. McCourt critically re-examines this idea, and argues that Britain's 'East of Suez role' was not an objective fact but rather 'a rhetorical construct'. Moreover, it was constantly reassessed until the Wilson government eventually accepted that it could no longer back it up.[32] Thus, it is contestable what exactly Britain's 'East of Suez role' meant, both as a military and as a political term.

In addition, the term 'East of Suez' deceptively conflated the diverse political arrangements between Britain and the various territories concerned. At one end of the spectrum, Hong Kong was still a Crown Colony of the British Empire, whereas Australia was already an independent member of the Commonwealth. Somewhere between the two ends lay the status of the Protected States of the Persian Gulf, which were independent in strict legal terms, even though their external affairs were under British control. The sentimental phrase 'East of Suez' could obscure the complex reality and the ongoing changes by provoking nostalgia for past glories.

In fact, the term was useful precisely *because* it was so ambiguous. It could be used either to postulate Britain's role in the world, or to strategise its military arrangements. The problem today is that the academic literature tends to uncritically recycle the term, with the scholarly conclusions thereby becoming dictated by the public presentation of the contemporary policy-makers, or with the writers being tempted to over-rationalise the past. Even McCourt, who has produced by far the most critical work on the rhetoric of 'East of Suez', takes the policy-makers' presentation at face value when he assumes that Britain's policy towards the Gulf was part of a larger 'East of Suez' policy. By contrast, the following paragraphs will examine Britain's policy towards the Gulf by locating it in its own context, as well as in relation to the military and political 'East of Suez' policy.

An analysis of the Persian Gulf perhaps ought to begin by asking whether there were any discernible trends on the ground towards change. In October 1967, the Shah of Iran commented on the opposition forces on the southern shore of the Gulf: 'Each Sheikhdom ... seems to have some London School of Economics leftist leaders ready to manipulate the destinies of these desert principalities'.[33] It is unclear to whom exactly he was referring, but it is true that the mid-1960s saw some events that posed threats, potential or actual, to the status quo.

For example, on 24 June 1965 a coup took place in Sharjah. Somewhat surprisingly, the British welcomed the sudden military change. As soon as Shaikh Saqr bin Sultan, the old Ruler, was superseded by Shaikh Khalid bin Muhammad al-Qasimi and left Sharjah, Britain conveyed its readiness to deal with Shaikh Khalid as the new Ruler.[34] Its official line was that Shaikh Saqr had been deposed by his family due to 'his neglect of his subjects, misgovernment of the State, extravagance and his dissolute way of life'.[35] The report from Glen Balfour-Paul, the Political Agent in Dubai, to the Foreign Office, took the view that 'Members of the ruling family of Sharjah, acting in the interests of the people, have decided that Sheikh Saqr bin Sultan al-Qasimi has shown by his scandalous behaviour and neglect of the welfare of his people that he is no longer worthy to be the Ruler of Sharjah.'[36] However, a closer look at the background gives a slightly different reading.

A month before the coup took place, Sayed Nofal, the Assistant Secretary General of the Arab League, visited the Gulf to discuss plans to provide aid and open new offices in the region. Not only did he manage to persuade the rulers of 'Ajman, Ra's al-Khaimah, Umm al-Qaiwain, Sharjah and Fujairah to write letters assuring that they would welcome aid, he also got assurance from the rulers of Sharjah and Ra's al-Khaimah that they would be willing to accommodate Arab League offices in their territories.[37] Nofal's robust diplomacy was perceived as an infiltration of Arab nationalism by the rulers of the larger members of the Protected States, namely Abu Dhabi, Dubai and Bahrain. Britain also took it as a challenge to its presence. George Thomson, the Minister of State of the Foreign Office, who was visiting the Gulf at that time, reported that the Arab League was posing a 'serious threat to our position'. He was so shocked that he looked back at the modality of British presence with a sense of regret.[38] From the other side, this was a testimony to how cost-efficient, and hence in certain ways successful, Britain's informal empire had been up to that point. Thomson remarked that Britain was using the Sharjah airfield 'dirt cheap at £30,000 odd per annum (compared to Aden and the Libyan subsidy)'.[39] In order to counter the Arab League offer, which was estimated to be around £900,000 per annum, ministers in London quickly started to discuss allocating aid of £1 million on top of the existing £200,000 via the Trucial States Development Fund.[40]

At the same time, Britain was displeased with the moves of Shaikh Saqr of Sharjah. Thomson noted that 'we must consider urgently how to deal with Saqr'.[41] Shaikh Saqr explained that he only agreed to the opening of the Arab League office because he thought that others had done so, but Thomson was not convinced.[42] He opined that if he did not withdraw his commitment to open an Arab League office, 'then we should consider ways of isolating Saqr when our own development programme gets under way' and Britain 'should be seen to be actively opposing Saqr in order to deter the smaller States from going ahead with the Arab League scheme.'[43] The documents that seem to record further details of the coup remain classified, but the evidence available suggests that Shaikh Saqr was conveniently removed from power when Britain was just about hoping for this. Glen Balfour-Paul, who was the Political Agent in Dubai, later asserted in his work that Britain gave 'encouragement' to the coup.[44] Whether Britain took some role in covertly initiating the coup or merely acquiesced in an internal revolt remains to be answered by the future opening of sources.

In the following year, there was also a coup in Abu Dhabi. Shaikh Shakhbut bin Sultan Al Nahyan had been the Ruler of Abu Dhabi for nearly 40 years, since 1928, when he was in his early twenties. There were mixed reviews on him. A British diplomat recalled him as 'a man of penetrating mind and also of much charm, when dealing with any matter other than business'.[45] During his reign, Abu Dhabi underwent its first wave of modernisation, although perhaps experiencing more of the difficulties thereof than the benefits. In the early twentieth century, the economy of the Gulf was heavily reliant on exports of pearls, but the Great Depression of 1929 damaged the global market of luxury products. Almost simultaneously, Japan started to penetrate the share of the Gulf producers by exporting cheap cultured pearls. Meanwhile, in 1935, the AIOC arrived to sign oil concessions with Abu Dhabi; but oil brought not only revenue but also tension. The most visible example of this was the international dispute over the Buraimi Oasis in 1952 to 1955. But at a more basic level, Shaikh Shakhbut was uneasy about negotiating with Western companies, which involved signing contracts and delineating land. He was also uneasy that the hope of wealth was attracting a new group of strangers to the land. Or at least he seemed apprehensive to his British interlocutors, and was so according to recent local accounts attributed to the current ruling family.[46] On the whole, he is remembered in such accounts as a traditionalist. At the same time, it is arguably also possible to take a more sympathetic view of him as a Bedouin leader representing local uneasiness about the Western model of modernisation. In fact, one of Britain's earlier documents seemingly issued before 1947 portrayed him in a much more favourable light, noting him 'to be sensible and clear headed in contrast to his exitable [excitable?] bedouin brothers'.[47]

At all events, by the mid-1960s Shaikh Shakhbut was deemed an impediment to development plans, such as the construction of water distillation plants, schools, power stations and roads. In June 1960, a British diplomat opined that he really should move on to build up the basis of an administration.[48] This seemed to have gradually improved by 1961, at least for the British, as suggested by one Arab adviser's letter to the British Political Agent. It noted how Abu Dhabi had developed from a small town to building roads and roundabouts in three places.[49] However, by 1966 Britain had become frustrated that he had 'managed to cancel, postpone or obstruct almost every development project submitted to him by his consultants', and believed he was determined to 'dissociate Abu Dhabi from the rest of the Trucial States'. And then, on 6 August, he was deposed. On the same day he was replaced by his younger brother, Shaikh Zayid bin Sultan Al Nahyan.[50]

What role Britain played in the coup is questionable. Already, on 22 December 1964, the Foreign Office was discussing the prospect of Shaikh Zayid succeeding Shaikh Shakhbut. The Political Resident Sir William Luce, who later played a leading role organising the political arrangements towards the full independence of the Protected States, was 'quite sure that so long as Shaikh Shakhbut is the ruler, federation including Abu Dhabi ... is out of the question, and there is no sign of his being ready to give any assistance to other States.'[51] According to *Arab Report and Record*, the Egyptian newspaper *Al-Ahram* reported that his reform plans had been frustrated by Britain, and Damascus Radio claimed that his deposing demonstrated that Britain could not tolerate even the mildest opposition.[52] There is no direct evidence that Britain initiated or helped the coup, but at the least it happily acquiesced in the change of leadership in Abu Dhabi.

Another episode that illuminates the nature of the British presence in the Gulf is the visit of Shaikh Khalifa, the Ruler of Qatar, to Bahrain. The two Protected States had a longstanding rivalry and border dispute. Luce, who was hoping to facilitate a rapprochement between the two parties, noted that the suspicion of Shaikh Isa, the Ruler of Bahrain, was so deep that even 'his lip service to the cause of Bahrain/Qatar friendship' was 'tempered by a flow of witticisms'. They included remarks such as, 'Sir William must be the happiest man here tonight', or 'You clearly find Shaikh Khalifa pleasant ... but can you see into his heart?'[53] This rather suggests that, at the level of rulers, the Protected States had more problems to solve between themselves than with Britain.

Similarly, in March 1965, demonstrators marched in the streets of Bahrain, and over the course of one year students demanded the release of people taken into custody. However, in the end, British officers believed the unrest to have been successfully contained.[54] On the whole, these episodes were seen as mild disturbances to the British presence in the Gulf.[55] Although in some ways they posed a potential threat to the status quo, the overall process assured that Britain's informal empire had a self-corrective mechanism built into it. During the 1960s, Britain was enjoying a largely peaceful state of affairs compared to the preceding decades.[56] Memoirs by and interviews with the British diplomats who resided in the Gulf at around this time confirm this point.[57]

With a structure in place that insulated London from local uprisings, the Wilson government continued to publicly express its commitment to the 'East of Suez' role. During a visit to the Gulf, Healey, the Defence Secretary, assured Shaikh Isa, the Ruler of Bahrain, that 'H.M.G. did not contemplate any change in their policy in the Gulf'.[58] The Defence White Paper published in February 1965 reaffirmed that it would have been 'politically irresponsible and economically wasteful' to consider withdrawal. Even though it admitted that British forces were 'seriously overstretched', it also stipulated that Britain's 'worldwide role' should be maintained as long as the local governments and peoples agreed.[59] Yet the fact that the White Paper had to be so apologetic about the 'East of Suez' commitment suggests that the government was aware of the pressures against it. In McCourt's words, Wilson's announcement in December 1964 that Britain should maintain its 'East of Suez role' had had the 'unintended effect of making it a matter of intense scrutiny and debate'.[60] Indeed, although the White Paper defended Britain's overseas commitment, it made certain concessions nonetheless by reducing military capabilities. It cancelled some projects related to the 'East of Suez' role, including the development of the fifth Polaris submarine, HS681 (a medium transport aircraft) and the replacement of P1154 (a supersonic combat aircraft).

Moreover, behind the public posturing there were more explicit proposals for change, even though they were limited in their impact. In 1965, Wilson and Michael Stewart, the Foreign Secretary, were discussing the option of withdrawing British protection from the Protected States, but they dropped it from the agenda in response to the change of situation following the coup in Sharjah.[61] Similarly, in December 1964, Wilson was told that the Ruler of Abu Dhabi had remarked to Sir William Luce, the Persian Gulf Resident, that 'he considered federation was a necessity'. However, instead of exploring the practicalities, he suggested that Britain should 'not come out openly for the time being with a formal plan for federation', which would provoke rivalries between the rulers and intervention from their neighbours.[62] By the same token, the rulers discussed possibilities of moving towards unity but the plans remained opaque. For example, in November 1965 the rulers of Qatar and Bahrain discussed the possibility of a unified currency, but 'the tyranny of Arab good manners precluded any serious

LABOUR'S CLINGING ON TO THE GULF, 1964-67

talks', at least according to Luce's observation.[63] In fact, the plan for a Gulf currency is still ongoing at the time of writing. Furthermore, it should be noted that discussions on British withdrawal or the transition of the Protected States towards unity at such an abstract level had been happening on and off since the 1930s.[64]

A signal to further change came in 1966, although again with limited consequences in the Gulf. The Defence White Paper of that year put forward the idea of some reduction in the 'East of Suez' commitment, on top of an additional cutback in military capabilities. Firstly, it announced that Britain would withdraw its troops from Aden. Aden was one of the largest ports of the British Empire, facing not the Persian Gulf but the whole Indian Ocean. It had been a Crown Colony until 1963, when it became the State of Aden within the Federation of South Arabia. Britain's attempt to unite Aden with its hinterland was likened to a 'Midnight marriage by [a] Justice of the Peace rather than [a] Church affair with trimmings', and it met with a widespread revolt organised by the National Liberation Front.[65] With the worsening of the conflict, the government was forced to consider accelerating the withdrawal from Aden; however, it should be stressed that the situation in Aden was not directly linked to Britain's presence in the Gulf. A Foreign Office official once noted, 'Maybe we should just cut our losses and leave, as we left Burma, concentrating on our interests elsewhere, as in the Gulf'.[66] Consequently, the White Paper of February 1966 declared that Britain would leave Aden by 1968, and would not maintain any forces there afterwards.

Furthermore, the paper announced the cancellation of orders not only for TSR2 –an aircraft designed for strike and reconnaissance roles – but also for CVA 01, a new aircraft carrier, whereas previously it had been expected that this 'together with HMS *Eagle* and HMS *Hermes* suitably modernized would give Britain a three-carrier fleet through the seventies' as 'the hub and the symbol of British power east of Suez'.[67]

Despite the withdrawal from Aden and the reduction of military capabilities, however, the Defence White Paper of 1966 announced no decrease in the level of engagement in the Persian Gulf.[68] In fact, the prevailing view was that the forces in the Gulf should be increased, so that Britain could continue providing protection to Kuwait after the withdrawal from Aden.[69] In short, the first Wilson government of 1964 to 1966 managed to cling on to Britain's traditional role in the Gulf.

Following the general election on 31 March 1966, Wilson had a substantially increased majority and was to remain in office until 1970. In July 1966, there was a serious financial crisis. Nonetheless, despite these changes in domestic politics and economic circumstances, the government clung to Britain's role in the Persian Gulf. In fact, in February 1967, the new Defence White Paper did not announce any major changes in overseas military involvement, but rather declared that a reduction in the overstretch of forces 'is now being achieved'.[70] Apparently, this posture did not convince many, as even the Cabinet Secretary noted that it was 'essentially a stalling White Paper'.[71]

The White Paper of 1967 was so indecisive that it provoked attacks on the government by Labour backbenchers. The Parliamentary Labour Party, in conjunction with its criticism of the government's support for the US in Vietnam, called 'for an earlier and more extensive reduction of Britain's commitments East of Suez than envisaged in the Defence White Paper'.[72] The revolt within the Labour Party was so intense that the Leader of the House of Commons was 'extremely alarmed by their mood'.[73] Shortly afterwards, the Cabinet decided to leave Malaysia and Singapore.[74] However, at this point, the forces in the Persian Gulf were not subject to change.[75]

Thus, by the first half of 1967, the Labour government had decided on the reduction of military capabilities and withdrawal from Aden, Malaysia and Singapore, but not from the Persian Gulf. For almost two and a half years after its inauguration, the government had been consistently committed to Britain's military engagement in the Gulf.

Up in the air

On 5 June 1967, the Six-Day War between Israel and the Arab states broke out. Two days later, a note issued by the Defence and Overseas Policy (OPD) Official Committee signalled a subtle change in British policy towards the Gulf. It unleashed the momentum that led to the implicit understanding within the Labour government that Britain would have to leave the Persian Gulf at some point. However, this was by no means an explicit decision, and the timeframe of withdrawal was kept vague.

Until that point, the assumption made by successive British governments was that 'we shall stay until satisfactory conditions [are] obtained for our departure', which implied 'a willingness on our part to stay indefinitely if need be'. Yet, as the note stated, the Labour government had increasingly been moving towards the assumption that 'we shall need in all circumstances to have withdrawn within a roughly definable period – by, say, the mid-1970s.' This new assumption implied 'a willingness on our part to leave under less than satisfactory conditions if need be'. Effectively, this meant that the OPD had decided to withdraw from the Persian Gulf – at least at the level of officials.[76]

The conclusions drawn at the ministerial level, however, were slightly more nuanced. On 3 July, an OPD meeting was held in the presence of Wilson, together with the Chancellor of the Exchequer and the Secretaries of State of the Foreign Office, the MOD and several other departments. The main focus of this meeting was the policy towards South East Asia, and no explicit decision was taken regarding the Persian Gulf. The participants accepted the assumption that Britain was not going to stay in the Gulf, but they were unclear as to the pace and modality of withdrawal. One could reasonably assert that, at this point, the Labour government had, at least subconsciously, reached an implicit understanding that it would need to pull its troops out of the Gulf *at some point* in the mid-1970s. However, this was not an outright decision.[77] Things were up in the air.

The subtle change in British policy coincided with the Six-Day War. The Arab defeat resulted in angry demonstrations in Bahrain, with the demonstrators surrounding the Political Agency. The tension was such that the British officers began to prepare for a military clash, until Shaikh Isa's speech persuaded the crowd to disperse.[78] However, back in London, the Labour government construed the implications of the crisis in various ways. One argument was that it 'had demonstrated the inability of our forces overseas to play any worthwhile role in a critical situation: indeed, by involving us in certain political commitments, it could be claimed that their presence in this area had been positively disadvantageous to our interests'. However, another thesis put forward contended that withdrawal from the Gulf would turn out to involve 'risks to our interests in Iran and the Persian Gulf and therefore to the sterling balances and our oil supplies'. In fact, from this point of view, 'the presence of our forces in the Persian Gulf and the maintenance of our commitments to the Central Treaty Organisation (CENTO) had proved of great importance to our interests in the supply of oil during the crisis in the Middle East, since they served to maintain our relationship with Iran'.[79] Thus, on the whole, the connection between the June War and the discussions related to British withdrawal was ambiguous.

In the meantime, in Washington, a Special State-Defense Study Group made a list of recommendations on strategy in the Middle East and the Horn of Africa. The report did not devote any space to independent analysis of the Persian Gulf strategy, instead discussing the region either in the context of a wider Indian Ocean policy or distinguishing between the Iranian ('Northern Tier') and southern shores ('Eastern Arab states'). Within this geographical conception, the study suggested that America should 'assist the British to remain in the Persian Gulf', while also encouraging Saudi Arabia to 'assume greater responsibility' and providing Iran with 'military and economic support' against the perceived Soviet threat.[80] On the whole, however, the US was standing aloof from the region. The expectation was that Britain would continue to assume principal responsibility for maintaining the stability of the region in the foreseeable future.[81]

Thus, in July 1967 there was no direct causality between the June War and the Labour government's implicit understanding regarding withdrawal from the Persian Gulf. Later, the rise in oil prices precipitated by the war would result in an economic crisis, which would eventually shape an important context concerning British withdrawal from the Gulf. However, at this earlier point such a remote link was unforeseen. Instead, as Dockrill points out, the understanding reached in July 1967 could be more appropriately understood as the outcome of a series of defence reviews over the preceding years, which were largely a consequence of the long-term retrenchment of the British economy.[82]

However, Dockrill also opens a debate when she goes on to claim that 'the withdrawal from the Persian Gulf was the "logical extension" of Britain's decision to withdraw from the Far East [i.e. Malaysia and Singapore]'.[83] Here, it is worth re-emphasising that, in July 1967, the government had reached only a vague consensus on its intention to withdraw from the Gulf *at some point* in the mid-1970s. Unlike in January 1968, it did not stipulate exactly when withdrawal would occur, nor did it take any steps towards making any public announcement of its intention. For example, in the OPD meeting on 3 July, those present assumed that, merely for costing purposes, Britain would withdraw from the Persian Gulf by 1975/76. At the same time, they noted that events in the region might affect the pace of withdrawal and, moreover, that the government could not 'exclude the possibility that we shall still have some tenuous obligations to the shaikhdoms of the Persian Gulf' after the mid-1970s.[84] In fact, the OPD paper issued on 7 June stipulated that no definite date should yet be appointed for the withdrawal, as this would increase the risk of instability.[85]

So, the terms of withdrawal from the Persian Gulf were deliberately kept vague. Moreover, in the mid-1960s Britain was having a hard time disengaging from Aden alone. The Labour government had learned from this experience that setting a rigid timeframe for British withdrawal and publicising it benefited only the local opposition groups. Hence, the deadline for withdrawal was deliberately discussed in round figures, and the deadline of the mid-1970s was only mentioned in that context. Making a public announcement was out of the question – at least until the Gulf rulers had recovered from the shock of the Aden episode.

LABOUR'S CLINGING ON TO THE GULF, 1964-67

Consequently, the Supplementary Defence White Paper issued on 18 July announced that, by 1970/71, Britain would have halved its forces in Malaysia and Singapore, and would have completely withdrawn them by the mid-1970s, mentioning nothing about withdrawal from the Persian Gulf.[86] Thus, in July 1967 the government had not yet taken any explicit decision on withdrawal from the Gulf, even though it had internally reached an implicit understanding on this. Indeed, the fact that anything had even been discussed was completely concealed from the public over the following months.

Two days after the Supplementary White Paper was issued, George Brown, the Foreign Secretary, stated in the House of Commons that the Protected States in the Persian Gulf still 'need our help and we propose to keep small forces there to meet our obligations', despite it being 'our long-term aim to create a situation in which these small States can stand on their own feet'. He went on to claim that, 'by maintaining what we are doing there, we are doing better than we would by getting out'.[87] Later, in early November, the Minister of State at the Foreign Office, Goronwy Roberts, visited the states of the Persian Gulf. During the tour, he assured 'the Rulers that the British presence would continue as long as it is necessary to maintain peace and stability in the area'.[88] Both domestically and internationally then, the Labour government was sending out messages that Britain would stay in the Gulf for an indefinite period, even as the situation on the economic front was deteriorating.

Meanwhile, the Six-Day War had led to a severe rise in oil prices, and by the autumn of 1967 large-scale offshore selling of the pound was generating a currency crisis.[89] It was looking increasingly untenable for the Bank of England to defend the pound. In order to secure a loan from the International Monetary Fund, on 18 November 1967 the Chancellor of the Exchequer, James Callaghan, announced that the pound would be devalued by 14.3%, from the previous US$2.80 to US$2.40. In fact, the devaluation option had been on the table as a solution to relieve the balance-of-payments problem ever since the Labour government took office. In July 1966, there was a similar financial crisis, arguably on a larger scale, but on this occasion Wilson rejected the devaluation option. Since Wilson had consistently claimed that the government could improve the economy while defending the pound, the eventual devaluation was all the more embarrassing. Even so, the government did not change its position over the Persian Gulf – until the Chancellor of the Exchequer was replaced.

Coming back to the original point, it needs restating that the aim of this and the next chapter is to critically re-examine the dominant view that the long-term relative economic decline convinced the government, by July 1967, that it should leave the 'East of Suez' area, including Aden, Malaysia, Singapore *and* the Persian Gulf. Thus, the conventional narrative rests upon three ideas:

(1) That the withdrawal from the Gulf was decided upon as part of the retreat from a larger area 'East of Suez';
(2) That the decision was taken by July 1967; and
(3) That economic pressure was the main driver behind the whole process.

The primary purpose of this chapter was to examine to what extent the Labour government's policy towards the Gulf was crafted as part of the 'East of Suez' policy and whether the withdrawal from the Gulf had been decided by July 1967. The findings illustrated here suggest negative answers to both of these points. During the first three years of his premiership, Wilson's Labour government kept referring to 'East of Suez' at a rhetorical level, thereby conflating Britain's commitment in the Persian Gulf, Aden, Malaysia and Singapore as governed by a coherent policy, although in the policy-making process the Gulf was largely separated from the other regions. Whereas the government had decided and announced its intention by July 1967 to withdraw from Aden, Singapore and Malaysia, it remained committed to the Persian Gulf. Now that the first two components are put in question, the next chapter will take up the third and put forward an original case with archival evidence.

Additionally, this chapter has examined whether any local considerations that moved Britain to leave the Gulf were emerging, or if there was significant ideological pressure pushing Britain out of the region. Whereas voices back in London were becoming increasingly hostile to Britain's imperial commitment overseas, during this period the Gulf was, at least in the eyes of the British officers there, largely at peace. Thus, by contrast with the other bases in the 'East of Suez', the Labour government was certainly still clinging on to the Gulf even after the devaluation in November 1967.

Glen Balfour-Paul contends that 'the question already at issue by the beginning of the 1960s was not whether, but when and how, withdrawal should be stage-managed'.[90] In analysing the British defence policy 'East of Suez' during this period, Philip Darby also argues that, 'As the debate wore on the disagreement came to centre not on withdrawal as an aim, but on how it should be carried out and at what rate, and what should be left at the end.'[91] However, the evidence presented in this chapter suggests that such considerations were largely absent from the Labour government's thinking as far as the Gulf was concerned. Problems such as how the withdrawal 'should be carried out and ... what should be left at the end' were mostly ignored.[92] These seemingly sensible questions were neglected because, ultimately, the withdrawal from the Gulf was not decided upon as a result of economic or foreign policy calculations, but rather for more short-term ulterior reasons, as will be demonstrated in the next chapter.

Notes

1 *Parliamentary Debates (Commons)*, vol. 704, cols 423–424.
2 Phillip Darby, *British Defence Policy East of Suez, 1947–1968* (London: Oxford University Press for the Royal Institute of International Affairs, 1973), p. 285.
3 'Premier Pledges Support for India', *Guardian* (11 June 1965), p. 1.
4 John Darwin, *The End of the British Empire: The Historical Debate* (Oxford: Basil Blackwell, 1991).
5 Meeting between Wilson, Brown and Callaghan, minutes by Armstrong, 16 October 1964, Prime Minister's Office (PREM) 13/32, compiled in S.R. Ashton and Wm. Roger Louis (eds), *British Documents on the End of Empire, Series A, Vol 5: East of Suez and the Commonwealth, 1964–1971*, Part 1 (London: The Stationery Office, 2004), pp. 1–3.
6 Nicholas Woodward, 'Labour's Economic Performance, 1964–70', in Richard Coopy, Steven Fielding and Nick Tratsoo (eds), *The Wilson Governments, 1964–1970* (London: Pinter, 1993), p. 75.
7 TNA, CAB 130/213, 'The Future Size of the Defence Budget', a memorandum by the Treasury and the Department of Economic Affairs, 13 November 1964.
8 TNA, CAB 130/213, 'The Future Size of the Defence Budget', a memorandum by the Treasury and the Department of Economic Affairs, 13 November 1964.
9 Darby, *British Defence Policy East of Suez*, p. 287.
10 Harold Wilson Papers, available at the Bodleian Libraries, University of Oxford, Oxford, Ref. 5625, Ms. Wilson c. 791, Holland to Lumsden, 10 January 1968.
11 *Parliamentary Debates (Commons)*, vol. 704, cols 423–424.
12 TNA, CAB 133/266, PMV(W)(64) 2nd Meeting, record of meeting held on 7 December 1964, issued by the Cabinet Office on 14 December 1964.
13 Darwin, 'Britain's Withdrawal from East of Suez', in Carl Bridge (ed.), *Munich to Vietnam: Australia's Relations with Britain and the United States since the 1930s* (Victoria: Melbourne University Press, 1991), p. 150.
14 TNA, PREM 13/103, note of conversation between Bruce and Wilson, 27 November 1964.
15 John Dumbrell, *A Special Relationship: Anglo-American Relations from the Cold War to Iraq*, second edition (Basingstoke: Palgrave Macmillan, 2006); David Reynolds, 'A "Special Relationship"? America, Britain and the International Order since World War II', *International Affairs*, 62:1 (1986), 1–20.
16 W. Taylor Fain, *American Ascendance and British Retreat in the Persian Gulf Region* (New York: Palgrave Macmillan, 2008), pp. 143–144.
17 Figure quoted by Sir Alec Douglas-Home on 24 January 1968 in the House of Commons. *Parliamentary Debates (Commons)*, vol. 757, col. 424.
18 TNA, CAB 148/80, 'Long-term Policy in the Persian Gulf', a note by the Secretaries, Defence and Oversea Policy (Official) Committee, 7 June 1967. The point is also confirmed by contemporary reports, including one written by a contemporary member of Chatham House Study Group on the Persian Gulf: A Correspondent, 'Oil in the Persian Gulf', *Oil in the Persian Gulf*, 20:7 (1964), 305–313; J.B. Kelly, 'The British Position in the Persian Gulf', *The World Today*, 20:6 (1964), 248.
19 National Archives and Records Administration, College Park, Maryland, USA

(NARA), Records of the Central Intelligence Agency (RG 263), Entry 29, Box 17, 'Soviet Strategy and Intentions in the Mediterranean Basin', 1 June 1967.
20 William Luce, 'Britain's Withdrawal from the Middle East and Persian Gulf', *Journal of the Royal United Services Institution*, 114:653 (1969), 8.
21 NARA, RG 263, Entry 29, Box 17, 'Soviet Strategy and Intentions in the Mediterranean Basin', 1 June 1967.
22 NARA, Department of State Central Files (RG 59), Central Foreign Policy Files, 1967–1969, Box 2418, POL 33, 'Persian Gulf Roundup', telegram from Dahran to Washington, 8 March 1967.
23 Roland Popp, 'Subcontracting Security: The US, Britain and Gulf Security before the Carter Doctrine', in Daniel Möckli and Victor Mauer (eds), *European-American Relations and the Middle East: From Suez to Iraq* (London: Routledge, 2011), pp. 171–186.
24 Dumbrell, *A Special Relationship: Anglo-American Relations from the Cold War to Iraq*, p. 77.
25 Jonathan Tepper, 'The Dollar, the Pound and British Policy East of Suez, 1964–67: Deals and Understandings between Wilson and Johnson' (unpublished MLitt thesis, Oxford: University of Oxford, 2004). Petersen puts forward the case that the Labour government was making official and explicit comments about its 'East of Suez' role in order to secure economic assistance from the US. Unlike Petersen, Dockrill argues that the Labour government did not try to extract economic assistance from the US in return for maintaining its overseas role. Tore T. Petersen, *The Decline of the Anglo-American Middle East, 1961–1969: A Willing Retreat* (Brighton: Sussex Academic Press, 2006); Saki Dockrill, *Britain's Retreat from East of Suez: The Choice between Europe and the World?* (Basingstoke: Palgrave Macmillan, 2002); Smith, *Britain's Revival and Fall in the Gulf*, pp. 220–221.
26 Richard Crossman, *The Diaries of a Cabinet Minister: Volume One, Minister of Housing, 1964–66* (London: Hamish Hamilton and Jonathan Cape, 1975), p. 354.
27 Even though Petersen himself admits that it 'is hard to explain the decision to leave the Gulf by anything other than domestic exigencies', he aggregates the withdrawal from the Persian Gulf into the whole 'East of Suez' retreat. He claims that the Defence Secretary, Denis Healey, was committed to withdrawal from the beginning of his tenure, and facilitated the decision by 'setting a ceiling of £2,000 million in annual defence expenditure at 1964 prices'. However, as this paper will demonstrate, the financial savings yielded by leaving the Persian Gulf were close to negligible compared to the overall budget. As his major source of evidence, Petersen refers to some interviews and memoirs in which Healey commented that he had been planning the retreat from the beginning. However, one should take into account policy-makers' potential incentives to make a retroactive justification and rationalisation of their actions. Even if one accepts Healey's later revelation at face value, this does not justify the conclusion that he represented the dominant voice within the Labour government. In an interview with Karl Pieragostini conducted in 1979, Wilson admitted, 'I think when we went into office there wasn't very much intention of a major pull-out from the East'. Petersen, *The Decline of the Anglo-American Middle East*, pp. 7, 66–77, 112–113, 127–128; Denis Healey, *The Time of My Life* (Harmondsworth: Penguin, 1989); Karl Pieragostini, *Britain, Aden and South Arabia: Abandoning Empire* (London: Macmillan, 1991), p. 114.
28 TNA, Ministry of Defence (DEFE) 25/130, 'Middle East Defence Policy', a personal note by Healey, 28 June 1965.
29 Darby, *British Defence Policy East of Suez*, p. 276.
30 Darby, *British Defence Policy East of Suez*, pp. 244–282.
31 Darwin, 'Britain's Withdrawal from East of Suez', p. 148.
32 David M. McCourt, 'What was Britain's "East of Suez Role"? Reassessing the Withdrawal, 1964–1968', *Diplomacy and Statecraft*, 20:3 (2009), 453–472. For a representative work on the constructivist approach in general, see Alexander Wendt, 'Anarchy Is What States Make of It: The Social Construction of Power-Politics', *International Organization*, 46:2 (1992), 391–425.

LABOUR'S CLINGING ON TO THE GULF, 1964-67

33 NARA, RG 59, Central Foreign Policy Files, 1967–69, Box 2418, POL 33, Persian Gulf, 'Security of Persian Gulf', telegram from Tehran to Washington, 25 October 1967.
34 TNA, PREM 13/3326, Dubai to Foreign Office, 24 June 1965.
35 TNA, PREM 13/3326, Foreign Office and Commonwealth Relations Office to various missions, 24 June 1965.
36 TNA, PREM 13/3326, Dubai to Foreign Office, 24 June 1965.
37 TNA, PREM 13/3326, Bahrain to Foreign Office, telegram no. 354, 16 May 1965.
38 TNA, PREM 13/3326, Bahrain to Foreign Office, telegram no. 355, 16 May 1965. He noted: 'Looking at the wretched condition of most of the sheikhdoms it seems to me that we have given disgracefully little over the years in return for the exclusive position and facilities we have enjoyed, much less for example than we would have given, if, what is in effect a colonial relationship, had been so in fact.'
39 TNA, PREM 13/3326, Bahrain to Foreign Office, telegram no. 355, 16 May 1965.
40 TNA, PREM 13/3326, Foreign Office to Bahrain, 26 May 1965.
41 TNA, PREM 13/3326, Bahrain to Foreign Office, telegram no. 355, 16 May 1965.
42 TNA, PREM 13/3326, Bahrain to Foreign Office, telegram no. 354, 16 May 1965.
43 TNA, PREM 13/3326, Bahrain to Foreign Office, telegram no. 355, 16 May 1965.
44 Balfour-Paul, *The End of Empire in the Middle East*, p. 121.
45 Jayanti Maitra and Afra Hajji, *Qasr Al Hosn: The History of the Rulers of Abu Dhabi, 1793–1966* (Abu Dhabi, UAE: Centre for Documentation and Research, 2001), p. 236.
46 Maitra and Hajji, *Qasr Al Hosn*, pp. 230–252.
47 BL, IRO, R/52/2/916, 'Shaikh Shakhbut bin Sultan bin Zayid, Ruler of Abu Dhabi', undated document with the watermark of 'Government of India'.
48 Donald Hawley Papers, available at the Palace Green Library, University of Durham, UK, HAW 49/1/1, from Middleton to Hawley, 6 June 1960.
49 Donald Hawley Papers, HAW 49/1/145, Bustani to Hawley, 11 October 1961.
50 TNA, PREM 13/3326, 'Deposition of Shaikh Shakhbut of Dubai', from Foreign Office and Commonwealth Office to Certain Missions, 6 August 1966.
51 TNA, PREM 13/3326, 'The Rulership of Abu Dhabi', a letter addressed to the Prime Minister with the seal of the Foreign Office, 22 December 1964.
52 'Ruler Deposed', *Arab Report and Record*, (1966, no. 15), p. 170.
53 TNA, FO 371/179805, Luce to Stewart, 8 November 1965.
54 'Student Demonstrations', *Arab Report and Record* (1966, no. 5), p. 50. In May 1966, it was reported that a grenade was thrown at police. 'Grenade Thrown at Police', *Arab Report and Record* (1966, no. 10), p. 110.
55 'Ruler Deposed', *Arab Report and Record*.
56 Christopher M. Davidson, 'Arab Nationalism and British Opposition in Dubai, 1920–1966', *Middle Eastern Studies*, 43:6 (2007), 879–892.
57 Interview with Sir James Craig, 13 October 2009; telephone interview with Mr. Julian Walker, 19, 21, 28 October 2009; Craig, 'Dubai and the other Trucial States'; Tempest, 'Qatar: A Strong New Bridge, 1967–2007'.
58 TNA, FO 371/179805, Tripp to Weir, 6 September 1965.
59 *Parliamentary Papers: House of Commons and Command*, Cmnd 2592, Statement on the Defence Estimates, 1965.
60 McCourt, 'What was Britain's "East of Suez Role"? Reassessing the Withdrawal, 1964–1968', pp. 459–460.
61 TNA, PREM 13/3326, Trend to Wilson, 25 June 1965.
62 TNA, PREM 13/3326, letter to Prime Minister, 22 December 1964. The letter was signed by 'PCGW'. The last paragraph that followed the argument remains classified.
63 TNA, FO 371/179805, Luce to Stewart, 8 November 1965.
64 Davidson, *Dubai*, p. 55; Abdullah El Reyes and Jayanti Maitra, 'Federation in the Making: Exploring the Historical Roots, Role of Leadership and the Voice of the People', conference presentation at the World Congress for Middle Eastern Studies, Ankara, 21 August 2014.

65 Simon C. Smith, 'Revolution and Reaction: South Arabia in the Aftermath of the Yemeni Revolution', *Journal of Imperial and Commonwealth History*, 28:3 (2000), 193–208.
66 TNA, FO 371/17975, B 1052/103, note by Arthur, 5 July 1965.
67 Darby, *British Defence Policy East of Suez*, pp. 298–289.
68 Cmnd 2901, Statement on the Defence Estimates, 1966: Part I, the Defence Review.
69 TNA, FO 371/177831, 'Report on Effects of Withdrawing from the Aden Base', 12 October 1964; CAB 148/22, 'Defence Review', 3 August 1965; CAB 148/41, minutes of OPDO (65) 24th meeting, 22 October 1965.
70 Cmnd 3203, Statement of the Defence Estimates, 1967.
71 TNA, PREM 13/1383, Trend to Wilson, January 1967.
72 Parliamentary Labour Party Archives, available at the Bodleian Library, Oxford, Card 259, Party Meeting Minutes, 22 February 1967.
73 Richard Crossman, *The Diaries of a Cabinet Minister, Volume Two* (London: Hamish Hamilton and Jonathan Cape, 1975), p. 256.
74 In terms of the withdrawal from Malaysia and Singapore, Whitehall officials were reaching a consensus by late 1965 that Britain would need to leave. Dockrill, *Britain's Retreat from East of Suez*, pp. 126–127.
75 For details of the changes of the Labour government's policy in South East Asia, see Phuong Pham, 'End of the East of Suez: The British Decision to Withdraw from Malaysia and Singapore, 1964 to 1968' (unpublished DPhil thesis, Oxford: University of Oxford, 2001), pp. 161–169.
76 TNA, CAB 148/80, 'Long-term Policy in the Persian Gulf', a note by the Secretaries, Defence and Oversea Policy (Official) Committee, 7 June 1967.
77 TNA, CAB 148/30, minutes of OPD (67) 25th meeting, 3 July 1967; CAB 129/131, 'Defence Expenditure Studies', a note by Trend, C(67)118, 4 July 1967; CAB 148/81, 'Defence Expenditure Studies', a note by the Secretaries, OPDO (67) 11 (Final), 25 July 1967.
78 Parsons, *They Say the Lion*, pp. 128–131.
79 TNA, CAB 148/30, minutes of OPD (67) 24th meeting, 26 June, 1967.
80 Report prepared by the Special State-Defense Study Group, undated (c. July 1967), compiled in US Department of State, *The Foreign Relations of the United States (FRUS) 1964–1968*, vol. 21 (Washington, D.C.: Department of State), pp. 49–59.
81 A CIA report on the Soviet influence in the Arab states during this period paid little attention to the Persian Gulf: NARA, RG 263, Entry 29, Box 9, 'Probable Soviet Objectives in Rearming Arab States', 20 July 1967.
82 Dockrill, *Britain's Retreat from East of Suez*, pp. 193–199.
83 Dockrill, *Britain's Retreat from East of Suez*, p. 213.
84 NARA, CAB 129/131, 'Defence Expenditure Studies', a note by Trend, C(67)118, 4 July 1967.
85 NARA, CAB 148/80, 'Long-term Policy in the Persian Gulf', a note by the Secretaries, Defence and Oversea Policy (Official) Committee, 7 June 1967.
86 Cmnd 3357, Supplementary Statement on Defence Policy, 1967.
87 *Parliamentary Debates (Commons)*, vol. 750, cols 2494–2495.
88 TNA, FCO 8/31, Roberts to Brown, 17 November 1967, compiled in S.R. Ashton and Wm. Roger Louis (eds), *East of Suez and the Commonwealth, 1964–1971: Part I, East of Suez*, British Documents on the End of Empire, series A, volume 5 (London: The Stationery Office, 2004), pp. 118–120.
89 Fain, *American Ascendance and British Retreat*, p. 164.
90 Balfour-Paul, *The End of Empire in the Middle East*, p. 143.
91 Darby, *British Defence Policy East of Suez*, p. 309.
92 Related to this point, in November 1964, D.C. Watt observed that it was in 'the British character ... not to waste energy on what the Americans call "contingency planning" but rather, in Kipling's words, "to deal with situations as they arise"'. D.C. Watt, 'Britain and the Future of the Persian Gulf States', *The World Today*, 20:11 (1964), 488.

CHAPTER THREE

Jenkins and the withdrawal decision, 1968

For three years after coming to power, Wilson's Labour government was committed to keeping the British informal empire in the Persian Gulf. They decided on withdrawing from Aden, Malaysia and Singapore, but little seemed to have changed on the Gulf front even after the devaluation in November 1967. While Downing Street hesitated, Sir William Luce published an article warning the government against a premature decision:

> It would be a mistake to lay down any specific period [for the withdrawal from the Persian Gulf] since there are many factors which could either hasten or delay progress; and certainly it should not be determined by any arbitrary or unilateral decision designed to effect a small saving in British defence costs or to satisfy opinion based on the artificial division of the world into east and west of Suez.[1]

In this article, which came out in July 1967, the British senior diplomat accepted that Britain might not be able to remain in the Gulf indefinitely, but he argued that the government should be careful not to decide to withdraw from the region for the wrong reasons nor with any explicit timeframe. Were these words of caution taken into account in the final stages of the process that led to the government's decision to withdraw from the Gulf? This chapter examines this question in some detail, asking who exactly took the decision, for what reasons, on what terms, and within what timeframe.

Jenkins, the Treasury and foreign policy

As we have seen in Chapter 2, Harold Wilson took no personal initiative to remove the British troops from the Persian Gulf after he became Prime Minister. He was not against the British presence in the Gulf, either owing to his ideological beliefs or because of practical calculations to secure American cooperation. His inner circle more or less shared his attitude. Although by July 1967 the OPD Official Committee had started considering withdrawal, the Cabinet did not take the issue seriously enough to discuss practicalities such as the timeframe or whether it should be preceded by an open announcement. The point, then, is just when the decision pertaining to these key issues was taken.

Even with the heightening of economic pressure and subsequent devaluation, a minister of state at the Foreign Office visited the Gulf and assured 'the Rulers that the British presence would continue as long as it is necessary to maintain peace and stability in the area'.[2] Thus, the decision to leave the Gulf – arguably 'the most momentous shift in our foreign policy for a century and a half' as the then Cabinet minister later put it – did not originate from the usual guardians of foreign policy, i.e. the Prime Minister, the Secretaries of Defence or Foreign Affairs, or their offices.[3] Instead, it was initiated by the Chancellor and the Treasury. Therefore, counterintuitive as it may sound, the main protagonist of the decision-making process was the new Chancellor of the Exchequer, Roy Jenkins, backed up by Treasury officials. The overall process followed three steps. Firstly, there were the internal consultations within the Treasury involving Jenkins and his staff. Secondly, the Treasury brought the issue to the government to persuade the Prime Minister, the Foreign Office and the MOD. Then, thirdly, the British government as a whole took the issue to the foreign governments involved. Here, we will start from the first level.

Roy Jenkins was born in 1920 into a Welsh trade-unionist and former mining family. Four years younger than Wilson, Jenkins had also studied at the University of Oxford. When Wilson formed his government in 1964, he nominated Jenkins Minister of Aviation, making him the youngest, albeit non-Cabinet, member of the government. The following year, he was promoted to Home Secretary, now becoming the youngest member of the Cabinet. Over the next three years, he initiated a number of social reforms, attempting to transform Britain into what he called a 'civilised society'. Given Jenkins's successful career as a politician, it was regarded as reasonable that Wilson should appoint him Chancellor of the Exchequer on 30 November 1967 after the devaluation turmoil.[4]

Despite somewhat similar career paths, the two politicians had contrasting views regarding Britain's world role. Jenkins recalls that, unlike Wilson, he had been against 'keeping Britain over-committed in the world' long before arriving at the Treasury.[5] Jenkins's coming to the Treasury triggered the discussions within the Labour government concerning withdrawal from the Persian Gulf.

JENKINS AND THE WITHDRAWAL DECISION, 1968

According to Jeffrey Pickering, the nomination of Jenkins as Chancellor marked a shift in the balance of power within the Labour government between those in favour of and those against Britain's overseas military engagement. Pickering emphasises the role of Jenkins in unleashing the Labour government's decision-making process regarding the withdrawal some time in December 1967 and January 1968.[6] Similarly, Darwin emphasises the role of Jenkins as the central force pushing for further reduction in overseas commitment.[7] However, Jenkins's memoir indicates that he never fully understood the particular implications of withdrawing from the Persian Gulf. He refers to the region only as 'East of Suez' and aggregates the Gulf with South East Asia.[8] Also, the declassified British government sources suggest that there was one week of silence after Jenkins took over the Treasury on 30 November. Only on 7 December did Jenkins state that some 'very big cuts' had to be made in defence, and even at this point he made no specific reference to the troops in the Gulf.[9]

It is unknown what was discussed off the record between Jenkins and the Treasury's senior officials during this one-week hiatus. The earliest evidence of the government's consideration on the matter during Jenkins's chancellorship notes that, on 4 December, the Principal Private Secretary to the Chancellor asked his junior staff to examine the possible effects of 'pressing for somewhat earlier military withdrawal from the Gulf'. However, this was only a discussion between the Treasury officials and does not suggest any involvement on the part of Jenkins.[10] It is debatable what level of coordination Jenkins and the officials reached during this period. On the one hand, a member of the government who later supported Jenkins as Minister of State and then Financial Secretary testifies that Jenkins 'soon established a good relationship with the civil servants at the Treasury'. On the other hand, Jenkins himself recalls that the 'Treasury at that time was less good at suggesting constructive action' and 'the one time in my ministerial career when I consider that I was badly advised on major questions was my first two or three months as Chancellor'.[11] On the basis of the existing evidence, it is difficult to assert whether it was Jenkins who initially raised the issue of making an explicit decision on the withdrawal or whether it was Treasury officials who proposed the idea to the new Chancellor.

In any case, on 7 December Jenkins and the officials agreed on the general idea of cutting defence expenditure. That said, at this point, they did not specify how this could be achieved.[12] So, officials started to consider a practical plan, beginning with a calculation of the cost of keeping forces in the Gulf.[13] Within a few days, on 11 December, they had concluded that withdrawal from the Gulf was the most desirable option. After comparing various potential options for reducing overseas commitment, including in Europe, South East Asia, Cyprus and Hong Kong, they concluded that the 'Persian Gulf is the most obvious candidate of all for withdrawal'. The fact that, at this stage, the Treasury officials were comparing the withdrawal from the Gulf to the hypothetical option of leaving Europe or Hong Kong backs up the point in the last chapter that they had not taken a *decision* in July.[14]

On 12 December, officials became confident enough to note that 'the presentational advantages of being able to declare that, with a few scattered exceptions, we aim to complete our withdrawal worldwide into Europe by say 1 April 1971 could be very great'.[15] By 14 December, Jenkins had agreed to the proposal of Treasury officials that withdrawal from the Persian Gulf had to be completed by 1 April 1971 and also that the decision should be publicly announced.[16] Although this was just an internal consensus within the Treasury, it created a momentum within the government towards taking an explicit decision and configuring the terms of withdrawal.

After Jenkins and the Treasury officials decided internally that Britain should leave the Gulf, they negotiated with the Prime Minister, the Foreign Office and the MOD. The negotiations started from 'a "softening up" lunch' between Jenkins and Denis Healey, the Secretary of State for Defence, on 14 December. Unexpectedly, Healey was understanding and took Jenkins's proposals 'without fainting or blustering'.[17] However, this should not be mistaken as implying that the MOD was totally happy about military retreat. On 21 November, the Chiefs of Staff of the MOD had come to Chequers and presented their views to Wilson and the main Cabinet members concerning defence and foreign policies, claiming that Britain's 'first priority should be the maintenance of oversea commitments'.[18] Later, the Chiefs of Staff would also express their concerns about the repercussions of the withdrawal from the Persian Gulf and the acceleration of withdrawal from South East Asia, arguing that the withdrawal would inevitably entail 'compulsory redundancies' and that the 'morale and discipline' of the forces would be at risk.[19]

After testing the water with the military, on 15 December Jenkins had a private discussion with Wilson for one and a half hours, which was recorded only in the papers of the Prime Minister's Office and not those of the Treasury. Without much hassle, Wilson also agreed to the withdrawal idea.[20] Following this, the Treasury's target was the Foreign Office. Knowing that they would be in charge of rearranging the complicated states system of the Gulf if the withdrawal were to be decided, the Foreign Office was more hesitant than the Prime Minister or the Defence Secretary. Yet, by 23 December, they too had accepted that withdrawal was inevitable, even though they resisted the particular terms, such as when to withdraw and whether to make a public announcement.[21] Once the internal consensus was built, the focus of the debate shifted onto how to push the proposal through the Cabinet and check the stances of the external actors.

There was also some discussion of the Soviet threat. On 21 December, the Permanent Secretaries of the three departments gathered to discuss the matter at a sub-ministerial level. The Treasury regarded the Foreign Office's proposal as 'inadequate'.[22] Meanwhile, the Foreign Office forwarded a note, originally submitted to Brown, to the Treasury. It argued that British withdrawal would create a power vacuum that would allow the Russians to come in. It could cause 'a historic change in the balance of power in the area bounded by the Mediterranean, the Red Sea and the Indian Ocean including the Gulf'. The Russians were already 'consolidating their power position and using the inter-Arab cold war as the means of doing it'; withdrawal would enable the Russians to further penetrate into the region and damage Western oil interests.[23] This was an exaggerated account, and it did not convince the Treasury to reconsider its plan.[24]

Meanwhile, in the Persian Gulf, there was no noticeable move towards pushing Britain out of the Gulf. There had been rumours on and off since October that Sayed Nofal of the Arab League was planning to visit the Gulf, ostensibly for fund-raising for war victims but with a hidden agenda to increase the influence of Arab nationalism, as had been tried in 1965.[25] Yet this visit did not materialise and nor there was any significant uprising.

On 4 January 1968, talk of withdrawal from the Persian Gulf was brought into the Cabinet for the first time. At this meeting, the Cabinet took an explicit, although internal, decision that Britain would not stay in the Gulf for an indefinite period. Hereafter, the debate in the Cabinet shifted from withdrawal per se to the particular terms of withdrawal, specifically about when to withdraw and whether to make a public announcement. The Cabinet also decided to consult various foreign governments in order to test the water before reaching the final verdict.[26] In short, between 14 December and the Cabinet meeting on 4 January, the Treasury by and large smoothly convinced the relevant departments about the necessity of the withdrawal, if not necessarily the terms thereof. Also to be noted is the split within the Cabinet. Crossman observed Wilson departing from the 'right-wing junta', which now only consisted of Brown, Healey and Stewart. They were defending the 'status barrier', which 'is as difficult to break through as the sound barrier: it splits your ears and it's terribly painful when it happens'.[27]

The day after the Cabinet meeting, Foreign Office officials started negotiations with the states of the Persian Gulf, which included Iran, Saudi Arabia and the recently independent Kuwait, together with the littoral Protected States such as Bahrain, Abu Dhabi, Dubai and Qatar.[28] Several days later, the government also consulted the US.[29] With the exception of Iran and Saudi Arabia, most of these foreign governments responded to the British plan with outrage. However, in the end, on 16 January, Wilson announced in the House of Commons that Britain had to 'come to terms' with its 'rôle in the world' and would withdraw from the Persian Gulf by the end of 1971.[30] Thus, it seems, at least on the surface, that the reactions from the foreign governments were not the main factor pushing Britain out of the Gulf. So, why exactly did Britain decide to withdraw?

Zayid's secret payment offer

It is clear from the last section that Jenkins and the Treasury initiated the movement towards withdrawal. One may assume that the Treasury's proposal for withdrawal from the Gulf derived from economic necessity after devaluation. Yet the linkage between the two was in fact remote. To begin with, Treasury officials reported on 7 December that, 'as regards the year 1968/69, cuts in defence expenditure were not likely to show results too quickly'. In fact, even the full cost of maintaining the troops was only £12 million in foreign exchange costs, and £25 million in budgetary costs.[31] This was an insignificant figure compared to the cuts in social expenditure that were being discussed simultaneously and which in the end amounted to £606 million.[32]

Moreover, the rulers 'begged' for the continuation of British support after withdrawal, even offering to pay for the maintenance of the British forces in the region.[33] A report on the discussion with the Ruler of Abu Dhabi, Shaikh Zayid, symbolises the level of their desperation:

> In order to secure indefinite continuation of British military presence he was prepared to contribute financially to its cost *whether publicly or secretly and in any way required by Her Majesty's Government*.[34]

Such a payment was not necessarily unusual in the British Empire, but the fact that he offered to pay *secretly* exemplifies how desperate he was. Bahrain even proposed a practical plan to waive the annual payments for British military facilities, whose net cost was £350,000 a year.[35] Bahrain was relatively poor amongst the four, but also the most vulnerable to the Iranian threat. The financial contributions from other states were presumed to be in 'straight cash'. British officials understood that these offers were 'clearly a most significant new factor'.[36] The Ruler of Qatar, Ahmad bin Ali Al Thani, put the point most plainly in his account:

> If it was true that Britain's financial position was such that she could no longer support her military forces in [the] Gulf, he and other Gulf Rulers, especially Sheikh Zaid [Ruler of Abu Dhabi], would be pleased to pay, each one according to his own ability, to maintain them.[37]

Taking a different tack, the rulers also tried to convince the British by suggesting that they 'would remove their sterling funds from Britain'.[38] As demonstrated in the previous chapter, when formulating the withdrawal plan, the Treasury officials had thought that removing their sterling funds would be the only option which the Persian Gulf rulers could resort to for retaliation; at this juncture, the rulers threatened just that.

The rulers' efforts to oppose British withdrawal were based upon their 'long friendship' and 'deep affection' towards Britain.[39] Yet, apart from these feelings of affinity, they had more substantial fears. On the one hand, each had multiple concerns in their region. In particular, they were deeply wary about Iranian ambitions. Although the Shah said that 'he had had no wish to make the Gulf an Iranian *mare nostrum*', his regional counterparts were suspicious.[40] Of course, the most profoundly threatened was the Ruler of Bahrain, who had a longstanding dispute with the Iranian claim over his territory. He was in 'profound shock' when he found out that Britain was planning to leave.[41] He argued that the island's economic and political future depended on continuing security. With the heightening of the perceived Iranian threat, he approached the King of Saudi Arabia and the US for protection. The other rulers were also suspicious of Iran,[42] as well as being afraid of the Saudis and the Russians.[43] In addition, they lacked confidence in their own abilities to run their respective states.

On top of these direct approaches, there was even a Conservative MP reporting to Wilson that Kuwait was implicitly offering to contribute financially to the keeping of British troops in the Gulf. On 10 January at the Kuwaiti Embassy in London, Peter Tapsell, a Conservative MP, met the minister-plenipotentiary who was the chargé d'affaires and temporarily in charge of their mission in the absence of the ambassador. The Kuwaiti chargé d'affaires implied that his country was ready to consider financial contributions to the maintenance of the British troops. The next day, the Conservative MP reported the case to Wilson, and the Prime Minister's Office sent a copy of the letter to the Foreign Office. The Foreign Office replied that the 'offers had clearly important implications'. Almost undoubtedly, the officials would have reported the news to Wilson and Brown, but the offer was not taken into account elsewhere during the Labour government's decision-making process.[44]

Had the withdrawal plan been mainly driven by economic concerns, such financial offers would have significantly affected the government's decision-making. However, in reality the financial offers from the Persian Gulf were not taken into consideration by the Treasury or in the Cabinet, and they were formerly declined on 30 January.[45] One may argue that the Labour government refused the offer because they did not want to create the image of British soldiers being turned into paid mercenaries. However, as Kelly points out, this was unlikely to have been the case considering that Britain had accepted contributions from 'the Western German government towards the cost of supporting the British Army of the Rhine' and 'the government of Hong Kong towards the maintenance of the colony's British garrison'.[46]

The actual reasons explaining why the Treasury initiated the discussion on the withdrawal from the Gulf were more political than economic, and Foreign Office officials thought that Jenkins was deciding on 'political grounds'.[47] Indeed, during a conversation with Treasury officials, Jenkins opined that some 'very big cuts' in defence expenditure would be needed as 'a necessary condition for making civil cuts on a substantial scale'.[48] Also, at a meeting with the Foreign Office, the MOD and the Commonwealth Office, he stated:

> It was already clear that there was practically no prospect of obtaining any further reduction in defence expenditure in 1968/69 and only a relatively small reduction in 1969/70 ... The immediate objective of the announcement would be to solve the problem of securing support for the required cuts in public expenditure as part of the economic measures which our situation necessitated.[49]

In the aftermath of devaluation, the Labour government was about to push through a set of highly contentious social policies. It was planning to restore prescription charges for the National Health Service (NHS), which had been abolished by the first Wilson government. It was considering postponing for four years the raising of the school-leaving age to 16. It was also putting restrictions on road expenditure and abandoning the promise made in the 1966 election campaign to construct 500,000 new houses.[50] The *raison d'être* of the Labour government was at stake. In the interest of persuading the relevant departments, Parliament and the public that these cuts were necessary, the Treasury believed that defence cuts would show that the government was trying its best on all fronts. Even though withdrawal from the Gulf would yield only a minor saving, what mattered was what it looked like rather than what it actually was.

JENKINS AND THE WITHDRAWAL DECISION, 1968

In geographical terms, the Persian Gulf was on the same side of the Suez Canal as Singapore and Malaysia. Since the withdrawal from those two countries had already been declared in July 1967, a further announcement of withdrawal, this time from the Gulf, would increase the impression that the government was making its best efforts to save money, even going so far as to withdraw from 'East of Suez'. In order to maximise the utility of this presentational device, the Treasury wanted to decide on a firm and early deadline for the withdrawal and make a public announcement of it. In short, the need to justify civil cuts precipitated the withdrawal decision. J.B. Kelly, F. Gregory Gause and John Darwin have briefly put forward this point, and the declassified official documents substantiate their argument.[51]

On 18 December 1967, Wilson told the House of Commons that 'the review will cover defence and overseas expenditure as well as home civil expenditure. The review as a whole is being related to what is essential in expenditure here at home, and to what is appropriate at a time when we have been, and are, reassessing Britain's role in the world. This must involve overseas policy.'[52] According to Darwin, these words also hinted that 'devaluation and the expenditure review had coincided with the climax of the negotiation of Britain's second abortive attempt to enter the EEC [European Economic Community]', which was announced on 20 December.[53]

Despite its far-reaching implications in international relations, the discussion leading to the explicit *decision* for withdrawal was primarily driven by domestic political motivations. The Labour government thus virtually ignored the opposition coming from the relevant Arab governments. Goronwy Roberts, who had assured the local rulers only a few months back that Britain would stay in the Gulf for the foreseeable future, was now asked to convey a message going back on his own words. The Foreign Office Arabists in London expected Roberts to resign, and they were 'stunned' when they knew that Roberts was to carry out 'double-dealing'.[54] The situation was even worse for the British diplomats stationed in the Gulf. They had to face the rulers, who were by no means going to be pleased. Anthony Parsons, a political agent in Bahrain, even came close to resigning; despairingly he noted, 'How could I now confront this volte-face and retain my honour?'[55]

Indeed, the reaction of the rulers was not far from that the Arabists had anticipated. As we have seen above in relation to the report in the Foreign Office, some of the states in the Persian Gulf not only offered to pay for the maintenance of the British troops but even desperately 'begged' for British support after the withdrawal.[56] They were deeply concerned by the potential opposition that could follow the British departure and threaten their supremacy, which had been heavily dependent upon British protection. According to what they had learned from observing the British departure from Aden, setting a rigid and tight deadline for withdrawal would only increase the risk of instability, and more so declaring that withdrawal officially.

The US also strenuously opposed Britain's withdrawal. Having enough trouble of its own trying to extract itself from Vietnam, the last thing that the US wanted to hear was that its principal ally was retreating from its imperial commitment. The US could not afford to fill the void left by British withdrawal and did not want to see any power vacuum in the context of the ongoing Cold War. When the British Foreign Secretary, George Brown, saw Dean Rusk, the US Secretary of State, on 11 January, Rusk said to him, 'For God's sake be Britain [sic]'.[57] However, this outright US opposition did not have any significant effect on British decision-making. In fact, Rusk was right when he sensed an 'acrid aroma of the *fait accompli*'.[58] Britain was not actually consulting the US on whether to withdraw; it was merely informing the US of a decision already taken. Also, in regard to the anti-imperial pressure on Britain in the UN, Balfour-Paul argues that by this point anti-colonial hostility towards Britain had been ebbing away, as Britain was no longer regarded as a serious imperial power. The findings here support this point.[59] The paradox was that Britain was making an important foreign policy decision not for reasons of international relations but in order to justify domestic social expenditure cuts.

Withdrawal from 'East of Suez'

The factors laid out in the last section help us to understand why the Labour government decided to withdraw from the Persian Gulf. However, they do not sufficiently account for the precise deadline for withdrawal, which was, ultimately, set for the end of 1971. Gause claims that bureaucratic politics played only a negligible role in the decision-making process concerning British withdrawal from the Gulf. The following section will explore the boundaries of this argument by looking into the processes through which the withdrawal timeframe was determined.

Between December 1967 and January 1968, there was a split within the Labour government over the deadline for withdrawal. On the one hand, the Treasury demanded that withdrawal be completed by 31 March 1971. In addition to the reasons illustrated above, Jenkins called for an even earlier withdrawal, for electoral reasons. He thought that the 'end of 1971' was 'over the dam' because it would be after the next general election.[60] At least in theory, if the Conservatives won the election they could reverse the decision. On the other hand, the Foreign Office and the MOD sought to buy time, and clamoured for the withdrawal to be delayed until 1972.

The Treasury was concerned only with the presentational effect of the decision, but the Foreign Office and the MOD were to be responsible for its execution. Completing the military withdrawal, and making the necessary diplomatic arrangements for the Protected States to achieve full independence in four years, would seem like a 'miracle' if this were to be achieved peacefully.[61] On top of the internal division, the Singaporean premier, Lee Kuan Yew, came to London to see Wilson and pressed for a delayed departure from South East Asia. Like the rulers of the Gulf, he was utilising British protection to maintain stability at home.[62]

The debate between the two camps continued until 15 January, the day before the withdrawal announcement. In the end, Wilson proposed a compromise. Although a decision in favour of delaying the final withdrawal until March 1972 would lack the presentational and catalytic advantages of adopting the date of a year earlier, this would not be so if Britain were to decide that the withdrawal should be completed by the end of the calendar year 1971. A decision along these lines would, moreover, have the advantage of demonstrating that there had been sufficient substance in the British undertaking to take account of the views of the foreign governments. At last, it was decided that withdrawal from the Gulf should be completed by the end of 1971 and, furthermore, that the withdrawal from South East Asia should be accelerated to coincide with this date. This was a political compromise between the Treasury, on the one hand, and the MOD, the Foreign Office and the foreign governments, on the other.[63] To this extent, one could argue that bureaucratic politics played some role in the decision-making process.

The next day, on 16 January 1968, Wilson announced in the House of Commons that Britain would withdraw all its troops from the Persian Gulf, as well as from Malaysia and Singapore, by the end of 1971. Simultaneously he also announced the social cuts as well as the reduction in military expenditure.[64] In the Cabinet and amongst the Conservative Party, there was a feeling that the announcement was 'a fig-leaf that had made the end of Empire acceptable at home and less revealing abroad'. It was thought that 'the form that the decision had taken symbolized the unpredictably rapid decline of British influence and inflicted an unnecessary loss of great-power dignity'.[65]

A week after the announcement, Secretary of Defence Denis Healey made the following comment on the BBC:

Well I don't very much like the idea of being a sort of white slaver for the Arab sheikhs. I think we must decide as far as the Gulf's concerned, what it's [sic] in our own British interests in the long run to do consistent with our commitments. And I think it would be a very great mistake if we allowed ourselves to become mercenaries for people who would like to have a few British troops around.[66]

The statement summarised the nature of Britain's withdrawal decision, perhaps too honestly. Healey had to apologise shortly thereafter.[67]

In reference to the 'pattern or puzzle' problem set out by John Darwin, can we comprehend the transformation from empire to a post-imperial international system as a planned and logical process, or was it an accumulation of a baffling series of retractions resulting in unintended consequences?[68] Whereas much of the literature on the end of the British Empire focuses on historical moments when Britain was, to a certain extent, pushed out by local oppositional groups, in the case of the Gulf the local rulers actually asked Britain to stay. Switching between different geographical conceptions helps us understand both the 'puzzles' and the 'patterns' of the end of empire. Dockrill argues that in terms of the nature and scope of Britain's withdrawal from 'East of Suez', the January 1968 decision 'made little difference to that which had been taken in July' 1967.[69] This was indeed a case for the reduction of military capabilities and the retreat from South East Asia; but these two chapters have together shown that, as far as the departure from the Persian Gulf was concerned, the decision-making process was more contingent, contested and fraught. In July, the government had only vaguely agreed upon the necessity to eventually withdraw from the Gulf, and it took another half a year for the government to convert the broad consensus into a practical and explicit decision.

The findings of the current chapter can be summarised as follows. After the devaluation of the pound in November 1967, the Treasury under Roy Jenkins needed to introduce large-scale cuts in social expenditure. Withdrawal from the Persian Gulf was chosen as one of the means to justify the Labour government's reversal of its social policies. The precise deadline for the withdrawal was set for the end of 1971, a timescale decided only the day before the announcement, as a compromise between the Treasury, which called for an earlier withdrawal, and the Foreign Office and MOD, which insisted on a later date. Despite the decision's far-reaching consequences in terms of international relations, the outright opposition from the US and the Persian Gulf States was almost ignored. Yet the government obscured the contingent and domestic nature of the policy by presenting it as an 'East of Suez' decision, emphasising that it was an economic policy intended to yield cuts in expenditure.

The day after the announcement, Jenkins addressed the House of Commons:

> We are no longer, and have not been for some time, a super Power [sic]. It does not make sense for us to go on trying to play a rôle [sic] beyond our economic strength ... the idea that these changes have been brought forward only as part of a package to appease some of my hon. Friends [sic] is absolute nonsense.[70]

The actual financial savings from the military withdrawal were, however, negligible compared to the social cuts that were announced simultaneously. Even Healey admitted that the 'foreign exchange cost of stationing troops abroad is offset by all sorts of gains we get in consequence but the objective of the decisions we took last week was not to reduce foreign exchange expenditure'.[71]

Drawing on extensive and original archival research, these two chapters have advanced the literature by examining the decision-making process of the British withdrawal from the Gulf, which has mostly been misleadingly aggregated as part of the 'East of Suez' decision.

At this point, it is useful to make a brief comparison with the other half of the 'East of Suez' decision, namely the decision to withdraw from Malaysia and Singapore. Phuong Pham, who has written a sophisticated account on the subject, emphasises the 'symbolism' of withdrawal. But there is a significant difference with the withdrawal from the Gulf. According to Pham, the 'strategic fundamentals' of the withdrawal from Malaysia and Singapore had been decided by July 1967, and once the withdrawal had been effectively decided the 'politics and presentation' of withdrawal came to the fore in the following months.[72] In the case of the Gulf, however, the 'politics of presentation' preceded the withdrawal decision and was precisely the key precipitator, if not the sole driver, behind it. These points reinforce the view that uncritical recycling of the policy-makers' rhetoric opens the door to an over-rationalisation of past events, particularly when that rhetoric is stained with an *ex post facto* justification of their decisions.

Notes

1 William Luce, 'Britain in the Persian Gulf: Mistaken Timing over Aden', *The Round Table*, 227 (1967), 282–283.
2 TNA, FCO 8/31, Roberts to Brown, 17 November 1967, compiled in Ashton and Louis, *East of Suez and the Commonwealth*, part I, pp. 118–120.
3 Patrick Gordon Walker, *The Cabinet*, revised edition (London: Collins, 1972), p. 122.
4 Roy Jenkins, *A Life at the Centre* (London: Macmillan, 1991); John Campbell, *Roy*

Jenkins: A Biography (London: Weidenfeld & Nicolson, 1983); Andrew Adonis and Keith Thomas (eds), *Roy Jenkins: A Retrospective* (Oxford: Oxford University Press, 2004).

5   Jenkins, *A Life at the Centre*, p. 225.
6   Jeffrey Pickering 'Politics and "Black Tuesday": Shifting Power in the Cabinet and the Decision to Withdraw from East of Suez, November 1967–January 1968', *Twentieth Century British History*, 13:2 (2002), 155–157.
7   Darwin, 'Britain's Withdrawal from East of Suez', p. 155.
8   Jenkins, *A Life at the Centre*, p. 223.
9   TNA, Treasury (T) 225/3066, a note on a conversation between Jenkins and Armstrong, 7 December 1967.
10 TNA, T 225/3066, Wright to Mackay, 6 December 1967.
11 Dick Taverne, 'Chancellor of the Exchequer', in Andrew Adonis and Keith Thomas (eds), *Roy Jenkins: A Retrospective*, p. 88; Jenkins, *A Life at the Centre*, p. 220.
12 TNA, T 225/3066, a note on a conversation between Jenkins and Armstrong, 7 December 1967.
13 TNA, T 225/3066, a note by Baldwin, 7 December 1967.
14 TNA, T 225/3066, Bancroft to Nicholas, 11 December 1967.
15 TNA, T 225/3066, Bancroft to Baldwin, 12 December 1967.
16 TNA, T 225/3066, a note by Baldwin, 15 December 1967.
17 Jenkins, *A Life at the Centre*, pp. 222–223.
18 TNA, CAB 130/213, MISC 17/1, 'Defence Policy', 21 November 1964, compiled in Ashton and Louis, *East of Suez and the Commonwealth*, pp. 4–7.
19 TNA, PREM 13/1999, Broadbent to Palliser, 11 January 1968; PREM 13/1999, record of meeting, 13 January 1968.
20 Jenkins, *A Life at the Centre*, pp. 223–224.
21 TNA, T 225/3066, Baldwin to Jenkins, 19 December 1967; FCO 46/43, Maitland to Brown, 19 December 1967; FCO 46/43, Gore-Booth to Brown, 19 December 1967; T 225/3066, Baldwin to Maitland, 20 December 1967; PREM 13/1999, minutes of meeting, 20 December 1967; T 225/3066, Bancroft to Baldwin, 21 December 1967; FCO 46/43, Garner to Brown, 22 December 1967; T 225/3066, Bancroft to Butler, 23 December 1967; FCO 46/43, record of meeting, 23 December, 1967.
22 TNA, T 225/3066, Bancroft to Baldwin, 21 December 1967.
23 TNA, T 225/3066, Gore-Booth to Brown. The document itself was not dated. Considering the sequence of the file, it was most likely forwarded to the Treasury on 21 December 1967.
24 On 23 December, the Treasury was still insisting on withdrawing from the Persian Gulf in 1968 or 1969. TNA, T 225/3066, Bancroft to Butler, 23 December 1967.
25 TNA, FCO 8/7, Bahrain to Foreign Office, 25 October 1967; Foreign Office to Bahrain, 26 October 1967; Bahrain to Foreign Office, telegram no. 697, 27 October 1967; FO to Cairo, 30 October 1967; Bahrain to Foreign Office, telegram no. 699, 27 October 1967; Weir to Brenchley, 31 October 1967; Graham to Balfour-Paul, 2 November 1967; Roberts to Balfour-Paul, 14 November 1967.
26 On Christmas Day, the Chancellor spoke to the Prime Minister and decided to hold an ad hoc inner Cabinet meeting. In this Cabinet meeting, two days later, the Foreign Office and the MOD agreed that the consultation with foreign governments would take place after 4 January. From the archival evidence it is not clear exactly which countries they meant to consult, whether the US, the Persian Gulf States, or others. But the answer was given on 4 January, the first Cabinet meeting in 1968. See TNA, PREM 13/1999, Note for the Record, Palliser, 27 December 1967; T 225/3066, Note for the Record, Baldwin, 27 December 1967; T 225/3066, 'Defence Expenditure', 27 December 1967; CAB 128/43 CC(68), '1st Conclusions', 4 January 1968.
27 Crossman, *The Diaries of a Cabinet Minister: Volume Two*, p. 639.
28 TNA, PREM 13/2209, Foreign Office to Tehran, 5 January 1968; Tehran to Foreign Office, 7 January 1968; Tehran to Foreign Office, 8 January 1968; Tehran to Foreign Office, telegram no. 87, 10 January 1968; Dubai to Foreign Office, 9 January 1968;

JENKINS AND THE WITHDRAWAL DECISION, 1968

Bahrain to Foreign Office, 9 January 1968; Kuwait to Foreign Office, telegram nos 14, 15, 9 January 1968; Bahrain to Foreign Office, telegram nos 29, 34, 37, 10 January 1968; Abu Dhabi to Foreign Office, 10 January 1968; FCO 46/43, Roberts to Brown, 11 January 1968.

29 TNA, PREM 13/1999, Johnson to Wilson, 11 January 1968; Washington to Foreign Office, 14 January 1968.
30 *Parliamentary Debates (Commons)*, vol. 756, col. 1580.
31 TNA, CAB 148/80, 'Long-term Policy in the Persian Gulf', a note by the Secretaries, Defence and Oversea Policy (Official) Committee, 7 June 1967; *Parliamentary Debates (Commons)*, vol. 754, Written Answers, col. 134; *Parliamentary Debates (Commons)*, vol. 735, Written Answers, col. 289.
32 *Parliamentary Debates (Commons)*, vol. 756, cols 1619–1620.
33 TNA, FCO 46/43, Roberts to Brown, 11 January 1968.
34 TNA, PREM 13/2209, Abu Dhabi to Foreign Office, 10 January 1968. Emphasis added.
35 TNA, PREM 13/2209, Bahrain to Foreign Office, telegram no. 37, 10 January 1968.
36 TNA, PREM 13/2209, Bahrain to Foreign Office, 9 January 1968.
37 TNA, PREM 13/2209, Bahrain to Foreign Office, telegram no. 34, 10 January 1968.
38 TNA, PREM 13/2209, Bahrain to Foreign Office, telegram no. 34, 10 January 1968.
39 TNA, PREM 13/2209, Abu Dhabi to Foreign Office, 10 January 1968.
40 TNA, PREM 13/2209, Tehran to Foreign Office, 8 January 1968.
41 TNA, PREM 13/2209, Dubai to Foreign Office, 9 January 1968.
42 TNA, FCO 46/43, Roberts to Brown, 11 January 1968.
43 TNA, PREM 13/2209, Bahrain to Foreign Office, telegram no. 34, 10 January 1968.
44 TNA, PREM 13/2209, Tapsell to Wilson, 11 January 1968; Palliser to Morphet, 11 January 1968; Maitland to Palliser, 11 January 1968.
45 TNA, FCO 8/1004, 'Annual Review of Bahrain', 4 January 1969.
46 J.B. Kelly, *Arabia, the Gulf and the West* (London: Weidenfeld & Nicolson, 1980), p. 51.
47 TNA, FCO 46/43, Gore-Booth to Brown, 3 January 1967.
48 TNA, T 225/3066, Jenkins and Armstrong, 7 December 1967.
49 TNA, T 225/3066, Baldwin to Maitland, 20 December 1967.
50 *Parliamentary Debates (Commons)*, vol. 756, cols 1577–1620.
51 Kelly, *Arabia, the Gulf and the West*, pp. 48–49; F. Gregory Gause III, 'British and American Policies in the Persian Gulf, 1968–1973', *Review of International Studies*, 11 (1985), 123; Darwin, 'Britain's Withdrawal from East of Suez', pp. 153–156.
52 *Parliamentary Debates (Commons)*, vol. 756, col. 923.
53 Darwin, 'Britain's Withdrawal from East of Suez', p. 36.
54 Alec Sterling, 'The End of British Protection, 1969–71', in Paul Tempest (ed.), *Envoys to the Arab World: MECAS Memoirs, 1944–2009*, vol. II, pp. 123–124.
55 Parsons, *They Say the Lion*, p. 134.
56 TNA, FCO 46/43, Roberts to Brown, 11 January 1968.
57 TNA, FCO 46/43, extract from a record of a meeting between Brown and Rusk, 11 January 1968.
58 TNA, FCO 46/43, extract from a record of a meeting between Brown and Rusk, 11 January 1968.
59 Balfour-Paul, *The End of Empire in the Middle East*, p. 152.
60 TNA, FCO 46/43, Gore-Booth to Brown, 3 January 1967.
61 TNA, FCO 46/43, a note on a conversation between Gore-Booth and Wilson, 10 January 1968.
62 Kuan Yew Lee, *From Third World to First: The Singapore Story, 1965–2000* (Singapore: Singapore Press Holding, 2000), pp. 56–62; Dockrill, *Britain's Retreat from East of Suez*, pp. 205, 220.
63 TNA, CAB 128/43 CC(68), '7th Conclusions', 15 January 1968; Barbara Castle, *The Castle Diaries, 1964–1970* (London: Weidenfeld & Nicolson, 1984), p. 357.
64 *Parliamentary Debates (Commons)*, vol. 756, cols 1577–1620. According to

Richard Crossman, the cancellation of 50 F-111 aircraft, which the government had decided to purchase in March 1967 at nearly £2.7 million each, saved some £400 million. Crossman, *The Diaries of a Cabinet Minister: Volume Two*, p. 278.

65 Darwin, 'Britain's Withdrawal from East of Suez', p. 156.
66 TNA, PREM 13/2218, extract from BBC TV *Panorama*, 22 January 1968.
67 He asked the British missions to deliver his apologies to Bahrain, Kuwait, Qatar, Abu Dhabi and Dubai. He wished 'to express regret for any offence he may unintentionally have given by the way in which he phrased certain remarks' during the programme. He also wished to express his appreciation for the 'spirit' in which the rulers of the Protected States made the offer to contribute financially to the maintenance of the British troops. See TNA, PREM 13/2218, Foreign Office to Bahrain, 23 January 1968.
68 John Darwin, 'British Decolonization since 1945: A Pattern or a Puzzle?', *Journal of Imperial and Commonwealth History*, 12:2 (1984), pp. 187–209.
69 Dockrill, *Britain's Retreat from East of Suez*, p. 204.
70 *Parliamentary Debates (Commons)*, vol. 756, col. 1797.
71 Healey's interview on television quoted by Sir Alec Douglas-Home on 24 January 1968 in the Commons. *Parliamentary Debates (Commons)*, vol. 757, col. 424.
72 Phuong Pham, *Ending 'East of Suez': The British Decision to Withdraw from Malaysia and Singapore, 1964–1968* (Oxford: Oxford University Press, 2010) p. 196.

CHAPTER FOUR

Dilemmas and delay, 1968–70

When Harold Wilson announced in January 1968 that Britain intended to leave the Persian Gulf by the end of 1971, the obvious implication was that the Protected States, even though they had adamantly opposed Britain's plan, would now have to become fully independent sovereign states within four years. Removal of British protection would require the rulers to be more accountable to their own societies, while at the same time they would have to defend themselves from potential threats from inside or outside their countries. In turn, regional powers like Iran and Saudi Arabia might capitalise upon this opportunity to increase their influence, while the US would need to ensure that independence would not become another source of turmoil, as was happening in Vietnam. In this contested theatre, the British needed to implement the withdrawal peacefully and gracefully, so that a mechanism could be left that would enable them to exercise some degree of influence after the retreat. The aim of the next two chapters is to examine the whole process of the implementation of the British withdrawal, which in the end accompanied the emergence of the UAE, Bahrain and Qatar in international society. Even though the British retreat was decided for short-term domestic reasons, it was going to have a more profound – even 'epochal' – effect than most could not foresee at the time.

Whereas various actors had different stakes in this process, they also shared a set of unresolved questions: In what form would the nine Protected States be independent, if at all? Would they be organised under one political body, or two, or three, or even nine separate units? What would happen to the territories that were disputed amongst the Protected States and with their neighbours?

Underlying these questions was a profound problem. The British imperial presence and the modality thereof had shaped the way in which these questions were put forward, but they were not the most essential cause of tension. The problem arose from the difference between the local tradition of diplomacy and social organisation on the one hand and the modern form of international relations based upon the notion of sovereignty on the other. In order to obtain full membership of the existing international society, the Protected States would have to subscribe to the idea of sovereignty. And mutual recognition and territorial exclusivity lay at its heart. Who would represent whom? Where and how would they demarcate their people, lands and water? These questions, which have disturbed almost all peoples in the world at some point in modern times, now loomed upon the southern shore of the Persian Gulf. At the same time, given the longstanding influence of the British Empire and the fact that the whole process was initiated from London in the face of opposition from the Gulf rulers, Britain's role in this crucial moment of transition was of paramount importance.

Taken from this perspective, the next two chapters not only possess a significant resonance for the histories of the Gulf and the British Empire but are illuminating for all those who are interested in the history of international relations. In particular, this chapter will look into the initial developments following Wilson's announcement in January 1968 and examine how effectively the local and external actors responded to the new situation. The first section will set out the main actors and their initial relationship, while the second will analyse how the local actors came together in order to take their own initiative towards unity, as well as the problems they encountered in doing so. The third section will analyse how Britain took a mediating role in overcoming one of the main problems by the spring of 1970, as well as looking at what remained to be solved.

Challenges and rivalries

Following Harold Wilson's announcement in January 1968 that British troops would leave the Persian Gulf by the end of 1971, four groups of actors had to quickly respond to the new situation. In the following paragraphs, the basic picture of the Gulf will be illustrated, with some statistical and geographical figures mentioned in a British report issued in 1967.[1]

The first and foremost group was the nine Protected States who had hitherto enjoyed British protection. Bahrain in the west, a collection of more than 30 islands totalling some 200 square miles, was not the richest but was certainly the most populous, with more than 180,000 inhabitants.[2] Internally, there was a tension between the Shi'ah and Sunni populations, and also opposition from the expanding educated class towards the ruling family. However, if one could assume some degree of social cohesion, the biggest problem was the Iranian claim that historically Bahrain had been its 14th province. It is not the purpose of this book to assess the historical grounds and legal basis of the Iranian case; the key point here is that, to Bahrain, Britain and many others involved, Iranian occupation of Bahrain after the British withdrawal seemed to be something more than a hypothetical prospect. This had to be avoided at all costs, and for the next few years it remained Bahrain's top priority.

East of Bahrain was Qatar, a peninsula of 8,000 square miles with a population of approximately 60,000. Unlike Bahrain, it did not face an imminent external threat to its survival, but nonetheless it had to decide in what form it was going to be independent. While maintaining close ties with Saudi Arabia in the south, its utmost concern was how to balance the power of Abu Dhabi in the east.

Abu Dhabi had a population of 30,000 and land of 26,000 square miles.[3] Minuscule compared to the regional powers, such as Iran and Saudi Arabia, it was nonetheless the largest, richest and most powerful among all the nine Protected States. Further east, there was Dubai, another potential contender for the leadership of the Protected States after the coming independence. Not as wealthy or as large as Abu Dhabi, it was still larger than the other states in the north, including Sharjah, 'Ajman, Umm al-Qaiwain, Ra's al-Khaimah, as well as Fujairah in the east. In these northern Trucial States combined with Dubai, a total of 80,000 people were living on a land of 6,000 square miles.

Surrounding these nine Protected States were their regional neighbours. This was the second group of actors, the most powerful being Iran to the north and Saudi Arabia to the south. Both had their own territorial and political ambitions. As mentioned earlier, Iran claimed that Bahrain had historically been its 14th province, and that it should therefore be amalgamated under its territory. It also disputed control of some other islands in the Persian Gulf. It was claiming sovereignty over the Greater and Lesser Tunbs against Ra's al-Khaimah, and it was disputing rights over the lands of Sirri and Abu Musa against Sharjah. Iran also had considerable influence in some of the Protected States, such as Dubai and 'Ajman. Saudi Arabia, on the other hand, had strong ties with Qatar but also had border disputes with Abu Dhabi and Oman over Buraimi, as well as some other territories. To Britain, it seemed that military action by Saudi Arabia over the Buraimi Oasis dispute was a possibility that could not be entirely ruled out, but the Saudis were less vocal in their claims compared to the Iranians' stance on Bahrain.[4]

In contrast to Iran and Saudi Arabia, the smaller neighbours largely stood aloof.[5] After the withdrawal announcement, Kuwait exchanged letters in May 1968 'providing for the severance on the 13 May 1971, after 72 years, of all formal political links between Kuwait and Britain', and thereafter limited itself to playing a mediating role between the Protected States, Iran, Saudi Arabia and Britain.[6] As far as Iraq was concerned, Britain suspected that it was encouraging migration from Basra to Dubai on dhows and, as 'usual, the Sultanate of Muscat and Oman was the odd state out'.[7]

The third group of actors involved comprised the extra-regional players, including the Americans, French, Japanese and the oil companies. The most powerful was obviously the US. Yet, after the Johnson administration failed in January 1968 to convince Wilson to reconsider the withdrawal plan, it did not show much willingness to take any further proactive role. Dean Rusk, the Secretary of State, opined in an internal telegram that the US government was 'naturally concerned re implications [of] British troop withdrawal from Gulf by end 1971'. Nevertheless, while they would be studying the question in detail in the coming months, they had 'no plan, general or specific, as to future'.[8] It is indeed true that Washington was not ready to devise an ambitious policy in this region. As mentioned earlier, in some documents they even betrayed a misunderstanding of the constitutional status of the Protected States and referred to them as 'protectorates'.[9] Knowing that their knowledge and capabilities in the region were limited, they wanted to keep away from complications. Washington had 'no interest' in 'replacing' the British or forming pacts and believed that the Protected States should themselves provide for the security of the Gulf after Britain's departure.[10]

The US hesitance to engage with the Gulf was a reflection of the perceived limited threat of the Soviets, the influence of which on the Protected States was believed to be indirect during this period.[11] For example, a study of Soviet foreign policy conducted by the Joint Intelligence Committee and issued at the end of December 1969 did not look into the Persian Gulf, and a similar study written three years later opined, 'We do not think that the Soviet Union could attain sufficient influence in the Middle East oil-producing countries to induce them to do substantial harm to their own interests by depriving western countries, their natural market, of significant quantities of oil.'[12] Soviet propaganda welcomed the British withdrawal and hinted at the USSR's intention to increase its influence in the Gulf, but it was not accompanied by significant political action. In May 1968, Soviet squadrons arrived in the Gulf for the first time and subsequently called at Iranian and Iraqi ports, but did not visit any place on the southern shore.[13] Indeed, as Roland Popp argues, America was 'subcontracting security' to Britain during this era.[14] A telegram from Dean Rusk remarked that they 'believe there will be continuing need for constructive and mutually helpful association' between Britain and the Protected States and they should keep 'encouraging British authorities to continue [to] do what they can [to] play meaningful role in Gulf'.[15]

Further to this point, the US was more concerned about its existing relationship with Iran and Saudi Arabia. Shortly after the British announcement, President Johnson told the Shah of Iran that 'The United States ... does not envisage that we would wish ... to replace the British military presence.'[16] Instead of agitating the ambitious Shah by taking over the British role, the US hoped to maintain the stability of the region by facilitating cooperation between Iran and Saudi Arabia. By May 1968, the National Security Council had come to the following conclusion:

> Hopefully, the Shah and Faisal will let their common interest overcome minor territorial disputes, but it won't be easy. Our policy is to stay out of the middle but to keep reminding both of them that the best way to keep Nasser and the Russians out is to work together.[17]

The following month it was suggested that this idea should be conveyed to the Shah when Johnson met him. Thus, it was proposed that Johnson should maintain that the US did *'not desire to replace the British in the Persian Gulf' but strongly hoped* that the Gulf States, especially Iran and Saudi Arabia, could 'cooperate to ensure the Gulf's security and progress'.[18]

In comparison to the government in Washington, American oil companies were more willing to take the opportunity to increase their presence in the region. Even prior to Wilson's announcement, some of them were actively drilling for oil.[19] In particular, the Bahrain Petroleum Company had something 'much closer than an ordinary business relationship' with Shaikh Isa, the Ruler of Bahrain, and its senior executives asked on multiple occasions for Washington to become more involved in protecting Bahrain from Iran.[20] The influence of American oil companies was also felt by the British. For example, when British officers took an RAF helicopter to Umm al-Qaiwain in order to celebrate the end of Ramadan, they found that the best landing site had been 'already taken by a smaller but newer and faster helicopter' belonging to Occidental Petroleum.[21]

The other Western countries had similar attitudes, although they were somewhat less pronounced. Avoiding direct involvement in the political machinations, Japan was developing its economic ties with the Protected States. By the end of 1969, 'the British share of imports remained stuck at 16% while the Japanese grew to 19%' in Dubai and the other five northern Protected States.[22] France was also slowly attempting to develop ties with Bahrain.[23] By this stage, the presence of external actors was already such that a British officer murmured that 'Ambassadors from all over the Middle East, messengers from the Shah in special jet aircraft [and] bankers with black leather briefcases' were all descending, not to mention the oil companies, 'tough and plushy by turns, exhaling the irresistible perfume of money'.[24]

The fourth actor to play a considerable role in the coming years was, of course, Britain. It discussed its interests in the Gulf in an internal document that stated that the country's policy in respect to the region had to take into account both short- and long-term interests. The former was thought to be 'to maintain stability and to retain the military and over-flying facilities necessary for an orderly withdrawal.' In regard to the latter, it was believed that, 'After 1971, the economic and strategic importance of the area will remain so great that it behoves us to promote conditions which will be the most promising for future stability after our withdrawal.'[25]

In essence then, Britain's goal was to leave in peace and to retain some informal influence after its retreat. Up to this point, Britain had enjoyed exclusive control over the formal external affairs of the Protected States and was also responsible for providing them with military protection. As a matter of principle, Britain did not interfere in internal matters – but it was nonetheless present at each important juncture of local life.

A British diplomat in Qatar recalls supervising the offloading of currencies between the Protected States, during which he was looking forward to a special treat that involved 'ample ice-cold refreshment on the bridge, accompanied at the Captain's table by a very hot curry followed by a choice of suet pudding, spotted dick, treacle tart or apple pie and custard'.[26] However, not everything was so sweet. By this time Britain's relationship with the local rulers had become more complicated than how retired diplomats tend to recall it.

The following are quotes from an internal report issued by the Political Agent in Dubai discussing the characters of some of the rulers. To his eyes, the Ruler of Fujairah appeared to be 'an incurable liar, bird-brained and chicken-hearted, stepping with dignity across the litter of rubbish outside his still unfinished palace on the shores of the Indian Ocean as the helicopter comes to a stop'. The Ruler of Umm al-Qaiwain was a 'sad wreck of a man who in his youth could break a coin in two between the fingers of one hand, unfailingly courteous even after I had to block his oil operations and deprive him of a million dollars'. The Ruler of 'Ajman was 'a figure of antique virtues and antique villainy too, roosting like a nomad in his ridiculous wedding cake of a palace and accepting with lecherous pride the curtsies of the ladies at the first mixed dinner party ever held in this tiny State'. Similarly, the Ruler of Sharjah was 'sustaining his soap-bubble economy with a bland smile, a faint hope of oil and not much else'.[27] Such a condescending and negative account of the local rulers is clearly not the best source on which to base an assessment of their actual personalities, but the tone of the report certainly serves to illustrate that by that time Britain was struggling to maintain a good working relationship with them.

Hence, the Protected States, regional actors, extra-regional powers and Britain had to work out how Britain was going to withdraw and what kind of order would follow. However, the relationship between them was hardly straightforward. In a nutshell, there were three contenders for the leadership of the Protected States. The first was Abu Dhabi, the largest of all the nine but with a longstanding dispute with Saudi Arabia. The second was Qatar, which enjoyed good ties with Saudi Arabia but had border disputes with Abu Dhabi and Bahrain. The third was Dubai, which had an established connection with Iran. So, at the three corners of the power triangle, were Abu Dhabi, the Qatar–Saudi alliance and the Dubai–Iranian alliance. The smaller states to the north of Dubai stood somewhere within this triangle and the three groups competed for their allegiance. A British diplomat once observed that, 'when Shaikh Zaid [of Abu Dhabi] heard that Shaikh Mohammed [of Fujairah] was thinking of going to Shiraz [in Iran] for medical treatment he quickly bought him a return ticket to Bombay instead'.[28]

In the meantime, Bahrain was preoccupied with its own survival. Another British officer recalls the time when he was driving on Muharraq Island in the north of Bahrain. Suddenly he 'found the road choked by a shouting mob of people from the town, carrying sticks and stones and running towards the airport'. One of them shouted, 'The Persians, the Persians, they have landed.' Baffled for a moment, eventually he 'saw a civil aircraft on the apron with a large tail fin emblazoned with a lion'. It was British Caledonian, a British private airline that existed between 1970 and 1988, but the lion was also the national symbol of Iran.[29] Just as some Bahrainis were fearful enough of Iran to mistake a British civil aircraft for the Iranian air force, suspicion was widespread and almost ubiquitous in the international affairs of the region. No one could easily foresee a realistic and peaceful solution that would provide an overarching platform for the full independence of the Protected States.

On the surface, it seemed that the two major obstacles were the policies of Abu Dhabi's Shaikh Zayid and the Iranian Shah's attitude towards Bahrain.[30] It appeared to Britain that their ambitions were disturbing the regional order. However, the fundamental source of contention lay much deeper than the everyday type of power struggle that is routinely observed in international relations. It derived from the need for the region to fully enter international society, which was characterised by the exclusive and mutual recognition of sovereign states delineated by strictly defined boundaries.

In practice, this had two major implications. Firstly, the idea of the exclusivity of sovereignty required that the Protected States could no longer stay in the grey zone where they were able to enjoy internal autonomy while outsourcing their military and external affairs to Britain. But in what form would they be fully independent states? Would they unite under one sovereign state, or divide into two, three or even nine separate states? The form of the independence of the Protected States was one of the most contested issues during the implementation of the British withdrawal.

Secondly, owing to the norm of territoriality that was an indispensable component of sovereignty, the Protected States now had to resolve the boundary disputes amongst themselves and with their neighbours. The most obvious one was the question of Bahrain, which Iran considered to be part of its territory. Iran also claimed sovereignty over some smaller islands, including Abu Musa, Sirri, and the Greater and Lesser Tunbs. Regarding the Tunbs, the dispute had not only been with Iran but also between Sharjah and Ra's al-Khaimah.[31] In addition to some other minor disputes, there was the still simmering conflict between Abu Dhabi, Oman and Saudi Arabia over the Buraimi Oasis. However, the problem of territoriality went far beyond a mere collection of boundary disputes. The local tradition of social organisation was such that, when a British diplomat drew a tentative map of the southern shore of the Gulf, there were a number of enclaves and areas with overlapping jurisdiction. Within the territory of Sharjah there was a piece of land claimed by 'Ajman; between Ra's al-Khaimah and Oman there were territories of 'Ajman and Dubai, and even some areas where 'Ajman and Oman jointly held control.[32] As we have seen, the map was so perplexing that it had been nicknamed 'Mr. Walker's jigsaw puzzle'.[33] There seemed, therefore, to be a fundamental tension between the idea of territorial exclusivity and the way in which the local societies, where migration was an integral part of life, had been organised.

In addition to these epochal changes, the Gulf was also going through an incremental transformation, essentially a competition for control and power. This manifested itself in three areas. First was the question of the power of central government. If some or all of the nine states were to be united into one, would they allow the central government to wield a large degree of influence over the constituent bodies, or would they only form a looser organ that would allow the member states to retain a somewhat larger degree of autonomy? The second point of contention was the leadership and power balance. Would the constituent members of the coming union be given equal constitutional rights? Or, if not, which would hold a larger degree of power? For example, according to one British officer, the policy of Shaikh Zayid, the Ruler of Abu Dhabi, 'based upon his rapidly mounting revenue from oil', was the building up of 'his own defence force on what appeared to his neighbours (and to ourselves) to be an unnecessarily large scale'. He was distributing money 'to the poorer Rulers and others outside his own territory in such a way as to arouse fears that he had expansionist aims and was insincere in his support of the U.A.E. as a union of equals'.[34] Related to this point, the third issue to be solved was the location of the capital, as clearly the state where the capital would be located would be in an advantageous position in the coming union.

To make matters even more complicated, there were issues pertaining to the region's communication networks. The telephone system linking the Protected States was still rudimentary during this period, which could be part of the reason why British diplomats had to take the role of mediator, facilitating negotiations between the regional actors.[35] Of course, this does not mean that the Protected States were totally isolated from modern means of transport and communication. Previously, the British Political Agent in Dubai could only speak to the Ruler of Sharjah after an 'hour's bumpy ride in a Land Rover across the mud flats' but, at this point, Sharjah was 'on an asphalt road and international telephone circuit'.[36] Dubai and Ra's al-Khaimah were also connected by a road that, as the Political Agent praised, 'now carries me there in 90 minutes on tarmac so smooth that it allows me to write out my telegrams on the way back'.[37] Nonetheless, on the whole the difficulty in transportation and communication contributed to the complexity surrounding the negotiations.

In short, the Protected States were going through fundamental transformations on multiple levels, yet they were deeply divided owing to the rivalries and fear among themselves as well as regarding external actors. The prospect of the regional actors finding a peaceful solution out of the chaos seemed remote. The brother of the Ruler of Bahrain had aptly depicted the lack of cooperation amongst themselves as an equation: '$0 + 0 + 0 + 0 = 0$'.[38] With these multiple sources of conflict and contention, the British policy was, 'We do not owe them more than a decent exit from the world stage, but I think we do owe even the least of them that much.'[39] The Gulf was deeply divided, and it appeared that Britain, having officially committed itself to leaving the region within four years, was one of the few who perceived a pressing need to bridge the gap.

Dubai agreement and procrastination

To Britain's surprise, however, a local initiative towards unity emerged before long. Shaikh Zayid of Abu Dhabi, the Ruler of the most powerful Protected State, met his rival Shaikh Rashid bin Sa'id Al Maktum of Dubai. He was once described by a British diplomat as 'the merchant prince with the happy knack of picking the right horses, briskly disposing of business with a wave of his little pipe in one hand and a lighted match in the other, reading my thoughts far in advance and barking out his instant decisions'.[40] Less than one week after Wilson's speech on the retreat, on 22 January 1968, the two began negotiations.[41] After another meeting on 18 February, they agreed:

> To form a Union comprising the two countries and having one flag and which shall be responsible for dealing with the following matters:
> a) Foreign Affairs.
> b) Defence and internal security in case of necessity.
> c) Services, such as health and education.
> d) Citizenship and migration.[42]

It is important to note that the rapprochement between the two old rivals, Abu Dhabi and Dubai, came from their own initiative. One American official noted that on 20 February the British Residency in Bahrain knew 'only what it heard on the radio' and that they were 'very surprised' at the announcement.[43] They thought that the fact that 'such arrangement could be made without British knowledge indicates how far and fast their influence has slipped' since Wilson's announcement a month earlier.[44] The next week, between 25 and 27 February, the rulers of all nine Protected States convened in Dubai in order to discuss the possibility of a union.[45] Qatar submitted a draft agreement, and they reached an official agreement on the final day:[46]

> (1) There shall be established a Union of the Arab Emirates of the Arabian Gulf of the contracting Emirates and it shall be called the 'Union of the Arab Emirates'.
> (2) The objectives of this Union shall be the strengthening of the ties between the member Emirates and co-operation between them in all fields, co-ordination of measures for their progress and development, respect of each for the independence and sovereignty [*siyadah*] of others, unification of their foreign policy and foreign representation and organisation of collective defence to preserve

DILEMMAS AND DELAY, 1968-70

their peace and security, and general consideration of their common interests to guarantee the achievement of their hopes and the aspirations of the whole great Arab nation.[47]

The term translated in the above quote as 'Union' was *ittihadah* in the original Arabic text.[48] Some translated it as 'confederation', and the documents of the US government tended to refer to what is translated here as the 'Union of the Arab Emirates of the Arabian Gulf' as the Federation of Arab Emirates. Such a difference in translation could result in various interpretations of the objective and nature of what was to become known as the Dubai Agreement.[49] For the purposes of this argument, the paragraphs below will follow the precedents in the British records.

In any case, this agreement caught Britain by surprise. The Assistant Under-Secretary of State of the Foreign Office confirmed to the US Embassy in London that Britain had played no role in the process. He was annoyed that Qatar had proposed a draft that became the basis of the agreement, calling it an act of either a 'political idiot or a wrecker'.[50] To Britain, the proclamation of the Dubai Agreement seemed 'entirely spontaneous'.[51] Given the many contentious issues involved, Britain thought the 'Rulers of the Protected States bestirred themselves surprisingly quickly to find a way forward'.[52] In the end, it accepted the local initiative, but it hoped that 'it remains their plan, not ours'.[53] Britain's official position was that it regarded it as important that the Protected States 'should work towards the closest practicable cooperation between themselves, but the precise forms of their cooperation or association are for them to work out for themselves' and that the agreement itself did 'not affect the existing relationships of the individual states concerned with Her Majesty's Government'.[54] Thus, the Dubai Agreement was a genuinely regional initiative to prepare for the British departure, and at this point there was some hope that it would be followed through.

Building up momentum, the rulers and their advisers soon started drafting a federal constitution and prepared a plan for a union defence force. Yet other issues such as 'the choice of capital and president, nature of representative institutions and control of security forces' remained up in the air at the end of 1968.[55] The rulers convened six Supreme Council meetings and their advisers had held numerous other meetings by the end of 1969; these have been documented in detail in the existing literature, but they produced little in the way of a substantive outcome.[56]

Initially, Britain was hoping to see an overarching political structure covering the nine Protected States as the 'best guarantee' of stability in the region, and Saudi Arabia was also pushing for the 'Union of Nine', which was thought to satisfactorily restrict the power of Abu Dhabi. However, by October 1969 the prospects for the single-state solution had become bleak. On the eve of the Deputy Rulers' meeting scheduled for 24 October, the Qataris – who were said to be 'determined to wreck' the meeting owing to their rivalry with Bahrain – 'rejected a plea from Shaikh Zaid that they should reach an accommodation with the Bahrainis', Britain observed in a later report. Thus the Deputy Rulers' meeting collapsed, and the Supreme Council meeting of the Rulers that was originally planned to follow was cancelled.[57]

One of the most telling accounts of this slow progress was that of Professor Charles Rousseau at the Paris Law Faculty, who was engaged by the government of Qatar to comment on the legal nature of the Dubai Agreement as an external expert. Rousseau considered that, 'subjecting the implementation of the Agreement to the approval of a study committee or an advisory committee, would be a disregard of the spirit of the Agreement, and an addition of a new provision thereto'. Moreover, 'such subjecting would in reality be considered a breach of the provisions of the Agreement, which would only have the effect of delaying and jeopardizing its implementation'.[58]

If Rousseau represented the international legal tradition, the slow progress of the rulers implies how the local customs of decision-making and social organisation were different from the norms of international society. In relative terms, Qatar was eager to take the lead and issued its provisional constitution as a tentative basis for the coming union.[59] However, on the whole, the Protected States' entry to international society did not look very promising.[60] One British diplomat's assessment of the Dubai Agreement was that it had 'offered the nine Rulers a satisfactory general objective in a perplexing period, discouraged fissiparous initiatives and muffled local rivalries during the last three years'. Yet it would 'have to develop into something much more robust than this' if it were 'to bear the weight of [the] responsibilities' that Britain proposed to unload upon it.[61] Thus, despite the euphoria that greeted the regional initiative, by this point it had become clear that the rulers had failed to achieve what they had committed so swiftly to do.

In order to understand the slow progress after the Dubai Agreement, it is useful to take a closer look at the local situation. During this period, they were experiencing rapid economic growth. In 1969 and 1970 in Dubai alone, at least three cinemas opened.[62] In 1969, 'Ajman also saw the opening of its first cinema, even though the Ruler allegedly said, 'I don't care much for the cinema: I prefer fighting.'[63] However, behind various development projects, the widening 'gap between rich and poor' was becoming an underlying source of social instability. In Dubai, for example, the Political Agent sometimes detected 'certain tension in the air amongst ordinary people discussing money'. He observed:

> The economy of Dubai and indeed of the Trucial States, rests on the lean backs of illegal immigrant labourers from Iran, Pakistan and Baluchistan who shovel sand or carry bags of cement for 7 riyals a day, or thirteen shillings ... At the other extreme are several hundreds of businessmen, many of them quite young, most of them from Europe or the Levant, who think nothing of spending £20 or £30 on a night's entertainment. And somewhere in between are the ever-growing numbers of Northern Arabs, particularly Palestinians, who ... crowd the Rulers' *majlises* [consultative assemblies], occupy many of the most powerful administrative posts and generally strike a discordant note.[64]

On top of the increasing economic discrepancy, the influx of migration was also disturbing the existing order favourable to Britain and the rulers. The Political Agent in Dubai did not hide his resentment of the transformation of the local societies:

> I am not being sarcastic when I say that some of my best friends are Palestinians, but I hate to see the northern Arabs invading the Trucial States with their bigotry, nepotism and greed. Even their white shirts and glottal stops offend my eyes and ears after two years amongst the long robes and deep-throated *quafs* of the Gulf ... Some [of the immigrants] bring talents that are needed here ... but others are natural material for NDFLOAG [the National Democratic Front for the Liberation of Oman and the Arabian Gulf] and its polysyllabic sister organisations. Indeed these may well be their agents.[65]

Alongside the military activities of NDFLOAG in northern Oman, there was also a military uprising in the province of Dhufar. Both revolts targeted the Sultanate of Muscat and Oman, which the British supported, but violence was spilling over beyond Oman and into various parts of the Arabian Peninsula. In Bahrain, nine cars were burnt in March 1968 and five in April, before the suspects were caught in May.[66] In Ra's al-Khaimah, the Ruler was in a longstanding dispute with some groups of the Shihuh, Za'ab and Khawatir tribes, and the Trucial Oman Scouts – a local military force under British command – were watching closely in order to prevent a flare-up.[67] On 17 July 1970, there was an assassination attempt on the Ruler of Sharjah, when a bomb exploded under his chair. According to the understanding of the British, the bomb had been passed on from 'a notorious political gangster' to a 'disgruntled policeman', who had carried it into the *majlis* of Sharjah. In less than a week, the Trucial States security forces arrested twelve NDFLOAG suspects (six of them in Abu Dhabi). By this point it was clear that there were 'organisations working systematically for the overthrow of the existing Governments, certainly with outside assistance'.[68]

It was very clear then that a significant portion of the population was influenced by Arab nationalism and not totally happy about Britain or the existing rulers. It was reported that 'Arab subversion' was starting to make an appearance in the form of 'leaflets, secret meetings, anonymous threatening letters, arms caches and a daily bundle of ominous reports from the Special Branches'. Many of these activities originated outside the Trucial States, and even outside the Gulf.[69]

As usual, the rulers could not aggressively oppose nor openly accept messages influenced by Arab nationalism. This situation also coloured their relationship with the Arab League. Anthony Parsons, the Political Resident, recalled a 'comic episode' when Sayed Nofal of the League paid a surprise visit to Bahrain in March 1968. The Ruler, Isa, coincidentally came across Nofal when the aircraft bearing him landed in Bahrain. Isa, 'suddenly realising that his presence together with a large assembly of notables would appear to Nofal to constitute either a welcoming party or a demonstration in favour of the Arab League, turned on his heel and withdrew hastily, much to the astonishment of those present'.[70]

Meanwhile, the Sultan of Oman was deposed in a coup. Some of the rulers of the Protected States entertained the idea of including the new Oman in the coming union, and Shaikh Zayid of Abu Dhabi paid a visit to Muscat on 9 August. However, on 20 October the new Prime Minister of Oman declared that it would not join the union, although he also stated that it might be prepared to form an association at a later date.[71] Thus, although Britain was not dragged into a civil war such as had happened in Oman, the social instability in the Protected States was increasing. At one point, Britain even considered establishing a new interrogation centre.[72]

Depending on how one judges the legality and legitimacy of these violent acts, they could be called 'insurgencies', 'riots' or 'resistance movements'. It is outside the scope of this chapter to discuss the terminology or to make a moral judgement on these activities, but it is clear that the legitimacy of both the British presence and the rulers was being challenged in an increasingly overt manner. It seemed to Britain that the aim of the opposition was to 'first get rid of the British, then get rid of the Shaikhs'.[73] In turn, Britain and the rulers were perceived to be collaborating with each other.

Acutely aware of these pressures from their own societies, the rulers were forced to distance themselves from the British by taking their own initiative towards independence. It was in this context that the Dubai Agreement was reached, but, as we have seen, from the beginning they were inhibited by rivalries between themselves. For example, the Ruler of Bahrain 'had little faith in the Union but his advisers and people, the latter seeing the Union as a means of popular participation in Government, were more optimistic'.[74] Social pressure was not enough to resolve the rivalries and mutual suspicions amongst the rulers. Some accused Bahrain and Abu Dhabi of not taking immediate steps towards arranging the practicalities for the formation of the union, while praising the Qataris for taking the lead.[75] It is debatable who exactly was frustrating the regional initiative, but it is inarguable that the rivalries amongst the rulers of the Protected States were preventing them from cooperating effectively.

Being unable to do more than assert the need for local unity, the rulers started to put the blame on Britain. To the British, they appeared to be turning a blind eye towards 'their own inability to agree among themselves or to sacrifice except *force majeure* any part of the sovereignty each tries so jealously to guard'.[76] As a British diplomat observed, 'there was just no steam in the boiler'. The dilemma, in a nutshell, was that 'We cannot protect them much longer, and at the moment they are taking no serious steps to protect themselves.' In December 1970 a British officer lamented, 'Now the hunting season is almost upon us, when the richer rulers disappear for weeks at a time under the disapproving scowls of the remainder, who of course would go too if only they could afford it.'[77] British diplomats were in a 'chicken-and-egg situation'; they could not force the nine-state solution upon the parties, but they also knew 'If our decisions depend on clear Arab decisions, we shall never make any,' even noting that 'the whole thing is an illusion'.[78] In the world outside the norm of self-determination was gaining much popularity, but the negotiations in the Gulf exposed its classic dilemma. For 'self-determination' to work, a coherent 'self' would need to be formed. Yet that process would most likely entail some considerable political sacrifice.

The slow, desultory and largely informal manner of negotiating substantial political matters appeared to Britain a sign of inefficiency and incompetence. But most likely the rulers were following their own political traditions. Not only did the Protected States need to transform their polities into something acceptable to the existing international society, the situation was asking them to change their customs of decision-making, the way in which they were going to transform their polities.

In response to this situation, they also started to prepare for more autonomous administration. For example, three young members of the local elite, at least one of whom was only 21 years old and freshly graduated from Baghdad University, were appointed in the Palace Office in Abu Dhabi. Britain now had to go through them for certain issues instead of directly talking to the Ruler. The Political Agent in Abu Dhabi murmured, 'The situation is one we will have to live with and make the best of, but the conclusion seems incontestable that during the period between now and military withdrawal there will be a gradual erosion of the overt link with the Ruler, upon which we have placed so much reliance.' By this point, Britain was so concerned about its decline of influence, it would 'watch out for any evidence there may be that these young graduates have been contaminated by Ba'athist policies'.[79]

Thus, Britain was frustrated that the Protected States were not moving fast enough or in the direction it wanted, but it could not afford to pass the buck back to the rulers. It had already officially committed itself to leave the region. The problem was how to bring the rulers together:

> If we want to achieve a smooth and orderly withdrawal of our forces in 1971 and to sustain thereafter our very important economic and political interests in the Protected States as well as to secure our requirements in the Sultanate, we must do our utmost to show that we have not turned our back on the Gulf States and that we are acting as best we can in their interests.[80]

The Foreign Office officials back in London thought that in general terms they should take 'the solution most favourable to our interests, however poor its hope of success'. The question, though, was how exactly to proceed.[81] Advertising Britain's cooperation with the rulers would only infringe their legitimacy in the eyes of their societies. Like the rulers, who were caught between the need to assuage social frustration and the competition between themselves, Britain was also suffering something of a dilemma:

> The more we engage in discussion of the substance of the points at issue, the more difficult it becomes to cling to the position that it is for the Rulers to decide their own political future ... we have not the time, the resources or freedom of action that we had once but did not think to use.[82]

On the other hand, a constant theme in the memoirs of the British diplomats was their friendship with the local rulers and people. However, at this point Britain was becoming increasingly out of touch with a significant element of the local society, particularly recent immigrants who 'percolate nimbly through the loopholes in our visa system' or come in on dhows from Basra, 'disembarking at night on the beach just outside the city limits of Dubai'.[83] Perplexed by the situation, a British diplomat reported, 'H.M.G. [Her Majesty's Government], for their part, hoped at first that what appeared as the more practical aim of a federal Union confined to the Trucial States or failing that, of a loose confederation of all nine, would be the solution chosen'.[84] Yet the regional rivalries made both options impracticable for the time being. It was unclear where things were going.

During this period, on the one hand, the rulers had managed to reach the Dubai Agreement very quickly. Thereafter, due to social pressure, they were forced to at least pretend that they were trying to achieve what they had put forward. Yet, on the other hand, they were inhibited by rivalries between themselves from cementing a practical plan for the formation of a union of nine states as declared in the agreement. They passed the blame to Britain, but there was little that Britain could do either. There was still a long way to go before an orderly British withdrawal and a peaceful entrance of the Protected States into international society could be ensured. There was no direction, and the clock was ticking.

Bahraini settlement and British mediation

While some rulers of the Protected States could afford to keep blaming the British for the stalling of negotiations after the Dubai Agreement, for Bahrain the problem was more pressing. As expected, Iran was claiming that Bahrain had historically been its 14th province. In contrast to many other Protected States, for which the key issue was the form and modality of independence, for Bahrain the problem was an existential one. Unsurprisingly, when Wilson publicised the withdrawal decision in January 1968, the news was received with shock on the island:

> the announcement was greeted in all quarters with unqualified dismay, not so much because of the economic consequences ... but because no-one could see how, within the short space of three years, the multitude of explosive and intractable problems of the Gulf ... could be settled in such a way as to give Bahrain even a sporting chance of survival in stability and peace.[85]

In fear of the Iranian threat, Shaikh Isa, the Ruler of Bahrain, sought support from the Americans. Shaikh Isa was living in a 'small and unpretentious palace at Rifa'a'.[86] To one British diplomat's eyes, he was 'utterly lacking in solemnity and the glint of humour never left his eyes'.[87] He sat in open council (*majlis*) three times a day, seven days a week, allowing people to consult him on various matters.[88]

'They're finished', he lamented about Britain in despair, and asked for the Americans to intervene.[89] However, Washington was hesitant. Its position was that, 'We did not seek to judge the 30–40 territorial disputes around the world.'[90] In addition to the threat from Iran, the Soviets were also showing some interest in Bahrain. In March 1968, Moscow Radio commemorated Bahrain's student demonstration that had taken place in 1965.[91] Also, the Russians approached Shaikh Isa via Baghdad at least twice, asking for permission for a group of 12 men to visit Bahrain. Shaikh Isa was 'scared to death' and did not even acknowledge their request.[92]

With its own survival at stake, Bahrain had to walk a tightrope after the Dubai Agreement. Anthony Parsons, the Political Agent in Bahrain between 1965 and 1969, recalls that the younger generations and students opted for the Union of Nine, whereas the majority of people there, and Parsons himself, thought that Bahrain should go it alone, given its geographical and historical distance from the rest of the Protected States and its already somewhat proven ability to stand on its own two feet. Shaikh Isa had already established a small indigenous defence force in late 1967 in preparation for the eventual British departure.[93] Hence, even though Bahrain signed the Dubai Agreement in February 1968, because 'of Iranian opposition, Bahrain did not become the centre of Union activities and Bahraini enthusiasm waned'. In fact, from the beginning of 1968, Shaikh Isa seemed to be aiming for a mini-statehood, although he was aware of the need to pretend to accept the idea of the union.[94] Consequently, at the end of 1969, Britain observed that the Ruler of Bahrain was prepared to go along with the idea of the union, or at least pretend to, for another year.[95]

On the other side of the Gulf, the Shah of Iran was also playing his cards carefully. Roham Alvandi notes that, even though the Shah was loudly proclaiming his claims to Bahrain, he did so largely in order to assuage domestic opposition rather than as a prelude to the annexation.[96] This interpretation of the Shah's motives is supported by archival sources. The Amir of Kuwait observed that 'the Shah was seeking a way out with dignity'.[97] The British conveyed a similar view to that of the Americans: 'the Shah regards Bahrain as a "jewel in his crown", and he doesn't feel he can give it up unless a way is found to save Iranian face'.[98] Winston Churchill, the grandson, wrote in *The Times* that Iran's claim over Bahrain appeared to be rhetorical.[99] Rather than the land of Bahrain per se, the Shah seemed interested in finding a face-saving formula that would allow him to downplay Iran's claim over Bahrain without undermining his legitimacy in his own country.

In order to achieve this goal, the Shah initially insisted that the will of the Bahraini people must be shown by a plebiscite endorsed by the

DILEMMAS AND DELAY, 1968-70

UN, but Shaikh Isa of Bahrain 'flatly refused' for fear of 'dangerous communal disturbances'.[100] Bahrain was divided between the Sunni and Shi'ah populations, and it was feared that 'a plebiscite would undoubtedly cause serious intercommunal disturbances in Bahrain' by exacerbating the underlying tensions within the country.[101] Faced with these difficulties, Shaikh Isa kept up a complaint during this period to the British Political Resident, declaring: 'How I wish you weren't going.'[102]

Thus, both the Shah and Shaikh Isa implicitly shared the idea that both sides wanted a peaceful way out, but the pressures from their own societies prevented them from directly coordinating publicly. While the two main parties were caught in a dilemma between realpolitik diplomatic calculations and domestic politics, British Foreign Office officials were also divided between those who favoured the Arab and those who favoured the Iranian position. On the one hand, an Arabist, feeling a 'gnawing in my belly' about the situation, remarked that 'the *quids* do not match the *quos*', were the Shah to gain any of the islands.[103] On the other hand, the British ambassador to Tehran later lamented the antagonistic attitude of his fellow Arabists in the Foreign Office, proudly noting that he had managed to make some progress in ensuring that Iranian claims were not just brushed aside.[104] Indeed, later, when the formation of the UAE became clearer, the Tehran Embassy sent a series of telegrams protesting that the draft immigration arrangements were 'clearly less favourable to Iran than to Saudi Arabia for example'.[105]

Out of this dilemma, Britain seems to have proposed 'a package deal' at some point in the early stages, whereby Iran would abandon its claims to Bahrain and acknowledge the coming UAE in return for taking over Sirri and the two Tunbs but not Abu Musa. However, no direct written evidence of this deal has been found, and in any case the Shah did not accept it.[106]

Meanwhile, Kuwait was working closely with Bahrain, arranging special meetings between Iran and Bahrain and even at one point considering the option of forming a union with the latter. Helped by the mediation of Kuwait and Britain, the Iranian Deputy Foreign Minister and Shaikh Khalifah of Bahrain eventually held meetings in Geneva on 25 September and 20 December 1968.[107] In March 1969, Britain told the US that 'the Iranians had hinted that the settlement of the Tunbs and Abu Musa was a prerequisite to the solution of Bahrain', and that they 'felt that, if a satisfactory solution to the Bahrain issue could be found, the Arabs would not be too upset if the Tunbs or, for that matter, Abu Musa went to Iran'. Nevertheless, Britain feared that, if the smaller islands were given to Iran without a Bahraini settlement, 'the Arabs could say that the whole thing was an Anglo-Iranian plot to substitute Iranian influence for British influence on the Arabian side of the Gulf'. In order to avoid an allegation of collusion, the UK wanted to 'get Bahrain out of the way first and then get the other islands question settled'. Hence, at this point it seemed that there was still a long way to go before a workable arrangement could be made.[108]

However, an internal Foreign Office document issued towards the end of 1969 stated: 'Given the burial of the Iranian claim to Bahrain, the remedy [for the survival of the Protected States] in the last resort is in Arab hands.'[109] This line indicates that Iran had made some gesture to abandon its claim over Bahrain by this point, but from the sources it is not clear exactly how this happened. Another document issued about two months later, on 7 February 1970, suggests that Britain was aware that Iran was intending to take over the small islands in the Gulf. It stated that the 'solution of the Bahrain/Iran problem may continue to be delayed' and even after that Iran might not throw 'her weight behind the union of nine, either because she wants to get the little islands first or because she is not yet convinced that the nine suits her better than some other arrangement.[110] This is clearly predicated on the awareness that Iran was going to occupy the small islands at some point sooner or later.

The following month, on 25 March, the Foreign Office was appalled by an article in the *Daily Telegraph* about Bahrain and Iran that was so well informed that initially they feared leakage from an official source.[111] It is not known where the *Telegraph* got its information but what was clear was that Iran and Bahrain needed the help of external actors in order to reach a practicable settlement. Britain was suspected of having made a deal with Iran, effectively exchanging Bahrain for the smaller islands, and Kuwait had made an '[a]ctive and helpful contribution ... to the settlement of the problems of the Persian Gulf, especially the Iranian claim to Bahrain'.[112] However, it is not clear if there was such an explicit quid pro quo or if there was only an implicit agreement. It could also be the case that Britain had gradually come to terms with the Iranian takeover of the islands, but there is not sufficient evidence to fully support this line of argument either.

The final solution to the Bahraini problem was reached with the help of the UN. On 30 March 1970, U Thant, the UN Secretary-General, sent Vittorio Winspeare-Guicciardi, Director-General at Geneva, as a special envoy to Bahrain. W. Taylor Fain asserts that Winspeare-Guicciardi 'administered a plebiscite that found that the vast majority of Bahrainis wished to remain independent' of Iran, but his narrative is misleading.[113]

In fact, Winspeare-Guicciardi was sent to Bahrain on a fact-finding mission to assess the will of the people of Bahrain without holding a plebiscite, which Shaikh Isa, the Ruler of Bahrain, had consistently opposed out of fear of social disturbances. After consulting popular opinion, the mission concluded that the inhabitants wanted a fully independent Bahrain and, on 11 March, the UN Security Council endorsed the report.[114] By settling the dispute in this way Bahrain could secure its independence without disturbing its own population, and also the Shah could justify to his people that he had no choice but to give up Bahrain, even though it was believed that 'the conclusions reached by the good offices mission are the same that would have been reached by a plebiscite'.[115] Later, when the Ruler of Bahrain visited Tehran, a group of students circulated a letter criticising the Shah for giving up the 14th province of Iran, but they did not seem to represent the majority view, at least in British eyes.[116] Later, the Bahraini settlement was remembered as 'a striking example' of how the UN can be used as an instrument to settle international disputes peacefully and legitimately.[117]

Meanwhile, in January 1969, Richard Nixon moved into the White House as the 37th President of the United States. Six months later, during a tour of Asia, he witnessed the return of Apollo 11 in the Pacific Ocean. After demonstrating US power to the world, Nixon held a press conference in Guam and spelt out his overall policy towards Asia. This later came to be known as the 'Nixon Doctrine', which is conventionally understood to have formed the basis of the so-called 'twin pillars' policy, nominating Iran and Saudi Arabia as US regional proxies.[118]

The Nixon administration's initial policy towards the Gulf is blurry. In an undated note to Nixon, Henry Kissinger remarked that the Gulf 'will become increasingly difficult to cope with over the next two years', and in early July 1969 Kissinger had asked under the name of Nixon for a study of US policy on the Gulf.[119] However, what came out of the Interdepartmental Group by the end of that year was a 'disaster' that was 'not worth reading'.[120] In September 1970, the British Foreign and Commonwealth Office observed that Nixon 'will be most reluctant to set up' an American 'presence' in the Indian Ocean and the Persian Gulf, irrespective of what the British themselves might do.[121] Like its predecessor then, the Nixon administration was not ready to play a proactive role in the Gulf at this stage.

On 2 February 1972, the Deputy Assistant Secretary of Defense for Near Eastern, African and South Asian Affairs stated to a subcommittee of the House of Representatives:

> British ... importance is considerable ... The United States has assumed none of the former British military role or functions and has no intention

of seeking or appearing to replace the British presence in the Gulf. We do not plan to make any security commitments or to develop any special military relationship with any of the newly independent states of the Gulf.[122]

In contrast to the euphoria that greeted the Dubai Agreement in February 1968, neither Iran nor the Protected States could find an agreeable arrangement on their own in regard to the Bahraini problem, and the US was largely out of the game. The solution to the Bahraini problem as reached in early 1970 was largely a product of external intervention by Britain, Kuwait and the UN. This removed the first obstacle concerning the formation of a union of the nine states, but the other questions remained up in the air. On the whole, even though local efforts towards the creation of the UAE had provided 'a general objective' for the nine Protected States, as a British diplomat noted, 'the Ruler of Dubai told a visitor in my hearing: "Frankly speaking the UAE has produced nothing", and frankly speaking he is right'.[123]

At one level, the delay in any real practical moves after the Dubai Agreement was a symptom of the tension between internal pressure and external rivalries. On the one hand, the rulers of the Protected States were forced by their own societies to work on the regional initiative towards forming a single union, but on the other hand their longstanding suspicion and rivalries inhibited them from engaging with each other. However, at a deeper level, they were also caught in an impasse between their desire to follow their own political and social tradition and the pressing need to internalise the norms of international society.

In order to understand this point, the conceptual framework put forward by John Gerard Ruggie is helpful. He points out the ontological and epistemological differences among 'incremental, conjunctural, and secular or epochal time frames' to be used in the study of international relations. Within this 'typology, the "normal politics" studied by much of the international relations field falls into the incremental category, the Cold War exemplifies the conjunctural, and the modern system of states the epochal time frames'.[124] In this sense, the Protected States were experiencing an 'epochal' transformation, where the rules defining the players of the game were about to change. They were competing not only for the outcome of a couple of rounds of the game of international affairs, or the details of the rules of the game, but the fundamental rule specifying who exactly was qualified to play the game – i.e. sovereignty, characterised by exclusive mutual recognition between states defined by geographically delineated territories. The act of admitting a new player to the game has a more profound and long-lasting effect than the outcome of one or two rounds of the game, because it has ramifications that affect all the rounds that follow. The delay therefore needs to be understood in such a context; at a fundamental level, the Protected States were struggling to internalise the norm of sovereignty and a new form of decision-making.

Nevertheless, during these three years, on the whole Britain remained the central actor in the international relations of the Gulf. Regional efforts such as the Dubai Agreement were proposed, but substantial moves such as Iran's abstention from its claims to Bahrain did not crystallise without British mediation. At the end of 1970, the Political Agent in Dubai remarked self-importantly that 'British influence remained as strong' as it had ever been. He continued, 'This is largely a matter of confidence, and of self-confidence on our part. The rulers have no idea what we are going to decide about the future of the Gulf, but so long as we do not appear worried they are not worried either.'[125] In truth, the rulers' confusion partly derived from the Conservatives having taken over from Labour in June 1970. The next chapter will start by examining the Conservatives' volte-face with regard to the Persian Gulf.

Notes

1 TNA, FCO 49/10, 'Long-term Policy in the Persian Gulf', report by the Defence Review Working Party, 28 September 1967, compiled in Ashton and Louis, *East of Suez and the Commonwealth*, pp. 403–419.
2 *Abu Dhabi News*, vol. 2, no. 57 (22 July 1971), p. 9, reported that the population had risen to 216,000, according to the Department of Finance and National Economy of Bahrain. Bahrainis comprised 82.5%, and the major expatriates were Indians and Pakistanis (15,000), Omanis (10,000) and Iranians (5,000).
3 According to *Abu Dhabi News*, vol. 1, no. 1 (7 May 1970), p. 4, Abu Dhabi's size was 80,000 square kilometres (note: kilometres) and its population 60,000.
4 TNA, PREM 13/3326, a letter to Peter J.S. Moon from the Foreign and Commonwealth Office, 28 May 1970.
5 TNA, FCO 8/927, 'Persian Gulf: Annual Review for 1968', from Crawford to Stewart, 14 January 1969.
6 TNA, FCO 8/1031, 'Kuwait: Annual Review for 1968', from Graham to Stewart, 4 January 1969.
7 TNA, FCO 8/927, 'Persian Gulf: Annual Review for 1968', from Crawford to Stewart, 14 January 1969; TNA, FCO 8/1510, 'Dubai and the Northern Trucial States: Annual Review for 1970', by Bullard, 10 December 1970.
8 Telegram from the Department of State to the Embassy in Saudi Arabia, 24 January 1968, compiled in *FRUS, 1964–1968*, vol. 21, doc. 124, pp. 260–261.
9 NARA, RG 263, Folder 27, Box 17, Entry 29, 'Soviet Strategy and Intentions in the Mediterranean Basin', 1 June 1967.
10 NARA, RG 59, Box 2418, POL 33, from Department of State to Tehran, 29 January 1968.
11 NARA, RG 263, Entry 29, Box 5, National Intelligence Estimate No. 11-6-70, 'Soviet Policies in the Middle East and Mediterranean Area', 5 March 1970.
12 Cabinet Office, JIC (Joint Intelligence Committee) (A)(69)41, 'Final Report by the Joint Intelligence Committee (A) on Soviet Foreign Policy', 15 December 1969, compiled in G.H. Bennett and K.A. Hamilton (eds), *Documents on British Policy*

BRITAIN AND THE FORMATION OF THE GULF STATES

Overseas, Series III, Volume I: Britain and the Soviet Union, 1968-72 (London: The Stationery Office, 1997), pp. 200-205; Cabinet Office, JIC(A)(72)34, 'Final Report by the Joint Intelligence Committee (A) on Soviet Threat', 14 September 1972, compiled in *ibid*, pp. 513-530.

13 TNA, FCO 8/927, 'Persian Gulf: Annual Review for 1968', from Crawford to Stewart, 14 January 1969.
14 Popp, 'Subcontracting Security'.
15 Telegram from the Department of State to the Embassy in Saudi Arabia, 24 January 1968, compiled in *FRUS, 1964-1968*, vol. 21, doc. 124.
16 NARA, RG 59, Central Foreign Policy Files, 1967-1979, Box 2418, POL 33, Johnson to Rostow, 31 January 1968.
17 'The Situation in the Persian Gulf', Foster to Rostow, 21 May 1968, compiled in *FRUS, 1964-1968*, vol. 22, doc. 285.
18 Rusk to Johnson, 7 June 1968, compiled in *FRUS, 1964-1968*, vol. 22, doc. 290.
19 NARA, RG 59, Central Foreign Policy Files, 1967-1979, Box 2418, POL 33, various telegrams, January-February 1967.
20 'Bahrain Situation; US-Bahrain Relations', memorandum of conversation, 23 October 1968, compiled in *FRUS, 1964-1968*, vol. 21, doc. 157, pp. 323-325. Also see 'Bahrain Situation; US-Bahrain Relations', memorandum of conversation, 25 January 1968, compiled in *FRUS, 1964-1968*, vol. 21, doc. 126, pp. 264-265.
21 TNA, FCO 8/1510, 'Dubai and the Northern Trucial States: Annual Review for 1970', by Bullard, 10 December 1970.
22 TNA, FCO 8/1509, 'Dubai and the Northern Trucial States Review of the Year 1969', Bullard to Crawford, 30 December 1970.
23 TNA, FCO 8/1360, 'Bahrain: Annual Review for 1969', from Stirling to Crawford, 28 December 1969.
24 TNA, FCO 8/1510, 'Dubai and the Northern Trucial States: Annual Review for 1970', by Bullard, 10 December 1970.
25 TNA, PREM 13/3326, 'Persian Gulf: Union of Arab Emirates', Guidance Department to various missions, 19 July 1968.
26 Tempest, 'Qatar: A Strong New Bridge, 1967-2007', p. 133.
27 TNA, FCO 8/1510, 'Dubai and the Northern Trucial States: Annual Review for 1970', by Bullard, 10 December 1970.
28 TNA, FCO 8/1509, 'Dubai and the Northern Trucial States Review of the Year 1969', Bullard to Crawford, 30 December 1970.
29 Parsons, *They Say the Lion*, p. 136.
30 TNA, FCO 8/927, 'Persian Gulf: Annual Review for 1968', from Crawford to Stewart, 14 January 1969.
31 BL, IRO, R/15/2/625, various documents, 1948/49.
32 The situation largely continued after the independence of the Protected States. See the endpapers of Heard-Bey, *From Trucial States to United Arab Emirates*.
33 TNA, FCO 8/1509, 'Dubai and the Northern Trucial States Review of the Year 1969', Bullard to Crawford, 30 December 1970.
34 TNA, FCO 8/927, 'Persian Gulf: Annual Review for 1968', from Crawford to Stewart, 14 January 1969.
35 Heard-Bey, *From Trucial States to United Arab Emirates*, p. 363.
36 TNA, FCO 8/1510, 'Dubai and the Northern Trucial States: Annual Review for 1970', by Bullard, 10 December 1970.
37 TNA, FCO 8/1509, 'Dubai and the Northern Trucial States Review of the Year 1969', Bullard to Crawford, 30 December 1970.
38 TNA, FCO 8/1004, 'Annual Review of Bahrain', by Sir Stewart Crawford, 4 January 1969.
39 TNA, FCO 8/1510, 'Dubai and the Northern Trucial States: Annual Review for 1970', by Bullard, 10 December 1970.
40 TNA, FCO 8/1510, 'Dubai and the Northern Trucial States: Annual Review for 1970', by Bullard, 10 December 1970.
41 Riyad Nahib al-Rayyis, *Watha'iq al-Khalij al-'Arabi, 1968-1971: Tamuhat al-*

DILEMMAS AND DELAY, 1968-70

Wahdah wa Humum al-Istiqlal (Arabian Gulf Documents, 1968–1971: Attempts at Federation and Independence) (London: Riad El Rayyes, 1987), p. 25.
42 Sir Geoffrey Arthur Collection, Middle East Centre Archive, St Antony's College, Oxford, 'Union of Arab Emirates. Resolutions, Decisions, Joint Communiqués and Documents', file 1 (January 1968–November 1970), agreement between Zayid and Rashid.
43 NARA, RG 59, Central Foreign Policy Files, 1967–1969, Box 2083, POL 19, Dahran to Washington, 21 February 1968.
44 NARA, RG 59, Central Foreign Policy Files, 1967–1969, Box 2083, POL 19, Dahran to Washington, 21 February 1968.
45 Al-Rayyis, *Watha'iq al-Khalij al-'Arabi*, pp. 25–26; TNA, PREM 13/3326, a Foreign Office letter to Palliser, 8 March 1968.
46 Sir Geoffrey Arthur Collection, 'Union of Arab Emirates. Resolutions, Decisions, Joint Communiqués and Documents', file 1 (January 1968–November 1970).
47 The full original Arabic text of the agreement can be found in al-Rayyis, *Watha'iq al-Khalij al- 'Arabi*, pp. 27–29. It is also enclosed in: NARA, RG 59, Central Foreign Policy Files, 1967–1969, Box 2083, POL 19, Kamel to Griffin, 20 April 1968. The English translation above relies on TNA, PREM 13/3326, the Foreign Office letter to Palliser, 8 March 1968, with minor changes by the author.
48 Al-Rayyis, *Watha'iq al-Khalij al-'Arabi*, p. 27.
49 Sir Geoffrey Arthur Collection, 'Union of Arab Emirates. Resolutions, Decisions, Joint Communiqués and Documents', file 1 (January 1968–November 1970, 'Legal Opinion', by Charles Rousseau, 22 June 1968.
50 NARA, RG 59, Central Foreign Policy Files, 1967–1969, Box 2083, POL 19, London to Washington, 29 February 1968.
51 NARA, RG 59, Central Foreign Policy Files, 1967–1969, Box 2083, POL 19, 'British Views on Persian Gulf Shaikhdoms', from Department of State to various missions, 18 April 1968.
52 TNA, FCO 8/927, 'Persian Gulf: Annual Review for 1968', from Crawford to Stewart, 14 January 1969.
53 TNA, PREM 13/3326, Bahrain to Foreign Office, 29 February 1968.
54 NARA, RG 59, Central Foreign Policy Files, 1967–1969, Box 2083, POL 19, 'British Views on Persian Gulf Shaikhdoms', from Department of State to various missions, 18 April 1968.
55 TNA, FCO 8/927, 'Persian Gulf: Annual Review for 1968', from Crawford to Stewart, 14 January 1969.
56 The details of the meeting have been recorded in various sources, including Sir Geoffrey Arthur Collection, 'Union of Arab Emirates. Resolutions, Decisions, Joint Communiqués and Documents', file 1 (January 1968–November 1970) and file 2 (October 1970–January 1971). For a solid narrative, see Heard-Bey, *From Trucial States to United Arab Emirates*, pp. 345–354; Smith, *Britain's Revival and Fall in the Gulf*, pp. 79–98.
57 TNA, FCO 8/1563, Wright to Douglas-Home, 'The Union of Arab Emirates, November 1969 to July 1971', 26 July 1971; Slater to Allen and Acland, 'Union of Arab Emirates', 5 August 1971.
58 Sir Geoffrey Arthur Collection, 'Union of Arab Emirates. Resolutions, Decisions, Joint Communiqués and Documents', file 1 (January 1968–November 1970), 'Legal Opinion', by Charles Rousseau, 22 June 1968.
59 Ahmad Zakarya al-Shalaq and Mustafa 'Aqil al-Khatib, *Qatar wa Ittihad al-Imarat al-'Arabiyah "al-Tis'" fi al-Khalij al-'Arabi, 1968–1971: Dirasah wa Watha'iq* (Qatar and the Union of the 'Nine' Arab Emirates in the Gulf, 1968–1971: A Study and Documents) (Doha: Dar-al-Thaqafah, 1991).
60 Sir Geoffrey Arthur Collection, 'Union of Arab Emirates. Resolutions, Decisions, Joint Communiqués and Documents', file 1 (January 1968–November 1970), 'The Provisional Constitution of Qatar', promulgated in Doha on 2 April 1970.
61 TNA, FCO 8/1510, 'Dubai and the Northern Trucial States: Annual Review for 1970', by Bullard, 10 December 1970.

62 TNA, FCO 8/1510, 'Dubai and the Northern Trucial States: Annual Review for 1970', by Bullard, 10 December 1970.
63 TNA, FCO 8/1509, 'Dubai and the Northern Trucial States Review of the Year 1969', Bullard to Crawford, 30 December 1970.
64 In the same report the number of the overall European and American community was estimated to be over 1,000, not counting children. TNA, FCO 8/1509, 'Dubai and the Northern Trucial States Review of the Year 1969', Bullard to Crawford, 30 December 1970.
65 TNA, FCO 8/1510, 'Dubai and the Northern Trucial States: Annual Review for 1970', by Bullard, 10 December 1970.
66 TNA, FCO 8/1004, 'Annual Review of Bahrain', by Sir Stewart Crawford, 4 January 1969.
67 TNA, War Office (WO) 337/18, 'A Talk with Sheikh Khalid bin Saqr', report by Ash, 4 March 1969; 'Ras al Khaimah Quarterly Round-up: Jan–Mar 1969', report by Ash, 31 March 1969; 'The Ruler of Ras el Khaima and the Shihuh', report by Ash, 14 May 1970. Also, see 'Dispute with Tribes', *Arab Report and Record* (1968, no. 22), p. 370.
68 TNA, FCO 8/1510, 'Dubai and the Northern Trucial States: Annual Review for 1970', by Bullard, 10 December 1970.
69 TNA, FCO 8/1510, 'Dubai and the Northern Trucial States: Annual Review for 1970', by Bullard, 10 December 1970.
70 TNA, FCO 8/7, Parsons to Crawford, 23 March 1968.
71 Heard-Bey, *From Trucial States to United Arab Emirates*, pp. 358–359.
72 TNA, FCO 8/1510, 'Dubai and the Northern Trucial States: Annual Review for 1970', by Bullard, 10 December 1970.
73 TNA, FCO 8/1510, 'Dubai and the Northern Trucial States: Annual Review for 1970', by Bullard, 10 December 1970.
74 TNA, FCO 8/1004, 'Annual Review of Bahrain', by Sir Stewart Crawford, 4 January 1969.
75 Sir Geoffrey Arthur Collection, 'Union of Arab Emirates. Resolutions, Decisions, Joint Communiqués and Documents', file 1 (January 1968–November 1970), 'Why is the Establishment of the Union of the Arab Emirates Being Delayed?', translation of an article published in *al-Jaridah* (18 July 1969).
76 TNA, FCO 8/927, Eyers to Gent and others, 21 January 1969.
77 TNA, FCO 8/1510, 'Dubai and the Northern Trucial States: Annual Review for 1970', by Bullard, 10 December 1970.
78 TNA, FCO 8/1296, Bahrain to Foreign Office, 28 October 1970.
79 TNA, FCO 8/1509, 'Abu Dhabi: Annual Review for 1969', Treadwell to Crawford, 19 December 1969.
80 TNA, FCO 8/927, 'Persian Gulf: Annual Review for 1968', from Crawford to Stewart, 14 January 1969.
81 TNA, FCO 8/927, Eyers to Gent and others, 21 January 1969. The Foreign Office (which had merged with the Commonwealth Office on 17 October 1968 to become the Foreign and Commonwealth Office, but will simply be referred to by its previous name hereafter unless it is necessary to make a distinction), *The Diplomatic Service List, 1972* (London: Her Majesty's Stationery Office, 1972), p. iii.
82 TNA, FCO 8/1510, 'Dubai and the Northern Trucial States: Annual Review for 1970', by Bullard, 10 December 1970.
83 TNA, FCO 8/1510, 'Dubai and the Northern Trucial States: Annual Review for 1970', by Bullard, 10 December 1970.
84 TNA, FCO 8/927, 'Persian Gulf: Annual Review for 1968', from Crawford to Stewart, 14 January 1969.
85 TNA, FCO 8/1004, 'Annual Review of Bahrain', by Sir Stewart Crawford, 4 January 1969.
86 Parsons, *They Say the Lion*, p. 112.
87 Parsons, *They Say the Lion*, p. 114.

DILEMMAS AND DELAY, 1968-70

88 Parsons, *They Say the Lion*, pp. 116-117.
89 NARA, RG 59, Central Foreign Policy Files, 1967-1969, Box 2083, POL 19, Dahran to Washington, 5 March 1968.
90 'Bahrain Problem', memorandum of conversation, 12 December 1968, Johnson Library, National Security File, Saunders Files, visit of Amir of Kuwait, 11-12 December 1968, compiled in *FRUS, 1964-1968*, vol. 21, doc. 161, pp. 331-332.
91 'Warning from Moscow', *Arab Report and Record* (1968, no. 6), p. 70.
92 'Bahrain Situation; US-Bahrain Relations', memorandum of conversation, 23 October 1968, *FRUS, 1964-1968*, vol. 21, doc. 157, pp. 323-325.
93 Parsons, *They Say the Lion*, p. 135.
94 TNA, FCO 8/1004, 'Annual Review of Bahrain', by Sir Stewart Crawford, 4 January 1969.
95 TNA, FCO 8/1004, 'Annual Review of Bahrain', by Sir Stewart Crawford, 4 January 1969.
96 Roham Alvandi, 'Muhammad Reza Pahlavi and the Bahrain Question, 1968-1970', *British Journal of Middle Eastern Studies*, 37:2 (2010), 159-177.
97 'Bahrain Problem', memorandum of conversation, 12 December 1968, Johnson Library, National Security File, Saunders Files, visit of Amir of Kuwait, 11-12 December 1968, compiled in *FRUS, 1964-1968*, vol. 21, doc. 161.
98 'US-UK Talks: Persian Gulf', memorandum of conversation, 11 March 1969, compiled in *FRUS, 1964-1968*, vol. 21, doc. 71.
99 Winston S. Churchill, 'Iran's Search for Gulf Security When Britain Withdraws: The Quest for Peace in the Middle East', *The Times* (10 June 1969), p. 11.
100 TNA, FCO 8/927, 'Persian Gulf: Annual Review for 1968', from Crawford to Stewart, 14 January 1969.
101 'US-UK Talks: Persian Gulf', memorandum of conversation, 11 March 1969, *FRUS, 1964-1968*, vol. 21, doc. 71.
102 Patrick Wright, 'The Run-up to Independence, 1971', in Paul Tempest (ed.), *Envoys to the Arab World: MECAS Memoirs, 1944-2009*, vol. II, p. 118.
103 TNA, FCO 8/57, 'Persian Gulf Islands', by Craig, 7 June 1968.
104 Denis Wright, 'The Memoirs of Sir Denis Wright, 1911-1971', vol. 2 (unpublished memoir, Bodleian Library, Oxford), p. 418.
105 TNA, FCO 8/1563, Tehran to FCO, telegram no. 583, 12 August 1971; Dubai to FCO, telegram no. 264, 14 August 1971; Abu Dhabi to Bahrain, telegram no. 173, 14 August; Tehran to Bahrain, telegram no. 622, 27 August 1971.
106 Mattair, *The Three Occupied UAE Islands*, pp. 335-372.
107 TNA, FCO 8/1004, 'Annual Review of Bahrain', by Sir Stewart Crawford, 4 January 1969.
108 'US-UK Talks: Persian Gulf', memorandum of conversation, 11 March 1969, compiled in *FRUS, 1964-1968*, vol. 21, doc. 71.
109 TNA, FCO 8/1509, 'Abu Dhabi: Annual Review for 1969', Treadwell to Crawford, 19 December 1969.
110 TNA, FCO 8/1509, 'Annual Review for 1969', Bullard to Crawford, 7 February 1970.
111 TNA, FCO 8/1369, Caradon to Hayman, 25 March 1970.
112 TNA, FCO 8/1031, 'Kuwait: Annual Review for 1968', from Graham to Stewart, 4 January 1969.
113 Fain, *American Ascendance and British Retreat*, p. 186.
114 Husain al-Baharna, 'The Fact-finding Mission of the United Nations Secretary-General and the Settlement of the Bahrain-Iran Dispute, May 1970', *International and Comparative Law Quarterly*, 22:3 (1973), 541-552. Also, see United Nations Security Council Resolution 278 of 11 May 1970.
115 Al-Baharna, 'The Fact-finding Mission', p. 552.
116 TNA, FCO 8/1373, Drace-Francis to Philip, 22 December 1970.
117 Edward Gordon, 'Resolution of the Bahrain Dispute', *American Journal of International Law*, 65:3 (1971), 568.
118 *Public Papers of the Presidents of the United States: 1969-1974*, available at the

website of the American Presidency Project, www.presidency.ucsb.edu, 'Informal Remarks in Guam with Newsmen', 25 July 1969.
119 Kissinger to Nixon, undated covering memorandum, National Archives, Nixon Presidential Materials, NSC Institutional Files, Box H-156, National Security Study Memoranda, NSSM 66; National Security Study Memorandum 66, NSC Files, Box 365, Subject Files, National Security Study Memoranda, NSSM 43–103, compiled in *FRUS, 1969–1976*, vol. 24, doc. 73, p. 239.
120 'IG Paper on U.S. Policy in the Persian Gulf', Rodman to Kissinger, 31 December 1969, National Archives, Nixon Presidential Materials, NSC Institutional Files, Box H-156, National Security Study Memoranda, NSSM 66, compiled in *FRUS, 1969–1976*, vol. 24, doc. 76, p. 242.
121 TNA, FCO 7/1810, 'Anglo/United States Relations', brief by Foreign and Commonwealth Office, 23 September 1970.
122 'U.S. Interests and Policy Toward the Persian Gulf', Hearings before the Subcommittee on the Near East of the Committee on Foreign Affairs, House of Representatives, 92nd Congress, second session, pp. 6–7.
123 TNA, FCO 8/1509, 'Dubai and the Northern Trucial States Review of the Year 1969', Bullard to Crawford, 30 December 1970.
124 John Gerard Ruggie, 'Territoriality and Beyond: Problematizing Modernity in International Relations', *International Organization*, 47:1 (1993), 139–140.
125 TNA, FCO 8/1510, 'Dubai and the Northern Trucial States: Annual Review for 1970', by Bullard, 10 December 1970.

CHAPTER FIVE

The 'secret' agreement, July 1971

After Harold Wilson's withdrawal announcement in January 1968 up until the first half of 1971, the negotiations between the rulers of the Protected States remained fraught and contested. At the beginning, they had responded promptly by seeking a regional solution, but they could not follow it through. The failure of the initiative put forward in the Dubai Agreement could be explained partly by the rivalries between the rulers and their neighbours, but it was also due to the fundamental difficulty in realising the modernisation of international relations. Consequently, the crucial questions remained unresolved. How was Britain going to implement withdrawal from the Persian Gulf? How, if at all, were the Protected States going to emerge into international society? This chapter examines how these problems were settled during the later stages of British retreat.

On top of the empirical contribution, this chapter also attempts to address a more conceptual issue by suggesting that we need to critically re-examine the idea of 'decolonisation'. Although the application of the terminology here is disputable, given that the Protected States were never colonised per se, the narratives of the literature essentially correspond with the paradigm supporting this same idea. Focusing on Britain's informal empire in the Persian Gulf, the enquiry is therefore driven by one of the most typical questions of decolonisation: How was the outcome of the end of empire and the concurrent emergence of the new states determined?

There are two principal schools of thought in the literature. On the one hand, a group of scholars attributes the utmost importance to the role of the former imperial metropole. Wm. Roger Louis emphasises the crucial nature of the British role in explaining the largely peaceful British withdrawal and the emergence of new states. In particular, he portrays Sir William Luce, a special envoy to the Gulf, as a key mediator between the jealous rulers of the Protected States. This line of argument is helpful in order to understand the British perspective.[1] On the other hand, Frauke Heard-Bey and Simon C. Smith focus on the role of the local rulers. They trace the negotiations undertaken between the local rulers and demonstrate that the crucial turning point came in the summer of 1971. The important question concerns what brought about this change. Heard-Bey identifies a week-long period of negotiations in mid-July that could have been crucial, but she cannot assert this with certainty owing to limitations in the sources.[2] Taking Heard-Bey's case forward, Smith argues that Dubai's Ruler was persuaded by one of his advisers to compromise with Abu Dhabi and set aside their longstanding rivalry in order to move forward towards independence. This explanation is insightful, but it does not show why Abu Dhabi accepted negotiating with Dubai and what exactly happened during this crucial one-week period. After all, Smith mainly bases his inference on one report issued later, in December 1971.[3]

Although there are significant overlaps between the different approaches, there is clearly a discernible difference in terms of their emphasis. Whereas Louis's work highlights the British role, the narratives of Heard-Bey and Smith lean towards portraying the July negotiations as a success in regional settlement. The literature is thus essentially divided between those who emphasise the role of the former imperial metropole in deciding the outcome of decolonisation and those who hold that the formerly dependent territories took greater control over their own fate. This chapter revisits this debate by examining the role played by both Britain and the local rulers during the crucial stages of the withdrawal.

Drawing on interviews with the British diplomat who was directly involved in the negotiations on the ground, as well as his memoirs and the declassified documents available from the British archives, on top of the Arabic sources, it puts forward a synthesised interpretation by illuminating the patterns of compromise and collaboration between Britain and the local rulers.[4] In addition, it reveals that a 'secret' agreement was signed at a crucial point between some of the key players and then handed over to Britain in confidence. As in previous chapters, the fluctuations in the ambivalent relationship between Britain and the Protected States remain an underlying theme. This chapter starts by introducing a new British government, and then examines the July negotiations in detail, before going on to the final days of the British withdrawal from the Gulf.

THE 'SECRET' AGREEMENT, JULY 1971

The Conservative volte-face

In the spring of 1970, whilst Iran's renouncing of its claim over the '14th province' was cheered on the streets of Bahrain, the British public was preparing for a celebration of democracy. Wilson's Labour Party had held power for two terms, over almost six years, and a general election was expected to be held soon. The reversal of some of his social policies over the past few years, including the domestic expenditure cuts announced simultaneously with the so-called 'East of Suez' decision, had undoubtedly undermined Wilson's popularity. Consequently, on 19 June, the Conservative leader Edward Heath became the new Prime Minister of the United Kingdom.

The general election of 1970 not only resulted in a change of leadership in Britain, it also represented the agony of the former world imperial power. If Wilson's two governments between 1964 and 1970 had been supported by a domestic demand for the expansion of the welfare state, his defeat in the general election reflected the constituencies' disappointment at its reduction. The public frustration extended to Wilson's foreign policies, a frustration the Conservatives did not hesitate to capitalise on. They opposed Labour's decision to depart from the Gulf from the outset, and the most enthusiastic advocate of this opposition was Sir Alec Douglas-Home.

Douglas-Home was born in 1903 into an aristocratic family, and was educated at Eton College. He finished his undergraduate education at Christ Church, Oxford, with third-class honours in modern history; however, he was talented in sports and played first-class cricket. He had been Prime Minister before Wilson, and would also later become Foreign Secretary in Edward Heath's government. While in opposition, in January 1968 he had maintained that, 'should Britain leave prematurely', the Gulf region would 'be torn by strife and trouble, and the Soviet would be only too ready to stir the pot'.[5] This exaggeration of the Soviet threat interestingly resembled the argument employed by the Foreign Office during the internal negotiations with the Treasury a month before. John Darwin even asserts that there was 'a strong element of play-acting' in the Conservatives' opposition to the Labour decision.[6]

Whether it was mere pretence or not, Douglas-Home stated that the Conservatives would 'consult the Governments of the Gulf as to what kind of progress will be helpful and practical, both for them and Britain'.[7] Similarly, Heath stated in the House of Commons that the Conservative position was that, given the 'present proof of Russian infiltration' and 'the profit and loss account of investment', 'when the time comes ... we shall ignore the time phasing laid down by the

BRITAIN AND THE FORMATION OF THE GULF STATES

Prime Minister' – i.e. Wilson.[8] He reiterated this point during his tour of Australia that began on 14 August 1968.[9]

Clearly then, the Conservatives opposed Labour's withdrawal policy. Whether that was for the domestic need to simply oppose the rival party's policy, for some calculation of Britain's self-interest, or owing to imperial nostalgia or even a sense of responsibility towards the formerly dependent territories and peoples, there was clear disagreement between the political elites of Britain. This generated some expectations among those who would like to see Britain stay in the region, such as Shaikh Isa, the Ruler of Bahrain, as well as caution and resentment from those who preferred its retreat, like the Iranian leaders. Therefore, it was no surprise for either side that, when the Conservatives came to power in June 1970, they explored the possibility of reassessing Labour's withdrawal decision. On 20 July, Douglas-Home stated in the House of Commons:

> Our future policy will not be determined finally until all concerned have been consulted ... If we are successful in forming the union of the Arab Emirates – and I hope we may be successful – it is for them to say, in consultation with Britain, what support they want.[10]

This was a curiously mixed message. On the one hand, he was reasserting his scepticism about Labour's decision, yet on the other he was now taking a softer stance by maintaining that the Conservatives would support the formation of new states and consult them before deciding what to do. It seemed that he was becoming aware of the difficulty of reversing Labour's decision, whilst trying not to contradict his previous espoused convictions. It was clear from the outside, as well as the inside, that Britain was troubled by the question of exactly when and how to retire from its former imperial commitments. Being unsure as to what would be the best solution to the Gulf question, the Conservative government commissioned a retired former diplomat, Sir William Luce, to provide one.

Luce was one of the most respected Arabists in the Foreign Office. His 'personal prestige and influence were great' in the Gulf region, a British diplomat recalled, and 'He had a remarkable gift of persuading other people to adopt his point of view without their feeling that they had been coerced or humiliated.'[11] A crucial and highly regarded pillar of Britain's informal empire, he had, 'perhaps to a greater extent than any of his predecessors, secured the love as well as respect of the rulers from Muscat to Bahrain and Qatar'.[12] This is at least partly because he was a true expert on the Gulf. Already in July 1967 he had warned the Labour government against announcing the withdrawal, as we have seen, by maintaining that it 'should not be determined by any arbi-

THE 'SECRET' AGREEMENT, JULY 1971

trary or unilateral decision designed to effect a small saving in British defence costs or to satisfy opinion based on the artificial division of the world into east and west of Suez'. When we look at what followed six months later, his cautions impressively resemble what actually happened. He had also foreseen 'many factors which could either hasten or delay progress', and hence had asserted it would be 'a mistake to lay down any specific period' for future withdrawal.[13] He proved to be right on this point as well. It was not just the decision to leave the Gulf but the fact that Wilson had announced it publicly and with a specific deadline that was posing a great problem to Britain at this stage. Now that the Conservatives had come to power, he was being asked to clean up the mess created by a policy that he had warned precisely against.

Thus, as a special envoy he was going to be dispatched to the Gulf in order to reassess with the local rulers whether Labour's decision should be reversed. But he was not optimistic. By the end of 1968 he had already come to the view that the die was cast. Wilson's announcement, he observed, had 'set in motion certain processes which cannot be put back', and he opined that Britain should not hope to keep any land-based forces after 1971.[14] Once again, his prognosis would turn out to be right.[15]

After negotiations with the rulers of the Gulf, Luce came to voice his conclusion that it would be impracticable to reverse the withdrawal momentum, particularly owing to the opposition from Iran.[16] Consequently, Douglas-Home admitted, on 1 March 1971 in the House of Commons, that the British withdrawal from the Gulf had to be continued. His excuse was that the Labour announcement in January 1968 had 'brought to the surface tensions which had hitherto lain dormant and led a number of countries which had previously accepted the British presence in the area to declare opposition to its continuance'. Despite these strong words, he could not justify why it took the Conservatives more than eight months to come to that realisation.[17] Denis Healey remarked, 'The House will understand the right hon. Gentleman's reluctance to admit that he was wrong for so long', although it should be recalled that Healey himself did not have an impressive record of understanding the nature of the British presence in the Gulf during his time as Defence Secretary.[18]

The whole episode added yet another layer of irony to the British policy towards the Gulf. Britain had made the decision to retreat against the will of the local rulers, but it was now forced to implement its decision due to pressure from the region. The rulers had been incapable of taking control of the situation, while Britain did not seem to have a clear idea of what it was doing. Underlying the Conservatives' dithering was the conflict between domestic politics and foreign

[99]

policy, as had been the case with Wilson's original announcement. The whole story needs to be understood in the context of this constant tension between the British government's relationship with the public and its relationship with the governments of the Persian Gulf.

Predictably, the Conservative volte-face produced little more than confusion and resentment in the region. The Conservatives came to power after criticising Labour's policies, but both parties had to realise that the momentum was out of Britain's hands. This was no longer everyday international politics. Neither was it going to simply end as a strategic rearrangement of military policy. It was more fundamental than that. It was about the termination of informal imperial control and the concurrent emergence of new fully independent states – what Ruggie would have called an 'epochal' shift.[19] Britain might have been able to move troops from one place to another effectively without consulting anyone, but deciding the new members of international society necessarily had to be a collective effort between the existing members and the new entrants. The 'epochal' shift could not be driven unilaterally either by Britain alone or by the Protected States themselves. And once it was announced, publicly, with a clearly defined timeframe, it could not be aborted easily. Neither Britain nor the Protected States seemed to be fully aware of these points and nor could they reverse the trend once it was set in place. Things had gone beyond the control of any single agent.

Zayid, Rashid and Britain's shuttle diplomacy

Meanwhile, the rulers of the Protected States were not making much progress either. The Iranian threat to Bahrain was removed, but they still could not follow through on the regional initiative set up with the Dubai Agreement in February 1968. 'The Ruler of Abu Dhabi slaughtered bustard in the desert of Sind; the Rulers of Qatar and Dubai disappeared to less distant, but more remote, hunting grounds in southeastern Iran', lamented a British diplomat. The most fundamental question, of what form the nine Protected States that were going to be independent would take, was still up in the air, along with the rearrangements on more practical issues such as police, immigration and trade.[20] The Gulf was filled with what Louis calls 'sloughs of jealousy and greed'.[21] On the one hand, they had to at least make the pretence with their own societies that they were doing their best to materialise the union; on the other hand, they were hesitant to cooperate with each other owing to longstanding rivalries. The conflicting motivations made it difficult for them to be open about their genuine intentions, and the air of ambiguity and suspicion proved to be a major obstacle to unity. Moreover, interventions by their neighbours were further complicating the situation. Kuwait and Saudi Arabia were pressing for the union of the nine states, while Iran was trying to prevent it by encouraging Dubai to go it alone. The usual aloofness of the US did not help to overcome the deadlock either. It was only on 9 June that the British Foreign Secretary concluded, in a letter to Faisal, that the option for the union of the nine must be abandoned and an alternative sought.[22]

The last British Political Resident in the Gulf later lamented the slow progress in the first half of 1971, saying 'the Arabs are more adept even than the rest of us at turning away from what they do not like'.[23] Whether this was a fair assessment or not, neither Britain nor the Protected States could any longer afford to keep passing the buck to each other. There was only half a year to go before the final deadline. Yet almost every actor involved was at best indecisive and at worst paralysed. The border disputes remained unresolved and, more importantly, nobody knew how, if at all, the nine Protected States were going to become independent. Frustrated by the reluctance of both the rulers and London to make practical progress, one British diplomat was working to bring everyone to the table – Julian Walker, who had come back to the Gulf.

During the 1960s, Walker was mostly outside the Gulf. Up until early 1970 he had believed everything to be on course for an orderly British withdrawal, but when he learned in London about the situation, his 'pleasant dreams vanished' and in January 1971 he returned as Political Agent in Dubai.[24] The scene was discouraging and he saw little progress in the first half of the year. Given that the British withdrawal had to be completed by the end of December, another major delay at this stage could bring disastrous consequences; by early June, he became convinced that if no one took the lead the rulers would simply 'disappear on their summer holidays'.[25]

Interestingly, during this crucial period Walker played a more pivotal role than William Luce. The personal diary of Luce has only scattered entries but supports this narrative.[26] As Louis illuminated, Luce played an important role in the earlier stages, but the evidence suggests that Walker was more directly involved in the crucial shuttle diplomacy during mid-July.[27] It should be noted that, during this period, Luce was staying in London and was not centrally involved in the crucial stage of the negotiations.[28] In a telegram dated 7 July, he mentioned that to his eyes it was 'not entirely clear what Suwaidi has in mind'. He thought it would be 'inappropriate' for Dubai and Abu Dhabi to reach a 'confidential understanding between themselves only' on matters related to 'the seven' states.[29] Similarly, there is no evidence to suggest that the regional powers such as Iran or Saudi Arabia played any direct role at this crucial juncture.[30]

After much correspondence and a number of negotiations with his seniors in Bahrain and London, as well as with the rulers of the Gulf, Walker managed to convince the rulers of the seven Protected States (excluding Qatar and Bahrain) to gather in mid-July for the Trucial States Council meeting. An English newspaper issued in Bahrain reported with a hopeful tone, 'Seven Move Towards Union.'[31] Thus, in the summer heat of 10 July 1971, the 33rd meeting of the Trucial States Council was convened.

The Council was a body consisting of the rulers of the Protected States set up by Britain in 1952.[32] Its primary goal was to promote economic development, but the underlying British intention was to assuage local frustration in order to prevent the spread of Arab nationalism in the region. It served not only as a development board but also as a forum at which the rulers would gather to discuss various issues.[33] Formally, the chairman was the British Political Agent in Dubai and, even after the chairman was elected annually from among the rulers from 1966, the British attended the meetings as an observer. British influence thus remained significant.[34]

The formal goal of the meeting was to discuss practical matters such as how to control migration, drugs, alcohol, issues of diplomatic immunity and so forth after the British departure.[35] Given their practices in negotiation and decision-making, it was unsurprising that they spent most of the time discussing the less contentious issues and refraining from addressing serious problems. It was only towards the very end of the meeting, on 13 July, that Shaikh Rashid, the Ruler of Dubai, and Shaikh Zayid, Ruler of Abu Dhabi, sat down to discuss the more fundamental issues.[36]

The precise development of events during this critical stage requires a careful investigation. On the surface, there were two clear turning points in July. The first was when the Trucial States Council was convened on 10 July and the second was when the formation of the UAE was publicly agreed on 18 July. That said, what happened between or even before these two dates seems to have been equally important. This was the crucial week when the map of the Persian Gulf States was effectively decided, and the details have evaded the scrutiny of previous studies. The sources contradict each other on some details, particularly as to who decided what and on which date.

To begin with, Julian Walker recalls that, in early summer, Shaikh Zayid and Shaikh Rashid agreed 'in confidence' that they should unite and that he had been 'informed of their agreement and welcomed it'.[37]

THE 'SECRET' AGREEMENT, JULY 1971

This would mean that the two rulers had decided, prior to the meeting of the Council, to work together for the UAE.[38]

Further to this point, Charles James Treadwell, the Political Agent in Abu Dhabi, reported on 8 July that he had heard from 'Adnan al-Pachachi that Shaikh Zayid was hoping to 'reach' a 'final agreement with Rashid' the following evening, and would 'propose consulting the other rulers in private sessions during the Trucial States Council meeting'.[39] Interestingly, before any agreement was reached between the rulers, Shaikh Zayid's advisers were considering the idea that negotiations should take place behind the scenes.

Among Shaikh Zayid's advisers, the most important of all was Ahmad Khalifa al-Suwaidi. Al-Suwaidi was born in 1937 in Abu Dhabi and was appointed Minister of Presidential Affairs in June 1971. He was described in a report issued later as 'a man of unusual charm' but 'only moderately intelligent'.[40]

Treadwell heard from al-Suwaidi that Shaikh Rashid 'saw a risk' that 'misunderstandings might arise following a purely oral agreement and wished to have the terms committed to paper and signed by the two rulers'. On the other hand, 'Abu Dhabi saw the point of this but feared that a document could fall into the wrong hands'. In response, Treadwell suggested that the document 'could be lodged for safe custody with either Political Agent' with no copy kept, which satisfied both al-Suwaidi and al-Pachachi.[41] So, Britain was mediating a secret agreement between the two major powers.

With these intentions in mind, al-Suwaidi contacted Mahdi al-Tajir, Shaikh Rashid's adviser. Al-Tajir was an influential adviser and a skilful businessman in Dubai. An internal brief issued by the Foreign and Commonwealth Office in 1976 notes, 'He is unpopular in Dubai and has few friends, but has proved himself more than a match of enemies ... He enjoys the power-game and is good at it. Can be a good friend or a nasty enemy. He can be brutally frank or deceptively smooth.'[42] A report by Walker describes how he would make suspicious remarks about other Arab advisers, such as regarding 'Adnan al-Pachachi, one of Shaikh Zayid's supposedly favourite advisers at that time.[43] By 1967, most of the meetings between the rulers of these Protected States were held in the house of Shaikh Rashid and brokered by al-Tajir.[44] Another document records complaints from British companies that he was marginalising their business. There were allegations that he was intending 'to launch as many projects as he can within the next year or so, pocket his commissions on all of these and then decamp to Europe or to the United States, where he already has substantial investments in property and other things'.[45] Later, Britain observed that by the mid-1970s he had 'amassed great wealth from his widespread business interests, some of it honestly'.[46] Of course, this is a one-sided narrative and, given that al-Tajir expanded his business extremely successfully thereafter and is still alive at the time of writing, the question remains a contentious one. However, at least to British eyes at that time, he seemed to be attempting to maximise his interest during the chaotic period of transition.

The negotiation took place on 9 July and also on the evening the next day, but no agreement was reached. On 9 July, Shaikh Zayid told Treadwell that he was 'against any form of public announcement' until the way was 'clear for one to be made'.[47] However, the level of confidentiality is debatable. A Kuwaiti newspaper was cited to have reported on 8 July that al-Suwaidi and al-Tajir had reached an agreement.[48]

From Dubai, Walker was reporting a similar development. In early July, he was working with Shaikh Rashid and al-Tajir on the vexed question of where exactly the balance of constitutional power between Abu Dhabi, Dubai and the other states could rest. After al-Tajir met al-Suwaidi on 8 July, to Walker's eyes the Abu Dhabi counterpart 'appeared confident that agreement would be reached'.[49] It is important to note that Walker was not directly present at all these meetings. On 11 July, he wrote that 'I have not learnt of the outcome yet'.[50]

The importance of these developments cannot be overstated. First, they imply that, at the adviser level, Abu Dhabi and Dubai had agreed prior to the opening of the Trucial States Council (i.e. the formal negotiation with the other Protected States) that they would try to secretly reach an agreement on what shape the coming new state would take; thus, the big two were planning to institutionalise their superiority before even consulting the others. Second, it is clear from the correspondence that the secret negotiation was not imposed upon them by Britain but was conducted essentially between Abu Dhabi and Dubai themselves. Although the whole momentum was initiated by Britain in January 1968 – for reasons that, as we have seen, had nothing to do with the Gulf – the solution was coming to crystallise as a local one. Third, Britain was trusted enough to be able to closely follow the behind-the-scene negotiations, so much so that Treadwell could propose that the coming written secret agreement should not be kept by the parties concerned but deposited in the hands of Britain. Meanwhile, Abu Dhabi Radio and Kuwait Radio reported gradual progress at the meeting, but they did not mention that more important negotiations were taking place offstage.[51]

Once the council was opened, on 12 July, al-Pachachi told Treadwell that Shaikh Zayid and Shaikh Rashid had 'resolved all outstanding matters in issue' such as deciding to locate the temporary capital in Abu Dhabi. They were expected 'to sign an agreement for a union of

THE 'SECRET' AGREEMENT, JULY 1971

the two emirates tonight'. Al-Pachachi assured Treadwell that 'no official statement will be made until the Union is complete', even though he thought that 'Leaks are however bound to occur.'[52] According to Walker's observation, the most important modifications to the provisional constitution were agreed on 13 July between al-Suwaidi and al-Tajir, the two main advisers to the rulers of Abu Dhabi and Dubai respectively, before they were presented to Walker the following morning.[53] Here, Abu Dhabi and Dubai agreed to be on an equal footing in the Supreme Council, and that only they would hold veto power. Shaikh Rashid and Shaikh Zayid's 'agreement' (*ittifaqiyah*), with a note declaring it 'secret' (*sirri*) on top, was officially signed on 15 July.[54] Its content was so sensitive that, as had been suggested by Treadwell a week before, only one original copy of the agreement was created and was handed over to Britain. I found the photostat of this copy, which Britain created and sent from Dubai to Bahrain, emblazoned with a cautionary note:

> As you know from our telegrams, the existence of this Agreement is known only to the two Rulers, their closest advisers and us. It should thus not be revealed to any other party.[55]

Indeed, it proved to be a well-kept 'secret' – none of the existing literature to my knowledge mentions its existence, let alone its content.

The agreement was essentially to establish a state comprising the seven members that make up the United Arab Emirates today, using as a basis the constitution draft recommended at the Deputy Rulers' meeting on 26 October 1970. I have tried to locate this draft, but could only find that the meeting on that day was observed by Britain to be a failure without any agreement reached.[56] It was agreed to achieve independence without Qatar and Bahrain, as soon as those states officially proclaimed their withdrawal from the nine-state solution. The agreement also had an annex, made of two parts. The first part of the annex was Abu Dhabi's and Dubai's proposals on amendments to the draft constitution of October 1970, and the second part was the other five states' response to the proposition.

In order to understand the sensitivity of the agreement, one needs to place it in its wider context. The key problem in the formation of the union was the balance of constitutional power. Colin Newbury points out that constitutional bargaining tended to play a critical role in deciding the outcome of decolonisation.[57] This was particularly the case with the Protected States, even though they were not colonies in the strictest legal sense. Since they were negotiating to become united as one new state, how each of them would be represented in the coming new state was of crucial concern to everyone. A useful analogy would be the UN. Alongside the egalitarian structure of the General Assembly, the Security Council invests power in five permanent members. Shaikh Zayid and Shaikh Rashid, the rulers of the two great powers of the Protected States, came up with a similar solution. They agreed to commit themselves to the coming UAE, provided that their countries alone would have veto rights and that the other Trucial States would not.[58]

Thus, it was agreed in 'secret' that a draft constitution to be proposed to the remaining five stipulated that 'matters of substance' (al-masa'l al-maudu'iya) at the 'Supreme Council' (al-majlis al-a'ala) were to be decided by a 'majority' (aghalabiyah) of five members, given that the five include both Abu Dhabi and Dubai.[59]

This had two major implications. First, it meant that Abu Dhabi and Dubai agreed essentially to be on an equal footing in the constitution. This was one of the defining moments of the British withdrawal and the formation of the UAE. Thus, the explanation for the reasons behind this agreement has direct ramifications for our understanding of the origins of the state of the UAE as well as the emirates of Dubai and Abu Dhabi today. Smith argues that al-Tajir, Shaikh Rashid's adviser, persuaded him to work together with Shaikh Zayid, claiming that Dubai could not afford to go it alone even though Abu Dhabi could.[60] This argument will be revisited later.

The second implication of the secret agreement was that Abu Dhabi and Dubai now had to persuade the smaller states to accept inferior constitutional status.[61] Obviously, this was not expected to be an easy task. Indeed, as Britain had observed over the deadlock of the Deputy Rulers' meeting in October 1970, the smaller five 'attacked the provisions on representation and voting which underlined their subordinate status' and 'were going to object fairly strongly to agreements that had been reached over their heads'.[62] In fact, Walker recalls that instead of sorting things out between the rulers themselves during the Trucial States Council meeting, Shaikh Zayid asked him to visit the rulers of the five smaller states after the meeting was dissolved and persuade them to sign up to the Abu Dhabi–Dubai initiative.[63]

In relation to this point, it may appear somewhat puzzling why the agreement stipulated that the decisions should be taken not only with the approval of Abu Dhabi and Dubai but also with the 'majority of five members'. The premise of the agreement was that the union was going to be formed with seven states, not eight or nine. Four members would have sufficed to create a majority. Why did they have to emphasise five? The direct answer to this question is not provided in the sources, but most likely it was aimed to assuage the anxiety of the smaller five, which had led to the breakdown in 1970. The stipulation of the 'major-

THE 'SECRET' AGREEMENT, JULY 1971

Why "majority of five"?

[majority out of 7] = 4

○ ○ ○ ○|○ ○ ○

Abu Dhabi + Dubai + [majority out of rest] = 5

● ● ○ ○ ○|○ ○

1 'Majority of five' in the secret agreement

ity of five' gave effective veto rights to the five smaller states after Abu Dhabi and Dubai, as shown in Figure 1.[64]

Thus, as much as Abu Dhabi and Dubai had the right to block a decision taken at the Supreme Council against their will, the remaining five smaller states (seven minus Abu Dhabi and Dubai) could also veto the decision if a majority of them (i.e. three out of five) could form a coalition against Dubai and Abu Dhabi. The stipulation of the 'majority of five' (Abu Dhabi plus Dubai plus three out of the remaining five) effectively gave the smaller five states a *collective veto right*.[65] There is no direct evidence that the stipulation was intended to give the third veto right, but that certainly seems to me to be the logical conclusion. Further to this point, although the main body of the agreement was explicitly stated to be a 'secret' one, the second half of the annex suggests that the practical amendments to the constitution, including the issues on the veto rights of the smaller five, were conveyed to the smaller five before the 'secret agreement' was reached. Thus the 'secret' agreement was also a result of a careful negotiation that had been taking place between Abu Dhabi and Dubai on the one hand and the smaller five on the other. And Qatar and Bahrain were out of the game.

In any case, at around the time the secret agreement was signed between Abu Dhabi and Dubai, the other members of the Trucial States Council started to discuss what their views were on the coming UAE.

[107]

BRITAIN AND THE FORMATION OF THE GULF STATES

Shaikh Saqr of Ra's al-Khaimah was the most resistant. Carrying 'the chip of past Qawasim greatness on his shoulders', as some observed, he reacted most strongly to an arrangement that gave clear superiority to Abu Dhabi and Dubai. The others also initially responded that the 42 members of the Union Council should be divided equally and that Abu Dhabi and Dubai should not be given veto rights in the Supreme Council.[66]

After the council was dissolved 'in mid-air' on 13 July, Julian Walker started his tour visiting the Rulers of Ra's al-Khaimah, 'Ajman, Fujairah, Sharjah and Umm al-Qaiwain, who had now returned to their respective homes. The son of the Ruler of Ra's al-Khaimah was first to come but had to withdraw after the first day owing to pressure from his father. As a result, Walker had to travel alone in his car between the capitals of the Protected States, which were not yet completely connected with paved roads.[67]

One should also note that the exact events leading to the signing of the secret agreement on 15 July still remain unclear to some extent. In some telegrams to London, Walker reported that on 14 July he had been briefed by al-Tajir and al-Suwaidi about the 'Abu Dhabi/Dubai modifications' and presented them to the 'Little Five', and that the 'Little Five' had continued discussions on the morning of the 15th. This may suggest that, before the rulers of Abu Dhabi and Dubai had signed the 'secret agreement', their advisers had already not only decided the content of it but also released it to the other prospective member states of the UAE.[68] Since even 'Mehdi [al-Tajir]'s enemies agree that he is a highly skilful negotiator', it is plausible that he played an important role in persuading Shaikh Rashid to make a realistic compromise with Abu Dhabi.[69] However, this line of argument, which conforms to the case put forward by Smith, does not explain the dynamics from the other direction – why Abu Dhabi accepted Dubai's offer. In fact, given that Abu Dhabi was indisputably the largest, wealthiest and most powerful among the Protected States, agreeing to be on equal constitutional status with Dubai was a major compromise on Shaikh Zayid's part. The question here then is why Shaikh Zayid accepted such a concession. Walker, who was on the ground working together with the rulers as Political Agent, later recalled in an interview that Shaikh Zayid simply decided to be generous. He also recalls the role taken by Shaikh Zayid's adviser, al-Suwaidi, as well as referring to the involvement of Shaikh Khalid, but there is not sufficient primary evidence in the British archives or the Arabic sources to further explore these points.[70]

On the whole, however, attributing the waning of such a longstanding rivalry to Dubai's realpolitik calculations or Shaikh Zayid's personal generosity appears to be overly simplistic. Here, one could also discern another contributing factor: that Shaikhs Rashid and Zayid both realised that time was running out. There is only circumstantial evidence to suggest that the two Shaikhs were feeling the pressure of time, but there is overwhelming evidence that Walker was in a hurry to finalise matters as soon as possible.[71]

On 14 July, the radio station 'Voice of the Arabs' broadcast from Cairo the announcement that a consensus had been reached about the formation of a federation of seven of the Protected States. Given that Ra's al-Khaimah was still refusing, the report was not entirely accurate; however, it did reflect how quickly informal negotiations leaked to the media.[72]

Meanwhile, Douglas-Home, the Foreign Secretary, was checking up with the British Embassy in Tehran, hoping that Iran would not interfere to disturb the still fragile developments on the southern coast of the Gulf.[73] Saudi Arabia was also aware that there were some 'secret talks' going on, but did not seem to know their exact content.[74]

After the hectic week on the southern shores of the Gulf, Walker had managed to convince everyone except the Ruler of Ra's al-Khaimah to come on board. Consequently, on 18 July 1971, the six Rulers of 'Ajman, Fujairah, Sharjah, Umm al-Qaiwain, Abu Dhabi and Dubai issued a communiqué proclaiming the formation of the UAE.[75] It should be noted that Britain was opting for the one-state solution and had referred to the UAE as the 'Union of Arab Emirates'; now, this was changed to the 'United Arab Emirates'.[76] The Arabists of the Foreign Office were using the famous Hans Wehr dictionary, discussing in detail how every piece of terminology in the provisional constitution should be translated.[77]

Beyond the semantics, it was now time for the rulers to sign an agreement and officially announce the UAE's formation. Fifty sheets were provided for the drafting of the communiqué, but after numerous efforts only two sheets were left. When the agreement was signed at a rectangular table, the room was packed with the press, and several photographers leapt onto the table for better shots.[78] The Ruler of Ra's al-Khaimah attended the meeting but did not sign the communiqué.[79] From the packed room, the participants were forced to get out via the French windows – a British diplomat recalls that it was a reversal of the joke that British imperialists tend to leave by the door and return through a window.[80]

Thus, the evidence suggests that the agreement reached on 18 July was a product of compromise and collaboration precipitated by the pressure of time. Since the whole process was beyond the control of any single agent, the agreement was not necessarily based on a fully thought-out grand design; rather, it was more of a haphazard accumulation of spontaneous efforts. It was not so much a British initiative led by senior diplomats such as Luce than a settlement that came out of compromises between local rulers encouraged by the shuttle diplomacy of Walker, a mid-level officer familiar with the intricacies on the ground. Each participant of the Trucial States Council meeting was pursuing his own interest, but the pressure of time compelled each to find a middle ground where they could all work together.

A couple of days later, Zayid, Rashid and Walker invited Saqr for dinner.[81] They tried to persuade him to sign up to the UAE. But this effort did not bear any fruit.[82]

Compromise and collaboration

This then was how the 18 July communiqué was produced. One should note, however, that the communiqué was only a declaration of intention rather than an act in itself. It proclaimed the intention of the six Protected States to form the UAE, but there remained two major issues to be resolved before the formation could be activated. The first was an internal problem. At this point, six Protected States had signed up to the UAE, but the communiqué left the door open for Ra's al-Khaimah, Bahrain, Qatar and even Oman to join. The second issue was more of an external one. The coming UAE would ideally have solved the border disputes with its neighbours, namely Saudi Arabia and Iran.

At first glance, these questions seem to concern regional matters. In theory, they had to be resolved by the local players; Ra's al-Khaimah, Bahrain and Qatar should have decided by themselves or with the other Protected States whether to join the UAE, and the coming UAE members should have been able to negotiate with Iran and Saudi Arabia over the territorial disputes. Soon after the agreement was reached, the rulers' advisers – including Mahdi al-Tajir, Ahmad al-Suwaidi and 'Adnan al-Pachachi – went on tour to Cairo, Tehran, Baghdad, Damascus, Beirut and London, explaining the agreement that had been reached to the respective governments.[83] Yet, in practice, Britain still had to play a mediating role, bridging the gap between the regional actors; once again, Britain was the crucial facilitator.

The biggest issue remaining was whether Bahrain and Qatar were going to join in. The communiqué had opened the door for them, but it was still an open question as to whether they would wish to enter.[84] Initially, Bahrain was frightened. By 10 July, Bahrain had informed Britain that it intended to provisionally end the special treaty relationship on 24 July and apply for membership of the UN immediately afterwards.[85] The carefully crafted communiqué proclaimed in July finally enabled them to be open about their intentions without being accused of disturbing the regional initiative. However, after the communiqué was issued on 18 July, the Ruler was not sure if Saudi Arabia would be happy if Bahrain did not join the UAE. Britain thought that Bahrain should immediately apply for UN membership, but Bahrain wanted to wait until the Saudi position became clearer.[86] The answer became apparent on 10 August when the Ruler of Bahrain informed the British Political Resident of his intention to seek immediate independence. The British feared that the Saudis might interfere, but King Faisal stayed silent. The First Secretary at the Italian Embassy in Tehran remarked that the Saudis 'really did not have a policy and were just continuing to wait and see what other people did – which was all that, in his experience, the Saudis were capable of doing'.[87]

Previously, Saudi Arabia had been pushing all parties concerned towards a one-state solution, but by this point it had no clear policy concerning the Protected States. On 8 July, a week before the July communiqué was signed, the British observed that Omar Saqqaf, the Saudi Foreign Minister, had persuaded the King to accept the possibility that the one-state solution was not going to be achieved. He had reportedly 'argued to King Feisal that a purely negative attitude of refusing to have anything to do with any policy other than one of establishing a Union of Nine (which had failed) would do great harm to Saudi Arabia's interest'. After this, the Saudi line softened.[88]

After the general retrocession of British jurisdiction in Bahrain on 31 July, the Ruler of Bahrain and the Political Resident exchanged letters and notes on 15 August terminating the special treaty relationship, replacing it with a Treaty of Friendship and thereby establishing Bahrain's full independence as a single state.[89] Similarly, on 24 August, the Deputy Ruler of Qatar informed the Acting Political Resident Agent in Doha of Qatar's intention to seek independence. The general retrocession of British jurisdiction in Qatar took place on 31 August. Since the Ruler of Qatar was on holiday in Geneva, the British Political Resident flew there to sign the Treaty of Friendship on 3 September. It was therefore established that Qatar was also going alone and would not join the UAE. Consequently, both of them were admitted to the UN on 21 September.[90]

During this period, Britain was carefully planning its communication with both Bahrain and Qatar so that each would know the other's move without directly revealing what the other had told Britain.[91] The British Political Resident observed that Bahrain and Qatar had never wanted the single overarching union; they were merely playing 'the Arab game of "after you" and were concerned only to escape the blame for breaking up the Union of Nine'. A telegram sent from the British

Embassy in Jeddah to the Foreign Office on 7 July, a week before the secret agreement was signed, maintained that all nine Protected States 'should pay lip service to the ideal of the nine' for the sake of assuaging Saudi Arabia. This meant Bahrain and Qatar assuring 'King Feisal of their determination to maintain close association with the other states and keep open the possibility of some formal link at a later date' and, in the case of the seven others, 'the inclusion in any declaration' of 'the hope that Bahrain and Qatar might join in the future and that in the meantime some close association might be worked out'.[92] The Foreign Secretary Douglas-Home agreed.[93] In fact, by 8 July the Political Agent in Abu Dhabi had heard from al-Suwaidi that Bahrain was planning to inform Saudi Arabia on 17 July of its intention not to join the UAE.[94] Interestingly, Bahrain had contacted Kuwait by 11 July before conveying the matter to Saudi Arabia, possibly to test the waters.[95]

Meanwhile, the Iranian position was complicated. On the one hand, it did not intend to 'discourage' the moves towards the political transformation. On the other hand, Britain knew all too well that it would immediately change its position if the island disputes were not dealt with in its favour.[96] Wary of Iranian suspicion, the Foreign Secretary thought it was not 'desirable for the Iranians to be given a blow-by-blow account of all twists and turns'.[97] The British diplomats posted in Iran took a different view. They thought that by informing the Shah about the developments, they could 'reduce his fear of a *fait accompli*' and 'the less will be the effect on him of misleading or malicious reports from the area'.[98] In the end, they were told not to inform Tehran about the talks between Abu Dhabi and Dubai that brought about their secret agreement.[99] Finally, the US had considered up to mid-July that the union of the nine states was simply a 'non-starter'.[100]

On the whole, these pieces of evidence suggest that, before the secret agreement or the communiqué were signed, it had already become clear to British eyes that Qatar and Bahrain were going to achieve independence separately and it was only a matter of how to publicise this without offending Saudi Arabia.

At the same time, Britain was also drafting some practical arrangements for the coming independence of the UAE. On the one hand, domestic issues such as policing, immigration and trade were only matters of practical detail once the overarching framework for independence had been set out. On the other hand, more fundamental issues – namely the boundary disputes – were unresolved. A British document mentions the 'Failure to resolve the dispute between Saudi Arabia and Abu Dhabi' in 1971. Cleary this refers to the Buraimi Oasis dispute, but the details remain sanitised.[101] Consequently, the British

THE 'SECRET' AGREEMENT, JULY 1971

officers thought it would be wiser to 'let sleeping dogs lie ... ignoring the boundary agreements in the termination process'.[102]

Throughout the whole period, the US was preoccupied with its business elsewhere. On 13 June, the release of the Pentagon Papers caused further controversy among the American public over the Vietnam War.[103] On 15 August, Washington announced its intention to effectively end the convertibility between the US dollar and gold – the announcement known throughout the world as the Nixon Shock. Whether to acknowledge the full independence of Bahrain and Qatar was a matter that had to be decided by the President but, in this climate, it was nothing more than a formality. Whatever Britain had arranged in this part of the world was good enough for the busy superpower to sign off without much reservation. Thus, on 14 July a memorandum was sent to President Nixon recommending that he acknowledge the sovereign status of Bahrain and Qatar in the case of their proclaiming independence, on the grounds that early diplomatic recognition would be in the United States' interest and also would not cause any significant problems with the remaining Protected States. Nixon approved it.[104] Within a few years, this decision would be put to the test over the oil shock.

Whilst the US was taking a hands-off approach in the Gulf, some oil companies were more carefully observing the local developments. For example, there was an unverified rumour that ENI, an Italian oil company that had concession rights in Saudi Arabia with Philips and Independent Oil, was approached by the Saudi government. It suggested that 'through their Abu Dhabi concession they should bring pressure to bear on the Ruler of Abu Dhabi to yield territory in the South of his sheikhdom which ENI would then be able to utilise under their Saudi contract'.[105]

At the same time, BP had started to prepare for the RAF's departure from Bahrain and possible retreat from Sharjah. Its main concern was that if the British troops were really going to be withdrawn by the end of 1971, particularly from Bahrain and Sharjah, BP would need to remove or reorganise necessary facilities for fuelling the civil and military services of the neighbouring countries. According to the records at the BP Archive, however, the MOD had only 'indicated' that the withdrawal would be carried out as announced.[106] By 17 August, BP was informed by the MOD that it would either persuade the Bahrain and/or Sharjah governments to 'sign an agreement' with BP 'on exactly the same conditions as we have with the M.O.D. at present', or at least help them 'get the best conditions possible under a new government'. Nevertheless, BP's fear was that 'whatever the M.O.D. say, once the withdrawal is completed and all the M.O.D.s rights revert to the two Governments the rulers can always issue an ordinance making all previous arrangements null and void and force new conditions on us'.[107]

Although BP was nervously trying to extract as much information as possible from the British government, the British withdrawal was almost set for the final stage. On 30 November, one day prior to the ceasing of British jurisdiction in the remaining five Protected States, Iranian forces landed in Abu Musa and the two Tunbs. However, the military clash was suspected to be a staged show. The seizure of Abu Musa had already been agreed with the Ruler of Sharjah, and the British troops had little desire to protect the Tunbs for only a day. After a 'skirmish' that killed three Iranian soldiers and one Ra's al-Khaimah policeman, the Iranian forces took over the islands.

As James Onley points out, in this way the Shah could divert the anger of Arab public opinion towards the incompetence of the British forces.[108] Some may even argue that Britain had made a quid pro quo with Iran so that Iran would approve of Bahrain's independence in exchange for the smaller islands. This line of argument will be revisited with new sources in the next chapter. For now, Britain's unenthusiastic reaction suggests that the Iranian action was not unexpected. Of course, Britain did not openly approve Iranian seizures of the islands, but the circumstances raised the suspicion that some kind of mutual understanding had been put in place before Iran took action. In anger against Britain, Libya nationalised its holdings of BP and Iraq expelled its British ambassador.[109]

Apart from the halfway staged Iranian takeover of the small islands, the British withdrawal was proceeding in an orderly manner. On 1 December, the six rulers of the remaining Protected States (except Ra's al-Khaimah) exchanged letters and notes terminating the special treaty relationship with the British Political Resident. The next day, the UAE was formed and proclaimed in Dubai. The six rulers elected Shaikh Zayid, the Ruler of Abu Dhabi, as their president. He then, 'amid scenes of enthusiasm and confusion', signed the Treaty of Friendship with the Political Resident.[110] The UAE was admitted to the UN on 9 December.[111] In purely legal terms the transfer of some of the legal responsibilities would still gradually take place until British jurisdiction finally ceased in Qatar, Bahrain and the UAE on 31 January, 15 February and 18 March respectively.[112] Also, a complete handing over of forces (i.e. the Trucial Oman Scouts) took until 22 December but, by and large, by 2 December the Protected States had become fully sovereign states. Such a smooth transfer of responsibilities was 'more than the most sanguine of us would have dared hope for when the year began', commented the Political Resident.[113]

THE 'SECRET' AGREEMENT, JULY 1971

Meanwhile, the withdrawal of British forces was gradually reaching the final stage. The RAF stations in Sharjah and Muharraq (in Bahrain) had closed by 15 December. The last British military ships to leave the Gulf were HMS *Intrepid* and HMS *Achilles*, which departed from Bahrain on 19 December. Britain was able to believe that 'nobody had anything but good to say of the way our soldiers, sailors and airmen had conducted themselves during their stay in the Gulf'.[114] As the British forces departed, one of the very final orders delivered from the British Foreign Service, so the last Deputy Political Resident recalls, was 'to ensure that all the official pianos in the Gulf were regularly tuned'.[115]

A month later, Britain's last Political Resident in the Gulf described Britain's departure and the emergence of the new states as 'the smoothest and most friendly parting that anyone could have wished for'.[116] It is certainly true that the British withdrawal was in the end conducted in an impeccably peaceful and orderly manner. Except for the minor clashes over the small islands, the military retreat took place in surprising silence. And despite the long period of procrastination interrupted by frequent holidays, the Protected States successfully came together and emerged into international society as fully sovereign states. The eight rulers (i.e. without that of Ra's al-Khaimah) reorganised themselves to form three separate states, and even Iran did not dispute their independence. The 150 years of Britain's imperial presence in the Persian Gulf was finally over, and a new order was in place.

This observation brings us back to our initial questions. First, how could the whole process have taken place so peacefully against all odds? The answer can largely be attributed to the compromise and collaboration between the main actors. The Conservatives' unnecessary and unsuccessful attempt to reverse Labour's decision made it clear to Britain that the momentum gained was irreversible. In addition to the pressure of time, underlying Walker's shuttle diplomacy in the summer of 1971 was the realisation that the whole process was beyond the control of any single actor. Thus, Abu Dhabi and Dubai compromised to come together, and 'Ajman, Fujairah, Sharjah and Umm al-Qaiwain accepted their leadership. Qatar and Bahrain had feared being swallowed up by Abu Dhabi and Dubai, but the successful formation of the UAE in the east allowed them to finally become clear in their intention to go it alone, avoiding allegations of disturbing the regional order.

This analysis leads us to the second question. How does the whole episode advance our understanding of decolonisation? As far as the Protected States were concerned, compromise and collaboration were essential, if not the only, requirements for their emergence into international society. In contrast to the literature, which emphasises either the British leadership or local initiative, the evidence suggests that the crucial resolution came about in a more haphazard manner, enabled by the collaboration between Britain, the Protected States and the regional actors. This finding brings us back to Louis and Robinson's thesis on the centrality of collaboration in the 'imperialism of decolonisation'.[117] Whereas their argument mainly revolves around the decolonisation of formal colonies, the finding here suggests that collaboration was also important during the dissolution of informal empire. It was a local answer for an imperial question.

Taking into account the longstanding rivalries among the Protected States, it may appear in retrospect that the failure of the 'Union of Nine' was predestined from the beginning, and it was naturally expected that the Trucial States would become the UAE and that Bahrain and Qatar would choose to be independent as separate states. However, a report issued in July 1971 demonstrates that, until at least October 1969, Britain was aiming for a one- rather than a three-state solution. With a somewhat self-comforting tone, it remarked that 'we were right to maintain a "correct" position for working for a Union of Nine', given the pressure from Saudi Arabia and Kuwait. It also noted, 'We could have perhaps given more practical advice on constitutional matters at an earlier stage, but the Union had its own Arab Constitutional advisers to hand.' Even discounting the possibility that the Deputy Political Resident had to justify his job to the Foreign Secretary, it is suggestive that Britain was no more in control of the course of events than were the rulers of the Protected States and their neighbours.[118] Indeed, the report was praised by his seniors.[119]

Notes

1 Wm. Roger Louis, 'The Withdrawal from the Gulf', in *Ends of British Imperialism*.
2 Heard-Bey, *From Trucial States to United Arab Emirates*, pp. 362–363.
3 Smith, *Britain's Revival and Fall in the Gulf*, pp. 103–104, 180n.
4 TNA, FCO 8/1761, Dubai to Bahrain and Abu Dhabi, 15 July 1971; telephone interviews with Julian Walker, 21, 28 October 2009; Julian Walker, 'Personal Recollections of the Rapid Growth of Archives of the Emirates', in *The Historical Documents on Arab History in the Archives of the World Conference* (Abu Dhabi: Centre for Documentation and Research, 2002), pp. 35–47; Walker, *Tyro on the Trucial Coast*.
5 *Commonwealth, European and Overseas Review*, 26 (1968), p. 9.
6 Darwin, 'Britain's Withdrawal from East of Suez', p. 155.
7 TNA, T 225/3066, Gore-Booth to Brown, undated, c. 21 December 1967; *Commonwealth, European and Overseas Review*, 26 (1968), p. 12.
8 *Parliamentary Debates (Hansard)*, vol. 756, cols 1970–1971.
9 *Commonwealth, European and Overseas Review*, 33 (1968), p. 6.
10 *Parliamentary Debates (Hansard)*, vol. 804, cols 13–14.
11 Sir Anthony Parsons, 'Foreword', in Balfour-Paul, *The End of Empire in the Middle East*, p. xviii.

THE 'SECRET' AGREEMENT, JULY 1971

12 Parsons, *They Say the Lion*, pp. 126–127.
13 Luce, 'Britain in the Persian Gulf: Mistaken Timing over Aden', pp. 282–283.
14 Luce, 'Britain's Withdrawal from the Middle East and Persian Gulf', p. 8.
15 It should be noted that, compared with his insight into diplomatic issues, Luce's arguments about Britain's naval presence were less perceptive. In the same lecture given at the Royal United Services Institute on 26 November 1968, he maintained that Britain should retain some naval presence in the Gulf. When he was asked by the audience to elaborate, he evaded the question and avoided 'a technical discussion of naval matters'. Luce, 'Britain's Withdrawal from the Middle East and Persian Gulf', pp. 8–9.
16 Louis, 'The Withdrawal from the Gulf', pp. 898–902. See also Fain, *American Ascendance and British Retreat*, pp. 186–190; Heard-Bey, *From Trucial States to United Arab Emirates*, pp. 356, 360–361; Smith, *Britain's Revival and Fall in the Gulf*, pp. 100, 103; Petersen, *The Decline of the Anglo-American Middle East*, pp. 52–58.
17 *Parliamentary Debates (Hansard)*, vol. 812, col. 1227.
18 *Parliamentary Debates (Hansard)*, vol. 812, col. 1229.
19 Ruggie, 'Territoriality and Beyond', pp. 139–140.
20 TNA, FCO 8/1804, 'Annual Review for the Persian Gulf for 1971', report by Sir Geoffrey Arthur, 24 January 1972.
21 Louis, 'The Withdrawal from the Gulf', p. 900.
22 Even then, on 27 June 1971, Kuwait was still asking Britain to press for the nine-state solution. TNA, FCO 8/1560, Sabah to Douglas-Home, 27 June 1971 (Arabic). FCO 8/1804, 'Annual Review for the Persian Gulf for 1971', report by Sir Geoffrey Arthur, 24 January 1972; Walker, 'Personal Recollections', p. 45.
23 TNA, FCO 8/1804, 'Annual Review for the Persian Gulf for 1971', report by Sir Geoffrey Arthur, 24 January 1972.
24 Walker, 'Personal Recollections', p. 44.
25 TNA, FCO 8/1761, Walker to Wright, 6 June 1971.
26 Papers of Sir William Luce Relating to Aden and the Gulf, available at Exeter University Library, UK.
27 Louis, 'The Withdrawal from the Gulf', pp. 898–902.
28 TNA, FCO 8/1761, Walker to London, 13 July 1971; Walker to London 15 July 1971; telephone interviews with Julian Walker, 19, 21 October 2009.
29 TNA, FCO 8/1561, FCO to Bahrain, telegram no. 319, 7 July 1971.
30 TNA, FCO 8/1761, various documents.
31 'Seven Move Towards Union', *Gulf Weekly Mirror* (4 July 1971), p. 1.
32 Barnwell, 'Formation and Function: British Institutions and Antecedents to a Federation of Arab Emirates'.
33 For a concise and perceptive analysis of the Trucial States Council, see Barnwell, 'Formation and Function: British Institutions and Antecedents to a Federation of Arab Emirates'. See also Christopher M. Davidson, 'Arab Nationalism and British Opposition in Dubai, 1920–1966', *Middle Eastern Studies*, 43:6 (2007), 56–58.
34 TNA, FCO 8/1762, Luce to Renwick, 31 March 1971.
35 TNA, FCO 8/1761, Walker to Wright, 22 June 1971.
36 TNA, FCO 8/1761, Walker to London, 13 July 1971; Walker to London 15 July 1971.
37 Walker, 'Personal Recollections', p. 45.
38 Walker reported to the Arabian Department on 8 July that Rashid was considering engaging in personal discussions about issues pertaining to military measures with Zayid beyond the council meeting. TNA, FCO 8/1561, Dubai to FCO, telegram no. 202, 8 July 1971; FCO 8/1561, Dubai to FCO, telegram no. 203, 10 July 1971.
39 TNA, FCO 8/1561, Abu Dhabi to FCO, telegram no. 96, 8 July 1971.
40 TNA, PREM 16/996, Dales to Wright, 27 April 1976.
41 TNA, FCO 8/1561, Abu Dhabi to FCO, telegram no. 96, 8 July 1971.

42 TNA, PREM 16/996, Dales to Wright, 27 April 1976.
43 TNA, FCO 8/1563, Walker to Wright, 14 August 1971; Walker to Green, 31 August 1971.
44 Davidson, *Dubai*, p. 60.
45 TNA, FCO 8/1510, 'Mehdi Tajir and the Dubai Government', Bullard to Weir, 18 May 1970.
46 TNA, PREM 16/996, Dales to Wright, 27 April 1976.
47 TNA, FCO 8/1561, Abu Dhabi to FCO, telegram no. 98, 10 July 1971.
48 'Seven Launch Gulf Summit', *Gulf Weekly Mirror* (11 July 1971), p. 1.
49 TNA, FCO 8/1561, FCO to Bahrain, telegram no. 319, 7 July 1971.
50 TNA, FCO 8/1561, Dubai to FCO, telegram no. 205, 11 July 1971.
51 TNA, FCO 8/1561, 'Rulers Meeting: Views Now Much Closer', BBC report, 12 July 1971.
52 TNA, FCO 8/1461, Abu Dhabi to FCO, telegram no. 99, 12 July 1971.
53 TNA, FCO 8/1561, Dubai to FCO, telegram no. 210, 14 July 1971.
54 TNA, FCO 8/1562, 'Ittifaqiyah', enclosed in letter from Coles to Everard, 19 July 1971.
55 TNA, FCO 8/1562, Coles to Everard, 19 July 1971.
56 For example, see FCO 8/1296, Abu Dhabi to FCO, 26 October 1970, compiled in A.L.P. Burdett (ed.), *Records of the Emirates, 1966–1971*, vol. 5 (Archive Editions, 2002), pp. 297–298.
57 Colin Newbury, 'Patrons, Clients and Empire: The Subordination of Indigenous Hierarchies in Asia and Africa', *Journal of World History*, 11:2 (2000), 262.
58 TNA, FCO 8/1761, Walker to London, 13 July 1971; Walker to London, 15 July 1971; telephone interviews with Julian Walker, 19, 21 October 2009.
59 TNA, FCO 8/1562, 'Mulahhaq al-ittifaqiyah al-muaqqadah baina hakim Abu Zabi wa Dubai', enclosed in a letter from Coles to Everard, 19 July 1971. The letter also includes the English translation of both the agreement and the annexed draft constitution.
60 Smith, *Britain's Revival and Fall in the Gulf*, pp. 103–104.
61 *Arab Report and Record* (1971, no. 14), p. 374.
62 FCO 8/1296, Bahrain to FCO, 28 October 1970; FCO 8/1296, undated enclosure, compiled in Burdett (ed.), *Records of the Emirates, 1966–1971*, vol. 5, pp. 303–306.
63 TNA, FCO 8/1761, Walker to London, 13 July 1971; Walker to London 15 July 1971.
64 Author's own collection.
65 I thank Roland Popp for pointing this out to me. All errors are mine.
66 TNA, FCO 8/1561, Dubai to FCO, telegram no. 217, 16 July 1971.
67 TNA, FCO 8/1561, Dubai to FCO, telegram no. 217, 16 July 1971; Walker, 'Personal Recollections', pp. 46–47.
68 TNA, FCO 8/1561, Dubai to FCO, telegram nos 212, 216, 15 July 1971.
69 TNA, FCO 8/1510, 'Mehdi Tajir and the Dubai Government', Bullard to Weir, 18 May 1970.
70 Even the most extensive compilation of Arabic primary sources gives only a commentary on this period. Al-Rayyis, *Watha'iq al-Khalij al-'Arabi*, pp. 647–655; telephone interviews with Julian Walker, 18, 19, 21 October 2009.
71 TNA, FCO 8/1761, various documents; Walker, *Tyro on the Trucial Coast*, p. 157; Walker, 'Personal Recollections', pp. 44–47. Also, telephone interviews with Julian Walker, 18, 19, 21 October 2009.
72 TNA, FCO 8/1561, 'Seven Gulf Rulers Reach Consensus: Cairo Report', BBC note, 14 July 1971.
73 TNA, FCO 8/1561, FCO to Tehran, telegram no. 369, 14 July 1971.
74 TNA, FCO 8/1561, Jedda to FCO, telegram no. 545, 16 July 1971.
75 TNA, FCO 8/1561, Dubai to FCO, telegram no. 225, 18 July 1971.
76 TNA, FCO 8/1562, 'al-Dustur al-Muaqqisa li al-Imarat al-'Arabiyah al-Muttahida', 18 July 1971; FCO 8/1563, Walker to Slater, 28 August 1971.
77 TNA, FCO 8/1563, Coles to Wright, 4 August 1971.

THE 'SECRET' AGREEMENT, JULY 1971

78 Patrick Wright, 'The Run-up to Independence, 1971', in Paul Tempest (ed.), *Envoys to the Arab World: MECAS Memoirs, 1944–2009*, vol. II, p. 120.

79 The Provisional Constitution included a space where the Ruler of Ra's al-Khaimah could sign, and also stipulated that Ra's al-Khaimah would be given six seats in the national council, even though it was not in force at that time. TNA, FCO 8/1563, Walker to Acland, 4 August 1971.

80 Wright, 'The Run-up to Independence, 1971', p. 120.

81 For an illustration of the culinary scene in the region, see Aida S. Kanafani, *Aesthetics and Ritual in the United Arab Emirates: An Anthropology of Food and Personal Adornment among Arab Women* (Beirut: American University of Beirut, 1983), pp. 11–40.

82 TNA, FCO 8/1561, Dubai to FCO, telegram no. 230, 20 July 1971; Dubai to FCO, telegram no. 233, 21 July 1971.

83 TNA, FCO 8/1562, note for meeting to be held on 27 July between Douglas-Home, Suwaid, Tajir and Pachachi, issued by Acland, 26 July 1971.

84 TNA, FCO 8/1804, 'Annual Review for the Persian Gulf for 1971', report by Sir Geoffrey Arthur, 24 January 1972; Walker, 'Personal Recollections', p. 46.

85 TNA, FCO 8/1561, Bahrain Agency to Bahrain Residency, 10 July 1971.

86 TNA, FCO 8/1561, Bahrain Agency to Bahrain Residency, telegram no. 46, 19 July 1971.

87 TNA, FCO 8/1563, from Tehran to Arabian Department, 6 August 1971.

88 TNA, FCO 8/1561, Jedda to FCO, telegram no. 528, 8 July 1971.

89 TNA, FCO 8/1804, 'Annual Review for the Persian Gulf for 1971', report by Sir Geoffrey Arthur, 24 January 1972. The Treaty of Friendship was drafted by Britain and was 'deliberately and inevitably insubstantial' so that even should the new states decide in future to terminate it, as many other arrangements as possible would remain in force. The most important part from the British point of view was Article 1(a), whereby the contracting parties were required to 'consult together on matters of mutual concern in time of need'. TNA, CAB 148/116, DOP (Defence and Oversea Policy Committee) (71)34, 'Policy in the Persian Gulf', memorandum by the Secretary of State for Foreign Affairs and Commonwealth Affairs, 18 June 1971.

90 Resolutions 2752 and 2753 adopted by the General Assembly during its 26th session, accessed at www.un.org/documents/ga/res/26/ares26.htm on 25 April 2011.

91 TNA, FCO 8/1563, Wright to Mansley, 6 August 1971.

92 TNA, FCO 8/1561, Jedda to FCO, telegram no. 527, 8 July 1971.

93 TNA, FCO 8/1561. FCO to Bahrain, telegram no. 321, 9 July 1971.

94 TNA, FCO 8/1561, Abu Dhabi to FCO, telegram no. 96, 8 July 1971.

95 TNA, FCO 8/1561, Bahrain Agency to Bahrain Residency, telegram no. 47, 11 July 1971; Kuwait to FCO, telegram no. 327, 11 July 1971.

96 TNA, FCO 8/1561, Tehran to FCO, telegram no. 505, 11 July 1971.

97 TNA, FCO 8/1561, FCO to Tehran, telegram no. 369, 14 July 1971. See also FCO 8/1561, FCO to Tehran, telegram no. 375, 15 July 1971.

98 TNA, FCO 8/1561, Ramsbotham to Parsons, 15 July 1971.

99 TNA, FCO 8/1561, FCO to Tehran, telegram no. 369, 14 July 1971. See also FCO 8/1561, FCO to Tehran, telegram no. 375, 15 July 1971.

100 Nixon Presidential Materials Staff, NSC Files, Country Files, Middle East, Box 632, 'U.S. Recognition of the Gulf States of Bahrain and Qatar', from Haig to President, 14 July 1971.

101 TNA, FCO 8/1804, 'Annual Review for the Persian Gulf for 1971', report by Sir Geoffrey Arthur, 24 January 1972.

102 TNA, FO 1016/907, Reeve to Elam, 13 October 1971.

103 *New York Times*, various articles (13 June 1971), pp. 1–2, 35–36.

104 Nixon Presidential Materials Staff, NSC Files, Country Files, Middle East, Box 632, 'U.S. Recognition of the Gulf States of Bahrain and Qatar', from Haig to President, 14 July 1971.

105 TNA, FCO 8/1563, Tehran to Arabian Department, 6 August 1971.
106 BP Archive, available at the University of Warwick, Coventry, UK, papers of the British Petroleum Co. Ltd and BP Trading Ltd, archival reference 5726, 'Eastern Agencies Cost and Profitability – Airfield Cost Reports', P.S. Hyem to K. McKern, 'Expected Cost to BP of the R.A.F. Withdrawal from Bahrain and Sharjah', 16 August 1971. I thank the BP Archive for granting me access to materials of © BP plc and © Abu Dhabi Petroleum Company Ltd.
107 BP Archive, papers of the British Petroleum Co. Ltd and BP Trading Ltd, archival reference 5726, 'Eastern Agencies Cost and Profitability – Airfield Cost Reports', P.S. Hyem to K. McKern and F.V.J. Collins, 'BP's Options for the Future of: Bahrain Fueller Depot [and] Sharjah Hydrant Fueller Depot', 17 August 1971.
108 TNA, FCO 8/1804, 'Annual Review for the Persian Gulf for 1971', report by Sir Geoffrey Arthur, 24 January 1972.
109 Onley, *Britain and the Gulf Shaikhdoms*, p. 23.
110 TNA, FCO 8/1804, 'Annual Review for the Persian Gulf for 1971', report by Sir Geoffrey Arthur, 24 January 1972.
111 Resolution 2794 adopted by the General Assembly during its 26th session, accessed at www.un.org/documents/ga/res/26/ares26.htm on 25 April 2011.
112 'The Bahrain Transfer of Jurisdiction Regulation 1972'; 'The Qatar Termination of Jurisdiction Regulation 1972'; 'The Qatar Execution of Judgments Regulation 1972'; 'The Bahrain Termination of Jurisdiction Regulation 1972'; 'The Trucial States Execution of Judgments Regulation 1972'; 'The Trucial States Transfer of Jurisdiction Regulation 1972'; 'The Trucial States Termination of Jurisdiction Regulation 1972', *The Persian Gulf Gazette*, 20:1 (1972), 3–9.
113 TNA, FCO 8/1804, 'Annual Review for the Persian Gulf for 1971', report by Sir Geoffrey Arthur, 24 January 1972.
114 TNA, FCO 8/1804, 'Annual Review for the Persian Gulf for 1971', report by Sir Geoffrey Arthur, 24 January 1972.
115 Wright, 'The Run-up to Independence, 1971', p. 121.
116 TNA, FCO 8/1804, 'Annual Review for the Persian Gulf for 1971', report by Sir Geoffrey Arthur, 24 January 1972.
117 Louis and Robinson, 'The Imperialism of Decolonization'.
118 TNA, FCO 8/1562, 'al-Dustur al-Muaqqisa li al-Imarat al-'Arabiyah al-Muttahida', 18 July 1971; FCO 8/1562, Coles to Reeve, 26 July 1971; FCO 8/1562, Wright to Douglas-Home, 'The Union of Arab Emirates, November 1969 to July 1971', 26 July 1971.
119 TNA, FCO 8/1563, Slater to Allen and Acland, 'Union of Arab Emirates', 5 August 1971.

CHAPTER SIX

Formal sovereignty and continuing collaboration, 1972

This chapter will examine the consequences of the British withdrawal from the Persian Gulf and the emergence of Bahrain, Qatar and the UAE. The impact of decolonisation in international relations has not been analysed in sufficient depth. Mohammed Ayoob explores the issue in relation to the security dimensions of the Third World. He argues that 'imperial powers bequeathed to their postcolonial successor regimes territorial entities that were composed of distinct ... ethnic groups or ... divided previously homogenous ethnic communities' into different states through a 'cavalier construction of colonial borders'. Consequently, these postcolonial states 'found themselves facing challenges of either a secessionist or an irredentist character' after independence. Leaving aside his dubious conception of a 'homogenous ethnic community', one has only to think about the Basque region in Spain, Ireland or Scotland to question whether such a problem is in fact unique to the Third World. Most critically, he fails to make a clear distinction between four different issues:[1]

(1) A resumption, or a continuation, of the issues that had existed prior to the arrival of the imperial power;
(2) The issues that were brought in by, or created through contact with, the imperial power;
(3) The issues that were created or exacerbated by the modality of the way in which the imperial power departed; and
(4) The issues created by a larger force of modernity or modernisation.

Making an analytical distinction between these interconnected issues helps us understand what is often called the 'legacy of imperialism'. Partly owing to the sense of guilt in the former metropole, or the insecurity of the postcolonial states, imperial powers are often condemned not only for their own conduct (2) but also for problems already existing at the time of their expansion into foreign territories (1), or that had been created by the way in which they left (3), or that were going to happen sooner or later regardless of the imperial presence, as long as the region concerned was going to experience modernisation (4).

For example, there had been various rival groups in the Persian Gulf before Britain established a foothold in the region in the nineteenth century (1). The treaty relations with Britain institutionalised some of those divisions (2), and subsequently some groups were marginalised when the three states achieved full independence in 1971 (3). However, irrespective of British presence or withdrawal, sooner or later the polities in the region had to choose between becoming sovereign states or being absorbed by existing ones. This was simply the process of, and reflection on, the modernisation of international relations. It was a global phenomenon, even though it carried a strong European colour (4). Other examples could be found in debates over 'ethnic', economic and other problems, but this chapter will focus on the issue of external sovereignty.

Further to this point, this chapter will critically re-examine the existing understanding of the relationship between decolonisation and the norm of self-determination. Mikulas Fabry asserts that 'for the last 200 years, recognition of new states has been tied to the idea of self-determination of peoples. In fact, recognition and self-determination have been ... two sides of the same coin.'[2] This line of argument suggests that the idea of self-determination significantly contributed to the new states being recognised as fully sovereign states. This chapter will ask if the norm did indeed play a pivotal role in the new states in the Gulf.

Another point of reference will be the argument put forward by Wm. Roger Louis and Ronald Robinson on the persistence of imperial sway. They contend that decolonisation did not demolish imperial associations but merely translated them into a less conspicuous guise. This idea was advanced with an emphasis on the co-option of nationalist movements by the Anglo-American alliance. This chapter will build upon Louis and Robinson's argument by illuminating the centrality of sovereignty throughout the whole process.[3] Whereas they fixed their attention on the players of the game, this chapter will look into the rules. After all, while the players alter over time, the rules tend to endure.

These points will be explored with a focus on the 1970s. This is partly because most government sources of the 1980s onwards remain classified. Another consideration is that the Islamic Revolution in Iran in 1978/79 fundamentally altered the regional dynamics of the Persian Gulf; something that deserves to be examined in a separate

FORMAL SOVEREIGNTY AND CONTINUING COLLABORATION

study. Of the various events that took place in the 1970s, four will be closely analysed: Ra's al-Khaimah's attempt to achieve independence in 1971/72, the oil shock in 1973/74, the UAE and Saudi Arabia's rapprochement in 1974, and the development of US policy on the Gulf during the Nixon era.

Saqr and the irrelevance of self-determination

By the end of 1971, 'Ajman, Fujairah, Sharjah, Umm al-Qaiwain, Abu Dhabi and Dubai had formed the UAE, while Qatar and Bahrain had achieved full independence separately. This meant that eight of the nine formerly Protected States had emerged into international society as fully sovereign states, but Ra's al-Khaimah was left out of the game. And Britain played a curiously mixed role in this episode.

When Britain's Political Agent Julian Walker was touring the coast of the Gulf persuading the other rulers to join the UAE in July 1971, he was initially accompanied by Shaikh Khalid bin Saqr al-Qasimi, the son of Shaikh Saqr bin Muhammad al-Qasimi, the Ruler of Ra's al-Khaimah. Yet Shaikh Saqr soon ordered his son to return and consequently Walker had to travel alone, persuading the other rulers to follow Dubai and Abu Dhabi's initiative. For a long time, Shaikh Saqr had appeared wary while Shaikh Zayid of Abu Dhabi was establishing himself as a leader of the Protected States. Shaikh Saqr once commented to a British officer of the Trucial Oman Scouts that 'the people did not love Sheikh Zaid, only his money'. He even 'made it quite clear that he disliked the Ruler of Abu Dhabi and would like to "do him down" should the occasion arise'.[4] Reciprocally, Shaikh Zayid claimed that Shaikh Saqr had 'an exaggerated idea of his own importance' since, during the earlier period of negotiations over the formation of the UAE, he was used as 'a cat's paw' by the Rulers of Qatar and Dubai 'whenever they wanted to sabotage the Union of Nine'. Still, Zayid contended, Ra's al-Khaimah 'would have to join the Union in the end'.[5] In any case, joining the UAE would not only entail working together with Abu Dhabi on a day-to-day basis but, more importantly, it would require that Shaikh Saqr accept the exclusive veto rights of Abu Dhabi and Dubai. Moreover, he also feared, rightly as it turned out, that the presidency would continue to be held by Abu Dhabi and not be rotated. The relatively limited power of the Supreme Council, which comprised the rulers of the constituting emirates, was also a source of his dissatisfaction.[6]

Shaikh Saqr also thought that Britain was not giving enough support to Ra's al-Khaimah in its territorial claim over the two Tunb islands versus Iran. Unlike Sharjah, which agreed that Iran would occupy part of Abu Musa, Ra's al-Khaimah was maintaining a harder stance over the boundary dispute. Feeding into these concerns was the hope of oil. The prospect of oil revenue was giving Saqr some confidence to compete with Abu Dhabi. The US Union Oil Company was drilling in Ra's al-Khaimah, and Shaikh Saqr was hoping that future revenue from oil would put his country on a par with Dubai and Abu Dhabi.[7] Although the first hole had to be abandoned in 1969 owing to technical difficulties, by the end of 1971 both the oil company and the Ruler were openly optimistic that there would be commercial-level quantities of oil.[8] Concerns were raised that the offshore drilling might infringe Iranian rights around the Tunb islands, but Shaikh Saqr was determined to go forward.[9] Thus, expecting the discovery of a significant oil reserve that would allow him not to 'kneel' to Abu Dhabi, Shaikh Saqr refused to join the UAE and sought independence.[10] His obvious first contact was Britain.

However, there is no evidence that Britain gave any serious consideration to Shaikh Saqr's request for approval of Ra's al-Khaimah's bid for independence. The relationship between the two had not been a straightforward one. Once, a British Political Agent in Dubai portrayed him as 'wall-eyed and enigmatic, parrying one question with another or trying to count up to 11 on the fat fingers of his Palestinian secretary to give me the numbers of his retinue for the trip to Muscat'.[11] Sir William Luce attempted to broker a deal over the two Tunbs whereby Iran would occupy the islands in return for financial compensation, but Shaikh Saqr declined.[12] The file that is most likely to contain the key papers in the British National Archives pertaining to the details of this negotiation is still classified. However, I have found a document that alludes to an arrangement made between Iran and Britain.

In a telegram sent from the FCO to Bahrain on 23 November, a Foreign Office official named 'Godber' outlines two timetables regarding the negotiation with Ra's al-Khaimah between 25 November and 1 December. In both scenarios, 'P A' (which presumably refers to the Political Agent in Dubai, Julian Walker) is scheduled to see the Ruler of Ra's al-Khaimah on 28 November, and give him the date of the 'L Day'. The 'L Day on Tunbs' was set as 30 November – the day when Iranian forces actually seized the island, just prior to the British forces' departure the following day.[13] The telegram refers to 'paragraph 3 of Bahrain Residency telegram no. 868' and 'paragraph 4 of Bahrain telegram no. 826', neither of which can be found in the same folder. Some other documents believed to be originally contained in the folder have been removed. It is not clear whether Walker actually told Saqr on 28 November of the 'L Day'. However, a later telegram records that by 25 November Walker had had some conversations with Saqr, who 'was reluctant even to discuss the Tunbs'.[14] Of course, the restricted evidence available does not reveal the full picture of what was negotiated between Iran and Britain. But it does suggest that Britain was not only aware of the 'L Day' but also that Iran was going to seize the island on 30 November.

Returning to the larger point regarding Ra's al-Khaimah's independence, circumstantial evidence suggests that Britain was at the very least uncomfortable with Shaikh Saqr's attempt to disturb the unity of the UAE, and at most determined from the beginning to refuse such a request.[15] Simon C. Smith interprets that Walker 'felt able to rebuff' Shaikh Saqr's request, based on a telegram issued on 26 November.[16] However, in this telegram Walker refers only to his conversation with Shaikh Saqr the day before, whereas Shaikh Saqr had been attempting since August to take a different course outside the UAE.[17] In fact, the negotiations taking place during this period were more complex than they may appear in retrospect.

After the formation of the UAE was effectively determined, Shaikh Saqr hinted to Walker that he might contact other countries, including Arab governments, for support for Ra's al-Khaimah's independence. Nonetheless, Walker did not expect that he would get any substantive support.[18] In August, Shaikh Saqr admitted that King Faisal of Saudi Arabia had sent him a letter urging him to join the UAE. Expecting that Shaikh Saqr would eventually have to do just that, Britain could afford to take a straightforward position; thus, it would terminate the Friendship Treaties, the date of which was eventually set for 1 December, and Ra's al-Khaimah would become a member of the new country. Shaikh Saqr, on the other hand, was clear that he did not want to follow suit but instead have Ra's al-Khaimah treated as an independent state. However, he also suggested that Britain should continue to provide military protection, and undertake certain administrative responsibilities such as control of visas and passports.[19] In essence, Ra's al-Khaimah wanted to be recognised as an independent state while maintaining some of the benefits of being part of Britain's informal empire.

There was no space for Britain to reconsider the termination of treaties or military withdrawal, but neither did it want to leave Ra's al-Khaimah high and dry.[20] When Shaikh Saqr and his son requested on 28 November that 'they set up a small consular office in London', Walker said, 'I would ask but personally saw no objections'.[21] Interestingly, in August, Walker had told Shaikh Saqr that Britain could not give him a letter 'authorising him to approach foreign powers for financial relief, so that he could avoid our present ban on establishing special relationships for the future'.[22] This implies that Britain was trying to keep Ra's al-Khaimah in its informal empire in its own way.

Seeing little hope in haggling with the British, however, by mid-September Shaikh Saqr had in fact turned his attention to the US. Britain was going to withdraw from the Gulf by the end of the year anyway, but he hoped that the US might take a different view of the issue. Thus he approached an American businessman called Robert Sheridan. Shaikh Saqr and his son Shaikh Khalid had been in close contact with Sheridan through previous business negotiations, and Shaikh Saqr asked Sheridan to convey a message to Washington asking for support for Ra's al-Khaimah's independence.[23] It is not clear exactly why Shaikh Saqr did not directly contact the US mission in Dhahran instead, and his oblique method of negotiation only provoked suspicions about his intentions.[24] Washington did not understand why Shaikh Saqr had asked a private businessman to act as an intermediary, and therefore proceeded with caution.

After failing to receive a positive response from Washington through private channels, Shaikh Saqr contacted the US directly, inviting it to build a military base in Ra's al-Khaimah. He also mentioned that he had been 'approached three times' by the Soviets in regard to refuelling facilities. He thus used the typical Cold War tactic of playing off rival superpowers against each other, but Washington was not convinced by this either. They reckoned that Shaikh Saqr's approach was an 'attempted end-run to avoid facing problems with Iran' and 'sacrificing his "sovereignty"' by participating in the UAE.[25] The US saw little reason to contemplate an option that even its imperial 'teacher' Britain would not take.[26] On 27 September, Lee Dinsmore, the US Consul General in Dhahran, told Shaikh Saqr that the US was not considering accepting his invitation to build military installations in Ra's al-Khaimah. Shaikh Saqr appeared 'crestfallen' and asked Dinsmore not to inform Britain about their negotiations. Dinsmore promised to keep the matter secret, yet revealed the whole story to Julian Walker on the same day.[27] Clearly the ex-imperial metropole mattered more to the US than a small polity in the Gulf seeking the right to self-determination. The Nixon administration could not afford to create further complications in the Gulf when it was having enough trouble in Vietnam.

Whether or not Shaikh Saqr was aware of the insincerity of the US, he continued to press the matter. While Britain had decided to terminate their treaty relations on 1 December, in early November Saqr's son Shaikh Khalid visited Washington and met the Assistant Secretary of State Joseph Sisco, in the presence of a representative of the Union Oil Company. The delegation from Ra's al-Khaimah asked for support for its bid for independence. 'Time was running out', noted a Lebanese adviser to Shaikh Saqr.[28] He stated that sovereignty is the 'primary issue' and Shaikh Saqr would not agree to any solution 'fussing' the question of sovereignty. He also mentioned that Ra's al-Khaimah had thought about the question of UN membership. He expressed his awareness of practical issues by remarking that gaining admission might be difficult, and the various problems should be tackled 'stage by stage'.[29] Ra's al-Khaimah's last-minute attempt, however, proved to be unsuccessful. On 27 November, Dinsmore conveyed a message from Sisco to Khalid, politely but firmly rejecting Ra's al-Khaimah's request.[30] Shaikh Saqr could only respond with 'resigned bitterness', and eventually he decided that the only option left for his country was to follow Abu Dhabi, in February 1972. Thus, it joined the UAE.[31] Only now was the formalisation of the model of sovereignty of the Protected States complete.

The episode prefacing Ra's al-Khaimah's participation in the UAE offers a stark contrast to the process whereby the other members of the Protected States achieved independence. Whereas Abu Dhabi and Dubai were essentially forced to become independent and only grudgingly took the negative option left behind by the imperial metropole's unilateral departure, Ra's al-Khaimah proactively sought independence and even tried to exploit superpower rivalries for its survival. Contrary to what would be commonly assumed, international society gave full sovereign status only to those who did not want it and refused it to the one country who appealed for the right to self-determination. These findings contradict the conventional understanding of the relationship between self-determination and decolonisation. We have seen Fabry assert that 'recognition and self-determination have been ... two sides of the same coin', but for the constituent member emirates of the UAE, self-determination was at best irrelevant and at worst detrimental in regard to recognition as a sovereign state.[32] In the final reckoning then, self-determination did not play a pivotal role in the decolonisation of this region, unlike the assumption in the wider body of literature.

Oil shock and rapprochement

Once the gate of sovereignty was closed, the new states departed from the hybrid international system combining imperialism and sovereignty and started to behave as fully sovereign states. The UAE, Qatar and Bahrain were now given legal status as independent states, assuming 'international legal sovereignty' in Stephen Krasner's words. None of them had sought this in January 1968 but, now that they had it, they could start to act upon it, which they did – and that transformation took place more quickly than expected.

On 6 October 1973, Egyptian and Syrian forces entered the territories held by Israel and the October War broke out. This of course accompanied the use of what is commonly known as the 'oil weapon' (*silah al-bitrul* or *silah al-naft* in Arabic). The 'oil weapon' was effectively an embargo with two elements – production was cut back and restrictions were put on exports. Following the outbreak of the war, the 'Gulf committee' of the Organization of the Petroleum Exporting Countries (OPEC), including Iran, Iraq, Saudi Arabia, Kuwait, Qatar and the UAE, announced on 16 October that it was to raise the posted price of oil by 70%, to US$5.11 per barrel. This came as a bombshell to the world, since up to that point it had been the major oil companies and not the producer governments that set the oil prices. However, more was to follow. The next day, the oil ministers from the members of the Organization of Arab Petroleum Exporting Countries (OAPEC) met in Kuwait and agreed on an immediate cut of 5% in their production level. Thus, the first half of the 'oil weapon' was launched by Algeria, Iraq, Egypt, Libya, Saudi Arabia, Kuwait, Oman, Qatar, Bahrain and Abu Dhabi,[33] and three days later came the second part, when Riyadh announced a complete embargo to the US, which was followed by Kuwait and the UAE.[34] The total ban on exports of oil was also extended to the Netherlands, Portugal, South Africa and Rhodesia, meaning that the 'oil weapon' caused wide and deep distress not only in the US but also in the Western world as a whole. Thus, the whole episode has been called the first 'oil shock'.[35]

The fact that the former Protected States of the Persian Gulf could launch such overt economic sanctions against Britain and, more broadly, the West seemed to signify a drastic shift in the international relations of the region. Previously, under Britain's informal empire, the external relations of the Protected States were delegated to Britain. Qatar and Abu Dhabi had joined OPEC in 1961 and 1967, respectively, and they had also joined OAPEC in 1970, together with Bahrain. At that time, however, they would not have been expected to ever act directly against British interests in the international scene. However, the 'oil weapon' decisively announced to the world that they had become independent polities. The actual shortage of oil in 1973/74 was not nearly as serious as had been imagined at the time, but it was received with great surprise. The fact that those states that had hitherto been looked upon as mere puppets could stand up to the West caused a deep and widespread psychological blow. They might have been unwilling to become independent only a couple of years before, but now they appeared in the theatre of global politics as independent actors. Not only had they attained the legal personality of independent states, but they were now able to express their autonomy through foreign or economic policy if they so wished. They had not become antagonistic to Britain at a substantive level, and in many ways they were eager to maintain a cooperative relationship with the West, but decolonisation had shifted the terms and modality of the alliance.

At the same time, their new status as fully sovereign states did not guarantee that the principle of non-intervention would always be observed. Stephen Krasner argues that the constituting states of international society hold the norm of non-interference, yet often break it at the same time.[36] In support of his view, sources suggest that the US was contemplating the possibility of compromising the territory of these states, even though it did not act upon it.

On 15 November 1973, James Schlesinger, the US Defence Secretary, told the Third Earl of Cromer, the British ambassador to the US, that 'it was no longer obvious to him that the United States could not use force' in the Middle East.[37] In response, the Assessments Staff of the Cabinet Office consulted the Foreign and Commonwealth Office and the MOD and prepared a paper to be presented to the Prime Minister and the top officials of both departments.[38] The report, drafted in December, remarked that in order to secure the oil supplies for western Europe, Japan and the US, under adverse circumstances the Nixon administration would consider, along with other options, seizing the oil fields of Kuwait, Abu Dhabi and Saudi Arabia. 'Occupation forces would be needed', and the US would hold the territories concerned, 'probably for a period of some ten years to give time for the west to develop alternative energy supplies'. In the case of military intervention in Abu Dhabi, 'the Americans might ask the United Kingdom to undertake this particular operation', since there were seconded British officers in the Abu Dhabi Defence Force. Alternatively, the US might 'replace the existing Rulers of Saudi Arabia, Kuwait and Abu Dhabi with more amenable men, and at the same time provide them with military support, both to maintain their authority at home and to defend themselves from foreign attack by more extreme Arab States', a strategy that bore a striking resemblance to that employed by the former British presence in the Gulf.[39] Schlesinger's recollection in a later interview largely corresponded with the British observation.[40] In short, the 1973 oil shock and the Anglo-American response represented opposing facets of the relationship between the former Protected States and the transatlantic alliance. One was the emerging tendency of the new states to act independently as fully sovereign states, and the other was the continuation of the hierarchical relationship, wherein the Anglo-American alliance might consider infringing the sovereignty of the Gulf States.

The oil shock is often remembered as the watershed of the Gulf region towards its prosperity. While there is much truth in the general idea, it should also be noted that the region had already started its march towards economic development prior to the increase in oil price. For example, the founding of the Arabic newspaper *Al-Wahdah* in August 1973 had demonstrated the increasing wealth of the Arab-speaking population in Abu Dhabi. Compared to the more established *Al-Ittihad*, the new paper targeted a more commercially orientated clientele, featuring advertisement of luxury goods such as BMW and Rolex.[41] Soon it also added a daily financial report of Merrill Lynch.[42] The oil shock accelerated this existing trend, but what enabled all the economic growth was the stable international order that had been established by 1971–72.

The new order also enabled the three new states to stabilise their relationships with their regional neighbours. In 1974, Saudi Arabia and the UAE signed a pivotal international agreement and subsequently established formal diplomatic ties. Since the emergence of the UAE in 1971, Saudi Arabia had refused to recognise its sovereign status, due to the dispute with Abu Dhabi and Oman over the Buraimi Oasis that had started in 1952. The literature has highlighted the 1974 agreement as a major breakthrough in the dispute, which accompanied the normalisation of Saudi–UAE relations. For example, Mattair asserts that Saudi Arabia renounced its claims to the Buraimi region in exchange for receiving 'a corridor to the Gulf between Qatar and Abu Dhabi, through the area of Khor al-Udaid, and most of the territory covering the Shaiba/Zararah oil field'.[43]

For the purpose of our discussion, what is more important than the seeming exchange of territories is the fact that the UAE could sign such an international agreement on a par with Saudi Arabia as sovereign states. This marked a sharp contrast with the initial stages of the conflict between 1952 and 1955.[44] In the Arbitration Tribunal set up in 1954, Abu Dhabi and Oman were represented by Britain in opposition to Saudi Arabia, which was supported by the US.[45] Abu Dhabi, as a constituting emirate of the UAE, could now negotiate the settlement directly with Saudi Arabia. Once again, such an occurrence signified the sovereign status of the UAE and the increasing importance of the regional dynamics of the international relations of the Gulf.

Furthermore, the 1974 agreement contains some oblique elements that the literature has tended to overlook. First and foremost, the 1974 agreement conceded to Saudi Arabia a large part of an area south of Buraimi, which had been considered to be Oman's territory. Even though Oman was going through a war in Dhufar at that time, and hence there was a degree of uncertainty regarding the future of the local regime, it is not entirely clear exactly why Shaikh Zayid of Abu Dhabi decided to sign an agreement that manifestly violated Oman's territory. Also, there is an issue of ratification. Alexander Melamid remarks that the agreement had not been ratified, but Article 9 stipulates that it would enter into 'force immediately on signature'.[46]

One may suspect the involvement of oil companies during these negotiations. I have been allowed to inspect some of the classified papers of the Iraq Petroleum Company. The IPC was closely observing the developments leading up to and during the Buraimi Oasis dispute through both the public media and the Foreign Office; none of the papers, however, directly suggest the company's proactive involvement in influencing the outcome.[47] Two decades later, however, a further question mark was placed over the perplexing history of the 1974 agreement. In 1993, Saudi Arabia registered the agreement with the UN. The Saudi intention behind publicising the secret agreement is unclear, but it implies that the dispute could be brought up again if Saudi Arabia wanted to do so in the future.[48]

On the whole, both the oil shock and the UAE–Saudi rapprochement demonstrated that the decolonisation of the Protected States had given them the status to act as independent sovereign states, although it did not insulate them from military threat from their neighbours and external powers, either perceived or actual. The Protected States were now undoubtedly fully fledged players in the game of international politics. They challenged some of the other players on certain occasions, but did not disregard the rules of the game. In essence, they accepted, and benefited from, the most fundamental rule of international society – sovereignty.

Informal empire decolonised

The previous sections have demonstrated that the period following the British withdrawal was characterised by the formalisation of the sovereign status of the UAE, Qatar and Bahrain. This process went in tandem with what Wm. Roger Louis and Ronald Robinson called the 'imperialism of decolonisation'. Louis and Robinson argue that the British Empire after the Second World War 'was nationalized and internationalized as part of the Anglo-American coalition'.[49] Whereas the previous chapters have demonstrated that sovereignty was the key device in the smooth and sustainable transformation of the imperial relationship, this section will examine in what areas the British and American influence was preserved during the 1970s.

First and foremost, the British influence remained significant at a linguistic and cultural, as well as a personal, level between the elites, and to a lesser extent among the general populace. Prior to the announcement in January 1968, the British Political Resident had stated, 'We must ... increasingly prepare ourselves for the post-1971 world in which our commercial and cultural relations with the Gulf will be dominant and in which we shall have to meet competition from many powers now virtually unrepresented here.'[50]

Yet, of course, the logical consequence of Britain's withdrawal from the region was that it could no longer exert overt imperial command as it once had. For example, while Britain imagined it was leaving the Gulf with grace and in order, in Ra's al-Khaimah the Iranian seizure of the Tunb islands was causing riots, an angry response to Britain's failure to protect them. Shops were damaged and an Iranian bank was set on fire.[51] By the same token, when a coup took place in Sharjah in 1972, Britain could only closely observe the situation as a third party. On 25 January, the Ruler of Sharjah was killed in an unsuccessful coup led by the former Ruler, who himself had been removed from power in 1965. The coup was contained after a battle that left five dead and seven wounded, and the ruling family elected Shaikh Sultan bin Mohammed, the brother of the assassinated Ruler, as the new Ruler by unanimous decision. The Foreign Office was told about an operation carried out by British ex-officers, but was not directly involved in the situation.[52] The incident raised concerns from backbenchers that it revealed the weakness of Britain's 'limited and spasmodic presence',[53] but the Conservative government claimed that it was largely an internal feudal problem.[54] Walker was convinced that Shaikh Saqr, the Ruler of Ra's al-Khaimah, had been involved behind the scenes;[55] however, the policy of the Foreign Office was that Britain had by this point become an 'outside referee' of such internal problems.[56]

On the northern shore of the Gulf, Britain took a similar attitude when Iran and Iraq were negotiating a solution to their regional conflicts, including the dispute over Shatt al-Arab. Britain stood outside the discussions, only collecting information from media sources and indirect official channels.[57] It was no longer the crucial hub or mediator of regional politics.

However, personal ties between the elites remained strong. When Britain and the UAE set up a joint committee in 1976, the main point that they discussed was Britain's selling of commercial aircraft; the UAE's interest lay in Britain's 'skills and expertise' in civil administration.[58] Britain continued to hold significant soft power even after its hard power withered away in the region. On 2 February 1972, the US Deputy Assistant Secretary of Defense for Near Eastern, African and South Asian Affairs remarked that British importance remained 'considerable' and that the US had 'assumed none of the former British military role or functions' and had 'no intention of seeking or appearing to replace the British presence in the Gulf'.[59] In fact, a study later issued by the Middle East Department of the Foreign Office in 1979 noted that Britain 'was struggling to maintain an "arm's length" distance' with the Gulf States due to '(a) our historical association and role in their transition to nationhood' and '(b) our continuing collaboration over national security matters and defence equipment'.[60]

The second point to be made is that the American influence in the region steadily increased during the 1970s but was qualitatively different from that which Britain had exercised. Instead of inheriting Britain's informal empire in the southern Gulf, the US took a more indirect approach to the maintenance of security in the whole of the Gulf region. The conventional understanding is that this line of policy crystallised as part of the Nixon Doctrine in the early 1970s. The Nixon Doctrine itself arose in 1969 as a response to US overcommitment in Vietnam, setting out that security matters in Asia should be taken care of by local actors. This was applied to the Gulf region in the early 1970s through the nomination of Iran and Saudi Arabia as the 'twin pillars', the two major regional proxies that would maintain the security of the region on behalf of the US.[61] This indirect approach is often compared with the Carter Doctrine that came about a decade later. Following the Islamic Revolution and hostage crisis in Iran and the Soviet invasion of Afghanistan, the then US President Jimmy Carter asserted in his State of the Union address:

> An attempt by any outside force to gain control of the Persian Gulf region will be regarded as an assault on the vital interests of the United States of America, and such an assault will be repelled by any means necessary, including military force.[62]

Thus, it appears that the indirect 'twin pillars' policy of the Nixon Doctrine nicely contrasts with the Carter Doctrine, but this narrative presents some problems. Firstly, there is some debate as to whether the Nixon Doctrine was actually a policy of the Nixon administration. For example, Jeffrey Macris contends that the Nixon administration's 'twin pillars' policy 'originated in early 1968 as the Johnson administration struggled to make quick decisions in a period of rapid political change'.[63] Advancing this line of argument even further, Roham Alvandi asserts that the US reliance on Iran and Saudi Arabia was inherited from the British during the Johnson era, and the Nixon administration adopted a policy of Iranian primacy by positioning Saudi Arabia as a junior partner.[64] Alvandi's thesis also leads to the question of whether Iran and Saudi Arabia were regarded as equal partners. The idea of Iranian supremacy during the Nixon era is particularly convincing where security matters are concerned. For example, the value of arms transfers from the US to Iran went up from US$103.6 million in 1970 to US$552.7 million in 1972, while those to Saudi Arabia increased only from US$15.8 million to US$312.4 million during the same period.[65] Nor did Saudi Arabia interfere in the Dhufar rebellion in Oman as proactively as Iran, or support the conservative regime in North Yemen as enthusiastically as Britain and the US expected.[66]

However, the more fundamental question is whether there existed a 'twin pillars policy' at all. On the one hand, Macris asserts that the term 'twin pillars' arose during the Nixon administration, although he does not give any documentary evidence.[67] On the other hand, Taylor Fain maintains that the term could not be found in the contemporary documentary record.[68] My experience in the archives chimes with Fain's findings, and the earliest usage of the term that I could identify was in a 1975 edition of *The Washington Post*. I corresponded with the author of the piece and asked how he came up with the term, but even he was not clear exactly when and how it came into use.[69] This finding suggests that it is debatable what exactly the 'twin pillars' policy was – whether it was a proactive and coherent policy, or mere rhetoric to mask a lack of policy that was only retrospectively applied in later years.

In asking why Macris and other authors have taken the terminology of 'twin pillars' as a given, his statement is particularly telling.[70] It noted, 'it is correct to associate the rise of the term 'Twin Pillars' with the Nixon administration, and especially with ... Henry Kissinger, who fleshed out the Persian Gulf policy and gave to it a philosophic underpinning'.[71] This statement is indicative of how significant Henry Kissinger was, not only for the policies of the Nixon administration but also for the forming of the historical understanding in later years. There is no evidence to assert that Kissinger intended to retroactively tailor the historical narrative regarding his policy towards the Gulf, but it should be noted that his influential memoirs were published in 1979, when a new momentum in international relations was unleashed with the revolution in Iran.[72]

On the whole, British involvement in the local affairs of the Persian Gulf declined following its withdrawal from the region, and the US did not replace Britain's imperial role. Even so, Britain and the US *in toto* continued to hold sway in the region throughout the 1970s. The cost-effective Anglo-American indirect presence was helped by the fact that the Gulf States were now formally independent. The formalisation of their sovereign status not only meant that the new states possessed equal legal status versus the former imperial metropole and superpowers, but it also enabled both Britain and the US to maintain an international order favourable to the West by means of consensus and collaboration, whilst minimising direct involvement and the use of coercive measures. The whole process entailed the rearrangement

FORMAL SOVEREIGNTY AND CONTINUING COLLABORATION

of the collaborative relationship that developed during the period of Britain's informal empire. Alexander Wendt and Daniel Friedheim's observation of the system of sovereign states is particularly telling:

> The contemporary states system embodies a tension between juridical equality and de facto inequality.[73]

The findings of this chapter suggest that the dissolution of Britain's informal empire and the full independence of the UAE, Qatar and Bahrain accompanied a rearrangement of their collaborative relationship by means of a formalisation of sovereignty.

Ra's al-Khaimah's ultimately unsuccessful move towards independence in 1971/72 made it clear that the key factor in achieving sovereign status in the Gulf was not the ideal of self-determination. The use of the oil weapon by the UAE, Qatar and Bahrain demonstrated that the new states were no longer mere clients of the former imperial metropole but had instead become capable and proactive players in international affairs. UAE's rapprochement with Saudi Arabia in 1974 confirmed that the regional dynamics had gained their own momentum. By the time Iran and Iraq signed the Algiers Agreement in 1975, Britain was happily staying outside the game. Similarly, the US remained aloof. Conventionally it has been believed that the Nixon administration appointed Iran and Saudi Arabia as the 'twin pillars' of the Gulf, but the evidence, or rather the lack thereof, casts some doubt on the assumption that there was such a coherent regional policy at that time. These findings correspond with Gregory Gause's argument that the Persian Gulf had its own regional dynamics in the 1970s, and they also indicate that the three new states had grown out of Britain's informal empire and joined the regional system.[74]

At the same time, a number of observers have remarked that Britain's influence remained considerable at cultural and individual levels. The ostensibly opposing impressions were in fact two sides of the same coin. Both reflected the fact that the UAE, Qatar and Bahrain had achieved full sovereignty. They had been admitted as full members of international society, and in return they accepted the norm of sovereignty. They sometimes acted against the apparent interests of the West, but they did not challenge the foundation of international society. The most disturbing act of sabotage imaginable to the members of international society, including Britain and the US, was the rejection of the norm of sovereignty. As Stephen Krasner points out, the norm of sovereignty (particularly the principle of non-intervention) is often violated, but as long as states bother to pay lip service, even while acting hypocritically, the idea of sovereignty continues to function as the constitutive norm of international society. Thus, more than the cultural influence, the most important and long-lasting influence of Britain's informal empire on the international relations of the Gulf was the consolidation of the system of sovereign states. Sovereignty institutionalised collaboration. Sovereignty standardised collaboration.[75]

Using the framework set out at the beginning of this chapter, the covert preservation of the imperial order – what Louis and Robinson call the 'imperialism of decolonisation' – needs to be understood not only as the transformation (3) of the former imperial relationship (2), but more importantly as a larger process of modernisation (4). It enabled the former Protected States' adaptation of the norm of the modern system of sovereign states and the existing members' acceptance of their participation. Suppose, for a moment, that the regional actors had rejected the norm of sovereignty altogether and refused to interact with the former metropole and other sovereign states as comparable legal personae with mutually exclusive territories. This would have disturbed the very foundation upon which international society rests. The effects would have been far more serious for Britain, and for the West, than if they had lost their influence in a region or two against the Eastern camp. The consolidation of the modern system of states, which was only completed with decolonisation, provided the fundamental basis for the development of the international society that followed and to which we now belong. Literature that tends to look at the region through the lens of the Cold War misses this profound point. Thus, the rearrangement of the imperial relationship was enabled by the formalisation of sovereignty. The two processes were interlinked, and together they implied that decolonisation rearranged the collaborative relationship that emerged out of imperialism and established it in a new pattern.

Notes

1 Mohammed Ayoob, *The Third World Security Predicament: State Making, Regional Conflict, and the International System* (Boulder: Lynne Rienner Publishers, 1995), pp. 34–39.
2 Mikulas Fabry, *Recognizing States: International Society and the Establishment of New States Since 1776* (Oxford: Oxford University Press, 2010), p. 9.
3 Louis and Robinson, 'The Imperialism of Decolonization', p. 487.
4 TNA, WO 337/18, 'A Talk with the Ruler', report by Ash, 4 March 1969.
5 TNA, FCO 8/1563, Bahrain to the FCO, 20 August 1971.
6 NARA, RG 59, Subject Numeric Files, 1970–73, Box 2632, POL TRUCIAL ST, Department of State to Dhahran, 'Ras al-Khaimah Requests U.S. Support', 8 November 1971.
7 TNA, FCO 8/1782, 'Ras al Khaimah', Drace-Francis, 30 July 1971.
8 TNA, FCO 8/1782, Coles to Everard, 15 February 1971; Walker to Elam, 24 October 1971.
9 TNA, FCO 8/1782, Walker to Wright, 10 May 1971; Drace-Francis to Walker, undated letter, c. August 1971.

FORMAL SOVEREIGNTY AND CONTINUING COLLABORATION

10 NARA, RG 59, Subject Numeric Files, 1970–73, Box 2632, POL TRUCIAL ST, Department of State to Beirut and Dhahran, 'Ras al-Khaimah Request for U.S. Support', 11 November 1971.
11 TNA, FCO 8/1510, 'Dubai and the Northern Trucial States: Annual Review for 1970', by Bullard, 10 December 1970.
12 Mattair, *The Three Occupied UAE Islands*, pp. 120–121, 469–470.
13 TNA, FCO 8/1567, FCO to Bahrain Residency, telegram no. 656, 23 November 1971.
14 TNA, FCO 8/1567, Bahrain Residency to FCO, telegram no. 897, 25 November 1971.
15 TNA, FO 1016/905 remains classified.
16 Smith, *Britain's Revival and Fall in the Gulf*, p. 105.
17 TNA, FCO 8/1567, Dubai to Bahrain, telegram no. 374, 26 November 1971.
18 NARA, RG 59, Subject Numeric Files, 1970–73, Box 2632, POL TRUCIAL ST, Dhahran to Secretary of State, 29 September 1971.
19 TNA, FCO 8/1563, Walker to Bahrain, telegram no. 230, 25 August 1971; FCO 8/1567, Dubai to Bahrain, 26 November 1971; Dubai to Bahrain, telegram no. 389, 28 November 1971.
20 Saqr also suggested that, should the termination of the Friendship Treaties be carried out, it would be on 24 December rather than 1 December. The issue was brought to the Foreign Secretary but declined by him. TNA, FCO 8/1567, Dubai to Bahrain, telegram no. 377; Bahrain to FCO, telegram no. 904; FCO to Bahrain, telegram no. 676, 26 November 1971.
21 TNA, FCO 8/1567, Dubai to Bahrain, telegram no. 389, 28 November 1971.
22 TNA, FCO 8/1563, Walker to Bahrain, telegram no. 230, 25 August 1971.
23 NARA, RG 59, Subject Numeric Files, 1970–73, Box 2632, POL TRUCIAL ST, Department of State to Dhahran, 'US Support for Ras al-Khaimah', 24 September 1971.
24 NARA, RG 59, Subject Numeric Files, 1970–73, Box 2632, POL TRUCIAL ST, Department of State to Dhahran and London, 'Possible Ras al-Khaimah Interest in Military Installations', 10 September 1971; Dhahran to Secretary of State, 11 September 1971.
25 NARA, RG 59, Subject Numeric Files, 1970–73, Box 2632, POL TRUCIAL ST, Department of State to Dhahran, 'US Support for Ras al-Khaimah', 24 September 1971.
26 TNA, FCO 46/43, record of meeting, 11 January 1968.
27 NARA, RG 59, Subject Numeric Files, 1970–73, Box 2632, POL TRUCIAL ST, Dhahran to Secretary of State, 29 September 1971.
28 NARA, RG 59, Subject Numeric Files, 1970–73, Box 2632, POL TRUCIAL ST. Dhahran to Secretary of State, 'Ras al-Khaimah', 30 November 1971.
29 NARA, RG 59, Subject Numeric Files, 1970–73, Box 2632, POL TRUCIAL ST, Department of State to Dhahran, 'Ras al-Khaimah Requests U.S. Support', 8 November 1971.
30 NARA, RG 59, Subject Numeric Files, 1970–73, Box 2632, POL TRUCIAL ST, Department of State to Dhahran, 'Ras al-Khaimah Request for U.S. Support', 30 November 1971.
31 NARA, RG 59, Subject Numeric Files, 1970–73, Box 2632, POL TRUCIAL ST, Dhahran to Secretary of State, 'Ras al-Khaimah', 30 November 1971.
32 Fabry, *Recognizing States*, p. 9.
33 Naturally, the event was reported widely in the Arab media but the level of detail varied considerably. The Egyptian and Lebanese press tended to report events in more detail than their Iraqi counterparts. See *Al-Ahram* (18 October 1973), p. 1; *Al-Hayat* (18 October 1973), p. 1; *Al-Jumhuriyah* (18 October 1973), p. 1.
34 F. Gregory Gause III, *The International Relations of the Persian Gulf* (Cambridge: Cambridge University Press, 2010), pp. 28–29.
35 For a more detailed account of the oil shock and the context leading up to the event,

see Daniel Yergin, *The Prize: The Epic Quest for Oil, Money, and Power* (New York: Free Press, 1992), pp. 588–612.
36 Stephen D. Krasner, *Sovereignty: Organized Hypocrisy* (Princeton, NJ: Princeton University Press, 1999), pp. 3–4.
37 TNA, PREM 15/1768, 'Middle East: Possible Use of Force by the United States', draft prepared by Assessments Staff, 13 December 1973.
38 TNA, PREM 15/1768, Note by the Assessments Staff, 12 December 1973.
39 TNA, PREM 15/1768, 'Middle East: Possible Use of Force by the United States', draft prepared by Assessments Staff, 13 December 1973. See also Owen Bowcott, 'UK Feared Americans Would Invade Gulf during 1973 Crisis: Heath Feared US Planned to Invade Gulf', *Guardian* (1 January 2004), home pages, p. 1; Glenn Frankel, 'U.S. Mulled Seizing Oil Fields in '73: British Memo Cites Notion of Sending Airborne to Mideast', *The Washington Post* (1 January 2004), A section, p. 1; Lizette Alvarez, 'U.S. Weighed Oil-fields Seizures during 1970's Arab Embargo', *International Herald Tribune* (3 January 2004), news section, p. 3. I thank the authors of the three articles, particularly Owen Bowcott, for helping me identify the documents concerned in the British National Archives. All errors are mine.
40 Jeffrey R. Macris, *The Politics and Security of the Gulf: Anglo-American Hegemony and the Shaping of a Region* (London and New York: Routledge, 2010), pp. 202, 288.
41 *Al-Wahdah* (6 August 1973), p. 1; (7 August 1973), p. 1.
42 *Al-Wahdah* (4 November 1973), p. 2.
43 Mattair, *The Three Occupied UAE Islands*, pp. 276, 279.
44 Hukumah al-Mamlakah al-'Arabiyah al-Saudiyah, *Al-Tahkim li Taswiyat al-Niza' al-Iqlimi bayna Musqat wa Abu Zabi wa bayna al-Mamlakah al-'Arabiyah al-Saudiyah: 'Ard Hukumah al-Mamlakah al-'Arabiyah al-Saudiyah*, 3 vols (1955); *The Buraimi Memorials 1955: The Territorial Dispute concerning Buraimi, Liwa and Khor al-Udayd: The Memorials Submitted to Arbitration by the Governments of Saudi Arabia and the United Kingdom*, 5 vols (Gerrards Cross: Archive Editions, 1987). For an analysis of the Saudi contention, see J.B. Kelly, *Eastern Arabian Frontiers* (London: Faber and Faber, 1964), pp. 207–259.
45 Cmd 9272, *Arbitration Agreement between the Government of the United Kingdom (acting on behalf of the Ruler of Abu Dhabi and His Highness the Sultan Said bin Taimur) and the Government of Saudi Arabia, Jedda, July 30, 1954* (London: Her Majesty's Stationery Office, 1954). The document contains both the English and Arabic versions of the agreement.
46 Alexander Melamid, 'The United Arab Emirates', *Geographical Review*, 87:4 (1997), 542.
47 File on 'Reports from Buraimi', archival reference 163969, containing various documents from 1934–52, and file on 'Saudi Arabia Boundary Dispute', archival reference 165331, containing various documents from 1953–56, both classified papers of the Iraq Petroleum Company Ltd, accessed at BP Archive, University of Warwick, Coventry.
48 For the authentic Arabic text, as well as English and French translations of the agreement, see 'Saudi Arabia and United Arab Emirates: Agreement on the Delimitation of Boundaries (with Exchanges of Letters and Map). Signed at Jeddah, Saudi Arabia, on 21 August 1974', in United Nations, *Treaty Series: Treaties and International Agreements Registered or Filed and Recorded with the Secretariat of the United Nations*, vol. 1733 (New York: United Nations), pp. 24–41. It was registered with the UN by Saudi Arabia on 9 September 1993. My thanks to Ms Rudina Jasini for her legal advice regarding the interpretation of the agreement. All errors are mine.
49 Louis and Robinson, 'The Imperialism of Decolonization', p. 494.
50 TNA, FCO 8/927, 'Persian Gulf: Annual Review for 1968', from Crawford to Stewart, 14 January 1969.
51 TNA, DEFE 13/1389, 'Repercussions in the Gulf', CDS to Secretary of State, 1 December 1971.
52 TNA, FCO 8/1925, various telegrams, 24 January 1972; Dubai to Abu Dhabi, 25

FORMAL SOVEREIGNTY AND CONTINUING COLLABORATION

January 1972; 'Report on Operations in the Period 24/25 January 1972', by Watson, 26 January 1972.
53 TNA, FCO 8/1925, Amery to Douglas-Home, 17 February 1972.
54 TNA, FCO 8/1925, Hudson to Andrew, 25 January 1972; Douglas-Home to Amery, 22 February 1972.
55 TNA, FCO 8/1925, 'Sharjah/Ras al Khaimah', Walker to Treadwell, 1 February 1972; Walker to Green, 7 March 1972.
56 TNA, FCO 8/1925, Treadwell to Walker, 6 February 1972.
57 TNA, FCO 8/2546, FCO 8/2547, various documents.
58 TNA, PREM 16/996, Weston to Wright, 22 April 1967; Dales to Wright, 27 April 1976; note of meeting between Callaghan and al Suwaidi, 28 April 1976.
59 'U.S. Interests and Policy Toward the Persian Gulf', Hearings before the Subcommittee on the Near East of the Committee on Foreign Affairs, House of Representatives, 92nd Congress, second session, pp. 6–7.
60 TNA, FCO 8/3281, 'UK Policy Towards Arabia and the Gulf in the Wake of the Iran Crisis', c. April 1979.
61 *Public Papers of the Presidents of the United States: 1969–1974*, available at the website of the American Presidency Project, www.presidency.ucsb.edu, 'Informal Remarks in Guam with Newsmen', 25 July 1969.
62 *Public Papers of the Presidents of the United States: 1977–1981*, available at the website of the American Presidency Project, www.presidency.ucsb.edu, 'The State of the Union Address Delivered before a Joint Session of the Congress', 23 January 1980, all internet details correct as at 21 November 2009.
63 Macris, *The Politics and Security of the Gulf*, p. 175.
64 Roham Alvandi, 'Nixon, Kissinger, and the Shah: The Origins of Iranian Primacy in the Persian Gulf', *Diplomatic History*, 36:2 (2012), 337–272; Roham Alvandi, *Nixon, Kissinger, and the Shah: The United States and Iran in the Cold War* (Oxford: Oxford University Press), pp. 28–64.
65 Gause, *The International Relations of the Persian Gulf*, p. 22.
66 Macris, *The Politics and Security of the Gulf*, p. 194.
67 Macris, *The Politics and Security of the Gulf*, p. 175.
68 Fain, *American Ascendance and British Retreat*, pp. 199–200.
69 Murray Marder, 'U.S. Ties Seen Continuing', *The Washington Post* (26 March 1975), p. 1. Present author's correspondence with Murray Marder, 6–7 April 2009.
70 For an example of other scholars who examine the term 'twin pillars' as a contemporary idea, see Gause, *The International Relations of the Persian Gulf*, p. 21.
71 Macris, *The Politics and Security of the Gulf*, p. 175.
72 Henry Kissinger, *The White House Years* (London: George Weidenfeld & Nicholson, 1979).
73 Alexander Wendt and Daniel Friedheim. 'Hierarchy under Anarchy: Informal Empire and the East-German State', *International Organization*, 49:4 (1995), 689.
74 Gause, *The International Relations of the Persian Gulf*, pp. 1–44.
75 For a pioneering study on the issue of standardisation, see Geyer, 'One Language for the World'.

CONCLUSION

> A map anticipated a spatial reality, not vice versa. In other words, a map was a model for, rather than a model of, what it purported to represent.[1]

This is a quote from Tongchai Winichakul's study of how the modern map of Thailand was created. He argues that the map, based on a delineation of boundaries in the modern sense, was not indigenous to the local traditions but rather discursively constructed in response to European influence. Such a notion presents a striking parallel with the way in which Britain's informal empire in the Persian Gulf laid the structural foundations of the international relations of the region.

This book has examined the British withdrawal from the Gulf, asking why Britain was able to leave the region so peacefully and why this departure was accompanied by orderly independence for Bahrain, Qatar and the UAE. The findings suggest that Britain was able to do so because of its enduring collaborative relationship with the local rulers, which was structured by the norm of sovereignty. It has become clear that the whole process was not so much pre-planned as an accumulation of incremental, and sometimes disjointed, decisions that were neither taken by a single central agent nor fully thought out from the beginning. Nonetheless, the norm of sovereignty, which was instrumentally brought in by Britain, provided a structure wherein the collaborative relationship was rearranged in a more sustainable form, within the guise of legal equality.

In the early nineteenth century, Britain sent military expeditions to the southern coast of the Gulf in order to secure a maritime route to India. Thanks to its subsequent military victory, London coerced the local forces into entering a series of treaties. These treaties were signed by those previously deemed to be 'pirates'. The primary aim of these unequal treaties was to establish a peace in the region that was favourable to British commerce and communication by subjugating the local societies and establishing Britain as the dominant external power. Yet the very act of signing these treaties implied that Britain had acknowledged the legal status of its counterparts. Consequently, the territories concerned – no matter how vaguely defined and inferior in terms of the actual relationship – were given the status of sovereign states. They became 'Protected States'. In the mid-twentieth century, the discovery of oil, or sometimes merely the hope thereof, prompted Britain to demarcate the borders between the nine Protected States of 'Ajman,

CONCLUSION

Fujairah, Ra's al-Khaimah, Sharjah, Umm al-Qaiwain, Abu Dhabi, Dubai, Bahrain and Qatar, resulting in an imperfect transplantation of the European idea of territoriality. In due course, these Protected States witnessed the independence of India and the nationalisation of the AIOC, as well as the Suez Crisis. They even experienced some nationalistic uprisings within their territories, but the foundation of Britain's informal empire remained intact.

In the Persian Gulf, in contrast with the oft-cited examples of decolonisation, such as the expulsion of France from Algeria or the 'winds of change' in Africa, the crucial impetus towards independence did not arise from the Gulf or even from wider international society. Nor was Harold Wilson expecting to initiate immediate substantial changes when he became Prime Minister in 1964. Conventionally, it is understood that Wilson's Labour government took the decision to withdraw from Malaysia, Singapore and the Gulf due to economic retrenchment and anti-imperialistic beliefs. This is commonly known as the 'East of Suez' decision, but the evidence suggests that it was actually an amalgamation of two separate decisions: one to leave Malaysia and Singapore, and the other to withdraw from the Gulf. The former was resolved upon by the early half of 1967 for the economic and social reasons mentioned above, whereas the latter was only decided between December 1967 and January 1968 as a consequence of domestic politics.

After the devaluation of the pound in November 1967, the Labour government was forced to reverse its own social policies. In order to justify the necessary reduction in social expenditure, it decided to withdraw from the Gulf in addition to the retreat from Malaysia and Singapore that had already been decided, and to present the two together as the withdrawal from 'East of Suez'. The timing of the departure was a source of great debate between the Treasury, which had been calling for an early retreat, and the Foreign Office and the MOD, which were asking for the maximum timeframe possible so as to enable an orderly implementation. Just one day before Wilson publicly announced it on 16 January 1968, the deadline for withdrawal was set for the end of 1971. The terminology 'East of Suez', which had long existed both as a romantic discourse and as a naval policy, masked the disjointed and incremental nature of the actual decision-making process – even from the eyes of later historians.

The rulers of the Protected States were notified of the news at the beginning of January, when the decision had almost been taken. They were shocked, partly because it went completely against what they had been officially promised only two months before. However, more importantly, they did not want to lose Britain's military protection, which had insulated them from local opposition and prospective intervention from neighbouring countries such as Iran and Saudi Arabia. They resolutely opposed Britain's plan. Shaikh Zayid bin Sultan Al Nahyan, the Ruler of Abu Dhabi, the largest Protected State, even offered to pay the necessary cost of keeping troops, and even to do so secretly if Britain so wished.

The US, exhausted by the Vietnam War, also tried to convince Britain to stay. But the Protected States reacted swiftly when it became clear that Britain intended go through with its original intention. In less than a week, Shaikh Zayid had met his rival, Shaikh Rashid bin Sa'id of Dubai. Together they set up a regional initiative to form a union of nine states, aiming to achieve full independence collectively; however, this plan turned out to be little more than window dressing, and the situation remained stalled for three years. In the meantime, the Conservatives returned to power in Britain and made an unnecessary and unsuccessful attempt to reverse Labour's decision, only to realise that the momentum towards the end of empire was irreversible. In this climate, Julian Walker, Britain's Political Agent in Dubai, convened the rulers in July 1971. Encouraged by Walker and also by their own advisers, Shaikh Zayid and Shaikh Rashid secretly agreed to come together to achieve a collective independence, provided that the other states would accept their leadership. This 'secret' agreement was signed behind closed doors. Only one copy of this ground-breaking document was produced, and I found its photostat not in the Emirates but in the British National Archive. After the secret agreement was reached, the Rulers of 'Ajman, Fujairah, Sharjah and Umm al-Qaiwain accepted inferior constitutional status within the new state, now named the United Arab Emirates, under the leadership of Abu Dhabi and Dubai. In contrast, Bahrain and Qatar opted out and declared their independence separately, with the agreement of Britain and the US. Ra's al-Khaimah also tried to go it alone, but Britain and the US forbade this and it grudgingly joined the UAE later, in February 1972. Thus, the call for self-determination did not play any discernible role either in Britain's decision to withdraw from the Gulf or in its implementation, which entailed the full independence of the UAE, Qatar and Bahrain.

The completion of the British withdrawal accompanied the consolidation of the system of sovereign states in the Persian Gulf. The implications of this transition were not felt profoundly until the oil shock in 1973, when the new states participated in launching the 'oil weapon' against the West. By this point, it was clear that these new states were no longer mere clients of the former imperial metropole but had become capable and independent players in international affairs. The UAE's rapprochement with Saudi Arabia in 1974 confirmed that

CONCLUSION

the regional dynamics had changed forever. By the time Iran and Iraq signed the Algiers Agreement in 1975, Britain was happily out of the game and the US too remained on the sidelines. Conventionally, it has been believed that the Nixon administration appointed Iran and Saudi Arabia as the 'twin pillars' of the Gulf, but a lack of hard evidence casts some doubt on the assumption that the US had crafted such a coherent regional policy at that time. Meanwhile, Britain's influence remained considerable at the cultural and individual levels. These ostensibly conflicting impressions reflect the fact that the UAE, Qatar and Bahrain had been admitted as full members of international society and that, in return, they had accepted the norm of sovereignty. They sometimes acted against the apparent interests of the West, but they did not challenge the foundations of international society. In other words, the transformation of their sovereign status from informal colonies to members of global international society not only meant that the new states possessed legal personalities equal to those of the former imperial metropole and superpowers, it also enabled both Britain and the US to maintain an international order favourable to the West by means of consensus and collaboration, whilst minimising their direct involvement and the use of coercive measures. In essence, the whole process entailed only a rearrangement of the collaborative relationship that had developed during the period of Britain's informal empire.

These findings suggest that Britain's informal empire preceding its withdrawal was fundamentally a hybrid of international society and imperialism. The following two figures are intended to illustrate how such a duality was constructed in practice.[2]

Figure 2 shows the multilayered structure of Britain's informal empire in the Persian Gulf. At one level, the nine Protected States were part of the British Empire (although only informally, as implied by the dotted line). Yet, by being components of the British Empire, they were also included in international society at another level. This hybrid system resulted in a complex web of diplomatic channels through which the Protected States could negotiate between themselves, as well as with other members of international society. Figure 3 illustrates how this worked in practice.[3]

We can see that, at a formal level, Britain acted on behalf of the Protected States (A > B > C), and the Political Residency or the local Political Agent also functioned as a hub for the negotiations between the Protected States themselves (A). These formal diplomatic channels are shown in Figure 3 in solid lines. At the same time, however, the Protected States frequently held less formal negotiations between themselves (D), as well as with other states (E), as represented by dotted lines.

BRITAIN AND THE FORMATION OF THE GULF STATES

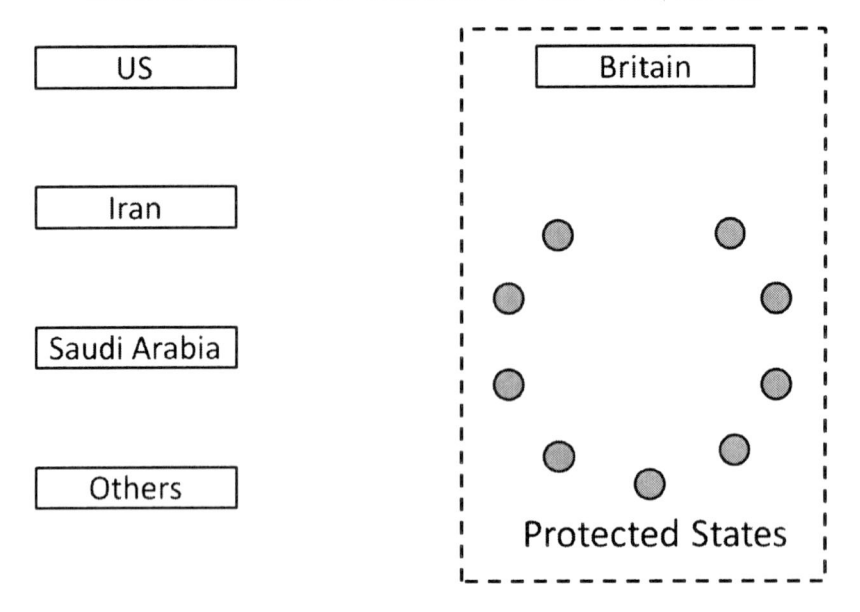

2 Duality of Britain's informal empire in the Persian Gulf

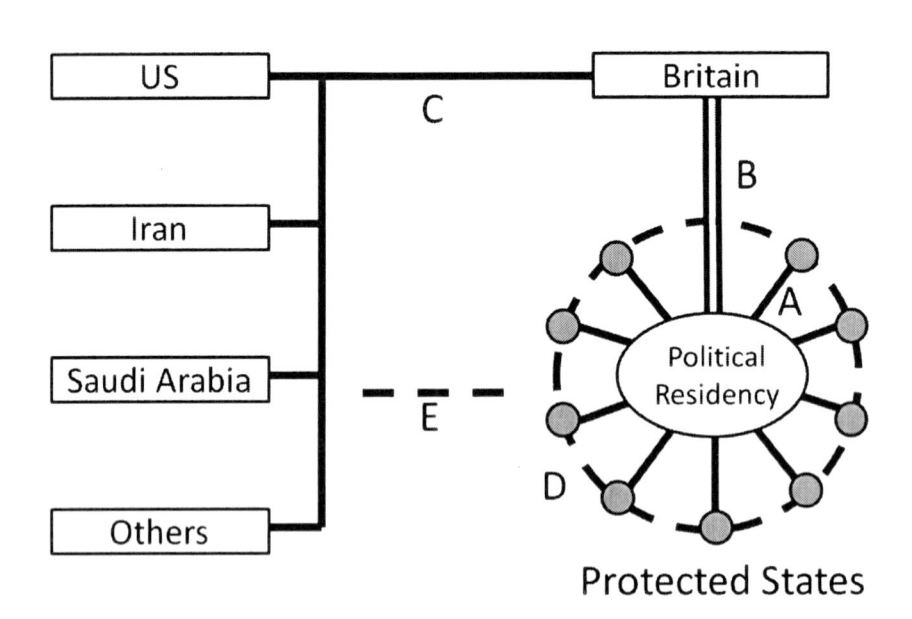

3 Multiple channels of diplomacy

[144]

CONCLUSION

Underlying this duality of negotiation channels was the opaque sovereign status of the Protected States. At one level, the Protected States were represented by Britain, but at another level they were also treated as virtual sovereign states precisely because of their relationship with Britain. The intriguing feature of this hybrid system was exemplified in the negotiations that took place in July 1971, in the run-up to the British withdrawal. The rulers of the Protected States had to be prompted by Walker to sit down and discuss the final arrangements towards the formation of the UAE, but at the last minute they also had to agree among themselves regarding their own fate. This book has explored this intricate process based on a reading of many different primary sources, some of which are used here for the first time.

Unlike the more famous examples of decolonisation, affairs in the Protected States remained relatively peaceful throughout the British withdrawal. Although the relationship between the Protected States and Britain was an asymmetric one in terms of their power, it was largely based upon consensus and coercive measures were avoided wherever possible. This remained the case after the British withdrawal, although in a much more subtle guise. The persistence of the collaborative relationship was underlined by a change in the structure in which it was embedded. With the formal independence of the UAE, Qatar and Bahrain, the formerly hybrid international system of the Gulf became unified under the globally standardised system of sovereign states. Of course, gaining the legal status of sovereignty did not guarantee that their borders would never be compromised. However, it did mean that no other entity but those states could be recognised as the legitimate actor to represent in international society the peoples in the territories concerned. Internally, this also meant that those in power were allowed to hold on to their position, although their regimes were not free from alteration. To that extent, it was a warranty for exclusivity. Moreover, in return for acting as fully sovereign states, they also came to share a larger stake with Britain and other members of international society in the maintenance of the status quo.

It is, however, misleading to state that Britain demonstrated its structural power through its withdrawal from the Gulf. The peaceful transition was enabled by a structural change in the sovereign status of the Protected States, but there was an intriguing absence of central will. There is no direct evidence that Britain consciously planned to transform the structure of the international system in the Persian Gulf in order to make it more resilient. Granting full sovereign status to the Protected States was the result of a perceived domestic necessity rather than a proactive foreign policy choice. Similarly, the norm of sovereignty had a strong appeal for the heads of the new states, since it enabled them to legitimately represent their peoples and territories; the more lasting effect, however, was that the entities of those states would remain in place in international society even if their regimes were altered or their borders violated. British economic retrenchment, and to a lesser extent local self-determination, no doubt played their part, but the most consistent thread in the entire story was the absence of a central agent. Neither Britain nor the new states drove the whole process with a central will or a fully thought-out plan. It was a series of ad hoc decisions and actions that often emerged through the negotiations between British diplomats and the Gulf rulers that unwittingly caused the region to take its current shape, yet even the protagonists could not fully conceive of the consequences of their own actions.

Today, it is almost taken for granted that, in the event of decolonisation, the formerly dependent peoples enter the postcolonial world by forming or joining independent states. It is rarely asked why they did not seek out any other option than to subscribe to the norm of sovereignty, which had a conspicuously European character at least at its origin. The relevance of our story to the global context should by now be obvious.

This book was not designed to make any generalisations. Its focus has been confined to the southern shore of the Persian Gulf, where there was not even a single colony in the constitutional sense. However, its focus on collaboration, or more specifically on the system of exclusive coexistence, allows us to understand why the norm of sovereignty had such a universal appeal, not just for the former metropole but also for those who sought to expel the imperial sway. The case therefore encourages us to examine sovereignty not just as a norm of independence but as one of collaboration, and to further explore how the modern world has been constructed through the intersections of various local contexts, but with the graft of a particularly European character.[4]

Notes

1 Winichakul, *Siam Mapped*, p. 130.
2 Author's own collection.
3 Author's own collection.
4 This argument builds upon Darwin's contention that the modern reconstructions in Asia under European influence 'meant the grafting of new political methods on to the original stock, not imposing an alien blueprint to which no one was loyal.' John Darwin, *After Tamerlane: The Rise and Fall of Global History of Empires, 1400–2000* (New York: Bloomsbury Press, 2007), p. 498. I thank Joydeep Sen for directing my attention to this line of argument; all errors are mine.

BIBLIOGRAPHY

Unpublished primary sources

The National Archives, Kew, UK (TNA)
CAB: Cabinet Office.
CO: Colonial Office.
DEFE: Ministry of Defence.
FCO: Foreign Office and Foreign and Commonwealth Office.
FO: Foreign Office.
PREM: Prime Minister's Office.
T: Treasury.
WO: War Office.

National Archives and Records Administration, College Park, Maryland, USA (NARA)
CREST (CIA records search tool).
Records of the Central Intelligence Agency (RG 263).
Central Files of the Department of State (RG 59).

Richard M. Nixon Presidential Materials Project, College Park, Maryland, USA
Files of the National Security Council, 1969–73.
HAK administrative and staff files.
National Security Council institutional files.

National Archives, Abu Dhabi, UAE
Qasr Al Hosn Papers.

Exeter University Library, Exeter, UK
Papers of Sir William Luce Relating to Aden and the Gulf.

Palace Green Library, Durham University, Durham, UK
Donald Hawley Papers.

BP Archive, University of Warwick, Coventry, UK
Papers of the Anglo-Iranian Oil Company.
Papers of British Petroleum Co. Ltd.
Papers of BP Trading Ltd.
Classified papers of Iraq Petroleum Company Ltd.

BIBLIOGRAPHY

British Library, London, UK (BL)
India Office Records.

Middle East Centre Archive, St Antony's College, Oxford, UK
Sir Geoffrey Arthur Collection.

The Bodleian Libraries, University of Oxford, Oxford, UK
CAB: Cabinet minutes (microfilm).
Denis Wright. 'The Memoirs of Sir Denis Wright, 1911–1971', unpublished memoir, 2 vols plus index.
Harold Wilson Papers.
Parliamentary Labour Party Archives (microfiche).

Internet (all accessed in December 2010 unless otherwise noted)
The American Presidency Project, www.presidency.ucsb.edu.
Declassified Documents Reference Systems (DDRS), http://infotrac.london.galegroup.com.
Digital National Security Archive (DNSA), http://nsarchive.chadwyck.com/home.do.
Presidential Recordings Program, http://millercenter.org/presidentialrecordings, accessed July 2015.
The Times Digital Archive, www.galeuk.com/times.
US Department of State, Foreign Relations of the United States (FRUS), http://history.state.gov/historicaldocuments, accessed July 2015.

Interviews and correspondence
Craig, James. Interview, 13 October 2009.
Marder, Murray. Correspondence, 6–7 April 2009.
Pelletreau, Robert. Correspondence, 3–4, 16 July 2009.
Walker, Julian. Interview, 29 August 2013; telephone interviews, 19, 21, 28 October 2009.

Published primary sources

Published official documents

Aitchison, C.U. *A Collection of Treaties, Engagements and Sanads Relating to India and the Neighbouring Countries*, vol. 11, Delhi: Government of India, 1933.

Arbitration Agreement between the Government of the United Kingdom (acting on behalf of the Ruler of Abu Dhabi and His Highness the Sultan Said bin Taimur) and the Government of Saudi Arabia, Jedda, July 30, 1954, London: Her Majesty's Stationery Office, 1954 (Cmd 9272).

Ashton, S.R., and Wm. Roger Louis (eds). *East of Suez and the Commonwealth, 1964–1971: Part I, East of Suez*, British Documents on the End of Empire, series A, volume 5, London: The Stationery Office, 2004.

Bennett, G.H., and K.A. Hamilton (eds). *Documents on British Policy Overseas,*

BIBLIOGRAPHY

Series III, Volume I: Britain and the Soviet Union, 1968–72, London: The Stationery Office, 1997.

Bullen, Roger, and M.E. Pelly (eds). *Documents on British Policy Overseas, Series I, Volume 4: Britain and America: Negotiations of the United States Loan, 3 August–7 December 1945*, London: Her Majesty's Stationery Office, 1987.

The Buraimi Memorials 1955: The Territorial Dispute concerning Buraimi, Liwa and Khor al-Udayd: The Memorials Submitted to Arbitration by the Governments of Saudi Arabia and the United Kingdom, 5 vols, Gerrards Cross: Archive Editions, 1987.

Burdett, A.L.P. (ed.). *Records of the Emirates, 1966–1971*, vol. 5, Archive Editions, 2002.

Commonwealth, European and Overseas Review, London: Conservative Political Centre.

The Diplomatic Service List, various volumes, London: Her Majesty's Stationery Office.

The Foreign Office List and Diplomatic and Consular Year Book, various volumes, London: Harrison and Sons.

Hukumah al-Mamlakah al-'Arabiyah al-Saudiyah (the Government of the Kingdom of Saudi Arabia). *Al-Tahkim li Taswiyat al-Niza' al-Iqlimi bayna Musqat wa Abu Zabi wa bayna al-Mamlakah al-'Arabiyah al-Saudiyah: 'Ard Hukumah al-Mamlakah al-'Arabiyah al-Saudiyah* (Arbitration for the Settlement of the Territorial Dispute between Musqat and Abu Dhabi on One Side and the Kingdom of Saudi Arabia on the Other: Submission from the Kingdom of Saudi Arabia), 3 vols, 1955.

Parliamentary Debates (Hansard): House of Commons Official Report, fifth series, London: Her Majesty's Stationery Office.

Parliamentary Papers: House of Commons and Command:
  Statement on the Defence Estimates, 1965 (Cmnd 2592).
  Statement on the Defence Estimates, 1966: Part I, the Defence Review (Cmnd 2901).
  Statement on the Defence Estimates, 1966: Part II, Defence Estimates (Cmnd 2902).
  Statement on the Defence Estimates, 1967 (Cmnd 3203).
  Supplementary Statement on Defence Policy, 1967 (Cmnd 3357).
  Statement on the Defence Estimates, 1968 (Cmnd 3540).
  Statement on the Defence Estimates, 1969 (Cmnd 3927).

Parry, Clive (ed.). *The Consolidated Treaty Series*, Dobbs Ferry, NY: Oceana Publications, various volumes, 1981.

The Persian Gulf Gazette, various volumes, London: Her Majesty's Stationery Office.

al-Rayyis, Riyad Nahib. *Watha'iq al-Khalij al-'Arabi, 1968–1971: Tamuhat al-Wahdah wa Humum al-Istiqlal* (Arabian Gulf Documents, 1968–1971: Attempts at Federation and Independence), London: Riad El Rayyes, 1987.

al-Shalaq, Ahmad Zakarya, and Mustafa 'Aqil al-Khatib. *Qatar wa Ittihad al-Imarat al-'Arabiyah "al-Tis'" fi al-Khalij al-'Arabi, 1968–1971: Dirasah*

BIBLIOGRAPHY

wa Watha'iq (Qatar and the Union of the 'Nine' Arab Emirates in the Gulf, 1968–1971: A Study and Documents), Doha: Dar-al-Thaqafah, 1991.

United Nations. *Treaty Series: Treaties and International Agreements Registered or Filed and Recorded with the Secretariat of the United Nations*, vol. 1733, New York: United Nations, 2000.

US Atomic Energy Commission. *The Nation's Energy Future: A Report to Richard M. Nixon President of the United States*, US Government Printing Office, 1973.

US Department of State. *Foreign Relations of the United States (FRUS)*, Washington, DC: US Government Printing Office, various vols.

Internet (accessed in April 2011)
United Nations, www.un.org/en/documents/index.shtml.

Periodicals
Al-Ahram, Cairo.
Arab Report and Record, London.
Gulf Weekly Mirror, Manama.
Guardian, London.
Al-Hayat, Beirut.
Al-Ittihad, Abu Dhabi.
International Herald Tribune.
Al-Jumhuriyah, Baghdad.
New York Times, New York.
The Times, London.
Abu Dhabi News, Abu Dhabi.
Al-Wahdah, Abu Dhabi.
The Washington Post, Washington.

Memoirs
Allfree, P.S. *Warlords of Oman*, South Brunswick: A.S. Barnes, 1967.
Benn, Tony. *Office Without Power: Diaries, 1968–72*, London: Hutchinson, 1988.
Benn, Tony, and Ruth Winstone. *Out of the Wilderness: Diaries 1963–67*, London: Hutchinson, 1987.
Brown, George. *In My Way: The Political Memoirs of Lord George Brown*, London: Victor Gollancz, 1971.
Burrows, Bernard. *Footnotes in the Sand: The Gulf in Transition, 1953–1958*, Wilton: Michael Russell, 1990.
Castle, Barbara. *The Castle Diaries, 1964–1970*, London: Weidenfeld & Nicolson, 1984.
Crossman, Richard. *The Diaries of a Cabinet Minister*, 2 vols, London: Hamish Hamilton and Jonathan Cape, 1975.
Dalton, Hugh. *The Political Diary of Hugh Dalton, 1918–40, 1945–60*, Ben Pimlott (ed.), London: Jonathan Cape, 1986.
Healey, Denis. *The Time of My Life*, Harmondsworth: Penguin, 1989.

BIBLIOGRAPHY

Jenkins, Roy. *A Life at the Centre*, London: Macmillan, 1991.

Kissinger, Henry. *The White House Years*, London: George Weidenfeld & Nicholson, 1979.

Lee, Kuan Yew. *From Third World to First: The Singapore Story, 1965–2000*, Singapore: Singapore Press Holding, 2000.

Nixon, Richard M. *Leaders*, New York: Warner Books, 1982.

—— *RN: The Memoirs of Richard Nixon*, London: Sidgwick and Jackson, 1978.

Parsons, Anthony. 'Foreword', in Glen Balfour-Paul, *The End of Empire in the Middle East: Britain's Relinquishment of Power in Her Last Three Arab Dependencies*, Cambridge: Cambridge University Press, 1991, pp. xv–xviii.

—— *They Say the Lion: Britain's Legacy to the Arabs: A Personal Memoir*, London: Jonathan Cape, 1986.

Tempest, Paul. 'Qatar: A Strong New Bridge, 1967–2007', in Paul Tempest (ed.), *Envoys to the Arab World: MECAS Memoirs, 1944–2009, Volume II*, London: Stacey International, 2009, pp. 130–137.

Walker, Julian. 'Personal Recollections of the Rapid Growth of Archives in the Emirates', in *The Historical Documents on Arab History in the Archives of the World*, Abu Dhabi: Centre for Documentation and Research, 2002.

—— *Tyro on the Trucial Coast*, Durham: The Memoir Club, 1999.

Wilson, Harold. *The Labour Government, 1964–70: A Personal Record*, London: Weidenfeld & Nicolson, 1971.

—— *The Governance of Britain*, London: Weidenfeld & Nicolson, 1976.

Wright, Patrick. 'The Run-up to Independence, 1971', in Paul Tempest (ed.), *Envoys to the Arab World: MECAS Memoirs, 1944–2009, Volume II*, London: Stacey International, 2009.

Miscellaneous contemporary documents

A Correspondent. 'Oil in the Persian Gulf', *Oil in the Persian Gulf*, 20:7, 1964, 305–313.

Kelly, J.B. 'The British Position in the Persian Gulf', *The World Today*, 20:6, 1964, 238–249.

Lorimer, John Gordon. *Gazetteer of the Persian Gulf, 'Oman, and Central Arabia*, vol. 1, Calcutta, 1915.

Luce, William. 'Britain in the Persian Gulf: Mistaken Timing over Aden', *The Round Table*, 227, 1967, 277–283.

—— 'Britain's Withdrawal from the Middle East and Persian Gulf', *Journal of the Royal United Service Institution*, 114:653, 1969, 4–11.

Shierlie, Anthony. *A True Report of Sir Anthony Shierlies Iourney Ouerland to Venice, Frō Thence by Sea to Antioch, Aleppo, and Bablion, and Soe to Casbine in Persia: His Entertainment There by the Great Sophie*, London, 1600.

Watt, D.C. 'Britain and the Future of the Persian Gulf States', *The World Today*, 20:11, 1964, 488–496.

BIBLIOGRAPHY

Secondary sources

Abdullah, Muhammad Morsy. *The United Arab Emirates: A Modern History*, London: Croom Helm, 1978.

Adonis, Andrew, and Keith Thomas (eds). *Roy Jenkins: A Retrospective*, Oxford: Oxford University Press, 2004.

Alvandi, Roham. 'Muhammad Reza Pahlavi and the Bahrain Question, 1968–1970', *British Journal of Middle Eastern Studies*, 37:2, 2010, 159–177.

—— 'Nixon, Kissinger, and the Shah: The Origins of Iranian Primacy in the Persian Gulf', *Diplomatic History*, 36:2, 2012, 337–272.

—— *Nixon, Kissinger, and the Shah: The United States and Iran in the Cold War*, Oxford: Oxford University Press, 2014.

Amin, Abudul Amir. *British Interests in the Persian Gulf*, Leiden: E.J. Brill, 1967.

Ayoob, Mohammed. *The Third World Security Predicament: State Making, Regional Conflict, and the International System*, Boulder: Lynne Rienner Publishers, 1995.

Balfour-Paul, Glen. *The End of Empire in the Middle East: Britain's Relinquishment of Power in Her Last Three Arab Dependencies*, Cambridge: Cambridge University Press, 1991.

Barnwell, Kristi N. 'Formation and Function: British Institutions and Antecedents to a Federation of Arab Emirates', conference paper presented at the 2010 annual British Scholar Conference at the University of Texas, Austin, 2010.

Bull, Hedley. *The Anarchical Society: A Study of Order in World Politics*, 3rd edn, Basingstoke: Palgrave, 2002.

—— 'International Theory: The Case for a Classical Approach', in Klaus Knorr and James N. Rosenau (eds), *Contending Approaches to International Politics*, Princeton: Princeton University Press, 1970, pp. 20–38.

Bull, Hedley, and Adam Watson. *The Expansion of International Society*, Oxford: Clarendon Press, 1984.

Cain, P.J., and A.G. Hopkins. *British Imperialism: Crisis and Deconstruction, 1914–1990*, London: Longman, 1993.

—— *British Imperialism: Innovation and Expansion, 1688–1914*, London: Longman, 1993.

Campbell, John. *Roy Jenkins: A Biography*, London: Weidenfeld & Nicolson, 1983.

Cassese, Antonio. *International Law in a Divided World*, Oxford: Clarendon Press, 1986.

Clark, Ian. *Globalization and Fragmentation: International Relations in the Twentieth Century*, Oxford: Oxford University Press, 1997.

Darby, Phillip. *British Defence Policy East of Suez, 1947–1968*, London: Oxford University Press for the Royal Institute of International Affairs, 1973.

Darwin, John. *After Tamerlane: The Rise and Fall of Global History of Empires, 1400–2000*, New York: Bloomsbury Press, 2007.

BIBLIOGRAPHY

——— *Britain and Decolonisation: The Retreat from Empire in the Post-War World*, Basingstoke: Macmillan, 1988.
——— 'Britain's Withdrawal from East of Suez', in Carl Bridge (ed.), *Munich to Vietnam: Australia's Relations with Britain and the United States since the 1930s*, Victoria: Melbourne University Press, 1991, pp. 140–158.
——— 'British Decolonization since 1945: A Pattern or a Puzzle', *Journal of Imperial and Commonwealth History*, 12:2, 1984, 187–209.
——— *The Empire Project: The Rise and Fall of the British World-System, 1830–1970*, Cambridge: Cambridge University Press, 2009.
——— *The End of the British Empire: The Historical Debate*, Oxford: Basil Blackwell, 1991.
——— 'An Undeclared Empire: The British in the Middle East, 1918–39', *Journal of Imperial and Commonwealth History*, 27:2, 1999, 159–176.
Davidson, Christopher M. 'Arab Nationalism and British Opposition in Dubai, 1920–1966', *Middle Eastern Studies*, 43:6, 2007, 879–892.
——— *Dubai: The Vulnerability of Success*, London: Hurst, 2008.
Davies, Charles E. *The Blood-Red Arab Flag: An Investigation into Qasimi Piracy, 1797–1820*, Exeter: University of Exeter Press, 1997.
Dockrill, Saki. *Britain's Retreat from East of Suez: The Choice between Europe and the World?*, Basingstoke: Palgrave Macmillan, 2002.
Dumbrell, John. *A Special Relationship: Anglo-American Relations from the Cold War to Iraq*, 2nd edn, Basingstoke: Palgrave Macmillan, 2006.
Dumett, Raymond E. (ed.). *Gentlemanly Capitalism and British Imperialism: The New Debate on Empire*, London: Longman, 1999.
El Reyes, Abdullah, and Jayanti Maitra, 'Federation in the Making: Exploring the Historical Roots, Role of Leadership and the Voice of the People', conference presentation at the World Congress for Middle Eastern Studies, Ankara, 21 August 2014.
Encyclopaedia of Islam, second edition, accessed through www.brillonline.nl on 25 March 2009.
Fabry, Mikulas. *Recognizing States: International Society and the Establishment of New States Since 1776*, Oxford: Oxford University Press, 2010.
Fain, W. Taylor. *American Ascendance and British Retreat in the Persian Gulf Region*, New York: Palgrave Macmillan, 2008.
Fisch, Jörg. 'Internationalizing Civilization by Dissolving International Society: The Status of Non-European Territories in Nineteenth-Century International Law', in Martin H. Geyer and Johannes Paulmann (eds), *The Mechanics of Internationalism: Culture, Society, and Politics from the 1840s to the First World War*, Oxford: Oxford University Press, 2001, pp. 235–257.
Gaddis, J.L. 'History, Theory, and Common Ground', *International Security*, 22:1, 1997, 75–85.
Gallagher, John, and Ronald Robinson. 'The Imperialism of Free Trade', *Economic History Review*, 6:1, 1953, 1–15.
Gause, F. Gregory. 'British and American Policies in the Persian Gulf, 1968–1973', *Review of International Studies*, 11, 1985, 247–253.

BIBLIOGRAPHY

―― *The International Relations of the Persian Gulf*, Cambridge: Cambridge University Press, 2010.
Geyer, Martin H. 'One Language for the World: The Metric System, International Coinage, Gold Standard, and the Rise of Internationalism, 1850–1900', in Martin H. Geyer and Johannes Paulman (eds), *The Mechanism of Internationalism: Culture, Society, and Politics from the 1840s to the First World War*, Oxford: Oxford University Press, 2001.
Gong, Gerrit W. *The Standard of 'Civilization' in International Society*, Oxford: Clarendon Press, 1984.
Gordon Walker, Patrick. *The Cabinet*, revised edn, London: Collins, 1972.
Haber, S.H., D.M. Kennedy and S.D. Krasner. 'Brothers under the Skin: Diplomatic History and International Relations', *International Security*, 22:1, 1997, 34–43.
Hawley, Donald. *The Trucial States*, New York: Twayne Publishers, 1970.
Heard-Bey, Frauke. *From Trucial States to United Arab Emirates: A Society in Transition*, new edn, London: Longman, 1996.
Holland, R.F. *European Decolonization, 1918–1981: An Introductory Survey*, Basingstoke: Macmillan, 1985.
Hourani, George Fadlo. *Arab Seafaring in the Indian Ocean in Ancient and Early Medieval Times*, Beirut: Khayats, 1963.
Hurewitz, J.C. 'The Persian Gulf: British Withdrawal and Western Security', *Annals of the American Academy of Political and Social Science*, 401:1, 1972, 105–116.
Iriye, Akira, and Pierre-Yves Saunier. *The Palgrave Dictionary of Transnational History*, Basingstoke: Palgrave Macmillan, 2009.
Jackson, Robert H. *Quasi-States: Sovereignty, International Relations, and the Third World*, Cambridge: Cambridge University Press, 1990.
Kanafani, Aida S. *Aesthetics and Ritual in the United Arab Emirates: An Anthropology of Food and Personal Adornment among Arab Women*, Beirut: American University of Beirut, 1983.
Kazim, Aquil A. *The United Arab Emirates, A.D. 600 to the Present: A Socio-Discursive Transformation in the Arabian Gulf*, Dubai: Gulf Book Centre, 2000.
Keene, Edward. *Beyond the Anarchical Society: Grotius, Colonialism and Order in World Politics*, Cambridge: Cambridge University Press, 2002.
―― 'International Law and Diplomacy in the European and Extra-European Worlds during the early Nineteenth Century', unpublished article, 2008.
Kelly, J.B. *Arabia, the Gulf and the West*, London: Weidenfeld & Nicolson, 1980.
―― *Britain and the Persian Gulf, 1795–1880*, Oxford: Clarendon Press, 1968.
―― *Eastern Arabian Frontiers*, London: Faber and Faber, 1964.
Khong, Yuen Foong. *Analogies at War: Korea, Munich, Dien Bien Phu, and the Vietnam Decisions of 1965*, Princeton: Princeton University Press, 1992.
Khuri, Fuad I. *Tribe and State in Bahrain: The Transformation of Social and Political Authority in an Arab State*, Chicago: University of Chicago Press, 1980.

BIBLIOGRAPHY

Kissinger, Henry. *The White House Years*, London: Weidenfeld & Nicolson, 1979.

Krasner, Stephen D. *Sovereignty: Organized Hypocrisy*, Princeton: Princeton University Press, 1999.

Lockhart, L. 'Hormuz', in *Encyclopaedia of Islam*, second edition, accessed through www.brillonline.nl on 25 March 2009.

Louis, Wm. Roger. *The British Empire in the Middle East, 1945-1951: Arab Nationalism, the United States, and Postwar Imperialism*, Oxford: Clarendon Press, 1984.

—— 'Introduction: Robinson and Gallagher and Their Critics', in Wm. Roger Louis (ed.), *Imperialism: The Robinson and Gallagher Controversy*, New York: New Viewpoints, 1976, pp. 2–51.

—— 'The Withdrawal from the Gulf', *Ends of British Imperialism: The Scramble for Empire, Suez and Decolonization*, London: I.B. Tauris, 2006, pp. 877–903.

Louis, Wm. Roger, and Ronald Robinson. 'The Imperialism of Decolonization', *Journal of Imperial and Commonwealth History*, 22:3, 1994, 462–511.

Macris, Jeffrey R. *The Politics and Security of the Gulf: Anglo-American Hegemony and the Shaping of a Region*, London and New York: Routledge, 2010.

Maitra, Jayanti. *Zayed: From Challenges to Union*, Abu Dhabi: Center for Documentation and Research, 2007.

Maitra, Jayanti and Afra Hajji. *Qasr Al Hosn: The History of the Rulers of Abu Dhabi, 1793–1966*, Abu Dhabi, UAE: Centre for Documentation and Research, 2001.

Mattair, Thomas R. *The Three Occupied UAE Islands: The Tunbs and Abu Musa*, Abu Dhabi: Emirates Center for Strategic Studies and Research, 2005.

McCourt, David M. 'What was Britain's "East of Suez Role"? Reassessing the Withdrawal, 1964–1968', *Diplomacy and Statecraft*, 20:3, 2009, 453–472.

Mendelson, M.H. 'The Application of International Legal Concepts of Sovereignty in the Arabian Context', *Geopolitics*, 3:2, 1998, 133–138.

Newbury, Colin. 'Patrons, Clients and Empire: The Subordination of Indigenous Hierarchies in Asia and Africa', *Journal of World History*, 11:2, 2000, 227–263.

Norton, Maureen Heaney. 'The Last Pasha: Sir John Glubb and the British Empire in the Middle East, 1920–1949', unpublished PhD dissertation, Johns Hopkins University, 1997.

O'Brien, Patrick. 'Historiographical Traditions and Modern Imperatives for the Restoration of Global History', *Journal of Global History*, 1:1, 2006, 3–39.

Onley, James. *The Arabian Frontier of the British Raj: Merchants, Rulers, and the British in the Nineteenth-Century Gulf*, Oxford: Oxford University Press, 2007.

—— *Britain and the Gulf Shaikhdoms, 1820–1971: The Politics of Protection*, Doha: Center for International and Regional Studies, School of Foreign Service in Qatar, Georgetown University, 2009.

BIBLIOGRAPHY

—— 'Britain's Informal Empire in the Gulf, 1820–1971', *Journal of Social Affairs*, 22:87, 2005, 29–45.

—— 'The Politics of Protection in the Gulf: The Arab Rulers and the British Resident in the Nineteenth Century', *New Arabian Studies*, 6, 2004, 30–92.

Osterhammel, Jürgen. 'Semi-Colonialism and Informal Empire in Twentieth-Century China: Towards a Framework of Analysis', in Wolfgang J. Mommsen and Jürgen Osterhammel (eds), *Imperialism and After: Continuities and Discontinuities*, London: Allen and Unwin, 1986, pp. 290–314.

Petersen, Tore T. 'Crossing the Rubicon? Britain's Withdrawal from the Middle East, 1964–1968: A Bibliographical Review', *International History Review*, 22:2, 2000, 318–340.

—— *The Decline of the Anglo-American Middle East, 1961–1969: A Willing Retreat*, Brighton: Sussex Academic Press, 2006.

—— *Richard Nixon, Great Britain and the Anglo-American Alignment in the Persian Gulf and Arabian Peninsula: Making Allies out of Clients*, Brighton: Sussex Academic Press, 2009.

Pham, Phuong. 'End of the East of Suez: The British Decision to Withdraw from Malaysia and Singapore, 1964 to 1968', unpublished DPhil thesis, University of Oxford, 2001.

—— *Ending 'East of Suez': The British Decision to Withdraw from Malaysia and Singapore, 1964–1968*, Oxford: Oxford University Press, 2010.

Pickering, Jeffrey. *Britain's Withdrawal from East of Suez: The Politics of Retrenchment*, Basingstoke: Macmillan, 1998.

—— 'Politics and "Black Tuesday": Shifting Power in the Cabinet and the Decision to Withdraw from East of Suez, November 1967–January 1968', *Twentieth Century British History*, 13:2, 2002, 144–170.

Pieragostini, Karl. *Britain, Aden and South Arabia: Abandoning Empire*, London: Macmillan, 1991.

Platt, D.C.M. 'The Imperialism of Free Trade: Some Reservations', *Economic History Review*, 21:2, 1968, 296–306.

Popp, Roland. 'Subcontracting Security: The US, Britain and Gulf Security before the Carter Doctrine', in Daniel Möckli and Victor Mauer (eds), *European-American Relations and the Middle East: From Suez to Iraq*, London: Routledge, pp. 171–186.

al-Qasimi, Sultan ibn Muhammad. *The Myth of Arab Piracy in the Gulf*, 2nd edn, London: Routledge, 1988.

Rahman, Habibur. *The Emergence of Qatar: The Turbulent Years, 1627–1916*, London: Kegan Paul, 2005.

Reynolds, David. 'A "Special Relationship"? America, Britain and the International Order since World War II', *International Affairs*, 62:1, 1986, 1–20.

Robinson, Ronald. 'The Excentric Idea of Imperialism, with or without Empire', in Wolfgang J. Mommsen and Jürgen Osterhammel (eds), *Imperialism and After: Continuities and Discontinuities*, London: Allen and Unwin, 1986, pp. 267–289.

—— 'Non-European Foundations of European Imperialism: Sketch for a

BIBLIOGRAPHY

Theory of Collaboration', in Roger Owen and Bob Sutcliffe (eds), *Studies in the Theory of Imperialism*, London: Longman, 1972, pp. 117–142.

Ruggie, John Gerard. 'Territoriality and Beyond: Problematizing Modernity in International Relations', *International Organization*, 47:1, 1993, 139–174.

Sartre, Jean-Paul. 'Preface', in Frantz Fanon, *The Wretched of the Earth*, translated by Constance Farrington, Harmondsworth: Penguin, 1967, pp. 7–26.

Sato, Shohei. 'Britain's Decision to Withdraw from the Persian Gulf, 1964–68: A Pattern and a Puzzle', *Journal of Imperial and Commonwealth History*, 37:1, 2009, 99–117.

—— 'Mapping for Modernity: An Arabist in Arabia, 1953–1955', *East Asian Journal of British History*, 2:1, 2009, 109–127.

Shlaim, Avi. 'Britain's Quest for a World Role', *International Relations*, 5:1, 1975, 838–856.

Slot, B.J. *The Arabs of the Gulf, 1602–1784: An Alternative Approach to the Early History of the Arab Gulf States and the Arab Peoples of the Gulf, Mainly Based on Sources of the Dutch East India Company*, Leidschendam: B.J. Slot, 1993.

Smith, Simon C. *Britain's Revival and Fall in the Gulf: Kuwait, Bahrain, Qatar, and the Trucial States, 1950–71*, London: RoutledgeCurzon, 2004.

——'Revolution and Reaction: South Arabia in the Aftermath of the Yemeni Revolution', *Journal of Imperial and Commonwealth History*, 28:3, 2000, 193–208.

Spruyt, Hendrik. 'The End of Empire and the Extension of the Westphalian System: The Normative Basis of the Modern State Order', *International Studies Review*, 2:2, 2000, 65–92.

—— *Ending Empire: Contested Sovereignty and Territorial Partition*, Ithaca: Cornell University Press, 2005.

Stivachtis, Yannis A. *The Enlargement of International Society: Culture Versus Anarchy and Greece's Entry into International Society*, Basingstoke: Macmillan, 1998.

Suzuki, Shogo. 'Japan's Socialization into Janus-faced European International Society', *European Journal of International Relations*, 11:1, 2005, 137–164.

Taryam, Abdullah Omran. *The Establishment of the United Arab Emirates, 1950–85*, London: Croom Helm, 1987.

Taverne, Dick. 'Chancellor of the Exchequer', in Andrew Adonis and Keith Thomas (eds), *Roy Jenkins: A Retrospective*, Oxford: Oxford University Press, 2004.

Tepper, Jonathan. 'The Dollar, the Pound and British Policy East of Suez, 1964–67: Deals and Understandings between Wilson and Johnson', unpublished MLitt thesis, University of Oxford, 2004.

Tidrick, Kathryn. *Heart-Beguiling Araby*, Cambridge: Cambridge University Press, 1981.

Yergin, Daniel. *The Prize: The Epic Quest for Oil, Money, and Power*, New York: Free Press, 1992.

Von Bismarck, Helene. *British Policy in the Persian Gulf, 1961–1968: Conceptions of Informal Empire*, Basingstoke: Palgrave Macmillan, 2013.

BIBLIOGRAPHY

—— 'The Kuwait Crisis of 1961 and Its Consequences for Great Britain's Persian Gulf Policy', *British Scholar*, 2, 2009, 75–96.

Watson, Adam. *The Evolution of International Society: A Comparative Historical Analysis*, London: Routledge, 1992.

Weber, Max. *Max Weber: Selections in Translation*, translated by E. Matthews, edited by W.G. Runciman, Cambridge: Cambridge University Press, 1978.

Wendt, Alexander. 'Anarchy Is What States Make of It: The Social Construction of Power-Politics', *International Organization*, 46:2, 1992, 391–425.

Wendt, Alexander, and Daniel Friedheim. 'Hierarchy under Anarchy: Informal Empire and the East-German State', *International Organization*, 49:4, 1995, 689–721.

Wight, Martin. *Systems of States*, Leicester: Leicester University Press, 1977.

Wilson, Arnold T. *The Persian Gulf: An Historical Sketch from the Earliest Times to the Beginning of the Twentieth Century*, Oxford: Clarendon Press, 1928.

Wilson, Graeme H. *Zayed: Man Who Built a Nation*, Abu Dhabi: National Center for Documentation and Research, 2013.

Winichakul, Tongchai. *Siam Mapped: A History of the Geo-Body of a Nation*, Honolulu: University of Hawaii Press, 1994.

Woodward, Nicholas. 'Labour's Economic Performance, 1964–70', in Richard Coopy, Steven Fielding and Nick Tratsoo (eds), *The Wilson Governments, 1964–1970*, London: Pinter, 1993.

Zahlan, Rosemarie Said. *The Making of the Modern Gulf States: Kuwait, Bahrain, Qatar, the United Arab Emirates and Oman*, revised and updated edn, Reading: Ithaca Press, 1998.

—— *The Origins of the United Arab Emirates: A Political and Social History of the Trucial States*, London: Macmillan, 1978.

INDEX

Note: The letter n following a page number indicates an endnote.

Abbas I, Shah 5–6
Abu Dhabi 22
  border disputes 69
  British withdrawal 142
  Buraimi Oasis dispute 74, 130–131
  coup 38, 39
  development 38–39
  Dubai Agreement 76, 82
  independence 69, 128–131
  leadership role 73
  Maritime Truce (21 May 1835) 9
  oil 16
  pearling industry 16
  Trucial States Council 103, 104–105
  wealth 130
  see also UAE
Abu Dhabi Defence Force 22
Abu Dhabi Radio 104
Abu Musa 69, 74, 85, 114, 123–124
Aden 35–36, 41, 44, 46
agriculture 20
Al-Ahram (Egyptian newspaper) 39
AIOC see Anglo-Persian Oil Company
aircraft 41, 66n.64, 132
aircraft carriers 41
airfields 21, 37
airlines 21, 73
'Ajman 18, 22, 37, 69, 78, 115, 123
  see also UAE
Algeria, French expulsion from 141
  see also Organization of Arab Petroleum Exporting Countries
Alvandi, Roham 84, 133
Anglo-American alliance 21, 129
Anglo-Persian Oil Company (later Anglo-Iranian Oil Company (AIOC)) 16, 38
Arab League 21, 37–38
Arab nationalism 21, 34, 37, 55, 80, 102, 122

Arab Report and Record 39
Arabian American Oil Company 17
Australia 36
Ayoob, Mohammed 121

Bahrain 56, 68–69
  airfield 21
  Britain, relationship with 22, 25n.48
  currency unification 40–41
  Dubai Agreement 81
  France, relationship with 72
  Friendly Convention (1861) 13
  independence 87, 111, 112, 114, 116, 123, 142
  Iran, relationship with 69, 73, 83, 86, 100
  military uprising (1968) 79
  Muslims 68–69
  oil 16, 135
  Political Residency 16
  population 89n.2
  Qatar, relationship with 39
  RAF departure 113, 115
  Second World War 15
  Six Day War demonstrations 43
  social continuity 14
  sovereignty 14, 127, 135, 143
  Soviet Union, relationship with 84
  UAE formation 110–111, 112
  United States, relationship with 71
  unrest (1965) 39
Bahrain Petroleum Company 71
Balfour-Paul, Glen 23, 37, 38, 46, 60
Banu Yas (Bani Yas) tribe 6
BI Line see British India Steam Navigation Company
BOAC (British Overseas Airways Corporation) 21
BP (British Petroleum) 16, 113–114

[159]

INDEX

Britain
  army 22, 34–35, 41, 51–52
  Dubai Agreement 77, 78, 81, 82, 85–86, 89
  economy 56
  general election (1970) 97
  Iranian seizure of Abu Musa 114
  navy 22, 35
  post-withdrawal 72, 115, 116, 123, 124–125, 131–133, 134–136, 143
  trade 8
  Treaties of Friendship 111, 125
  UAE, relationship with 103, 104, 105, 109, 132–133
  United States, relationship with 21, 32–35, 42, 43–44, 129
  welfare state 97
  withdrawal from Gulf States 99, 145
  see also Conservative governments; Labour government
British Caledonian (airline) 73
British Empire
  informal 23, 140, 143–144
  world wars, impact 20–21, 61, 63, 131
British India Steam Navigation Company (BI Line) 21
British Overseas Airways Corporation see BOAC
British Petroleum see BP
Brown, George 32, 45, 55, 60
Buraimi Oasis dispute 17–19, 38, 69, 74, 112, 130–131
Bushire (Iran) 16

Callaghan, James 32, 45
Carter, President Jimmy 133
Carter Doctrine 133
Central Treaty Organisation (CENTO) 43
Churchill, Sir Winston 35
Churchill, Winston (grandson) 84
cinema 15, 78
Cold War 22, 88
Commonwealth 20, 36
communication networks 75
  see also telegraph lines; telephone system

communism 33
Conservative governments
  (1962–64) 35, 89
  (1970–74) 97–100, 115, 132, 142
Crawford, William 19
Crossman, Richard 55, 66n.64
cultural policies, Second World War 15
currency unification 40–41
Curzon, George Nathaniel, Viceroy of India 15
CVA 01 aircraft carrier 41

Daily Telegraph 86
Damascus Radio 39
Darby, Philip 29, 46
Darwin, John 3, 30, 32, 35, 59, 97, 146n.4
Davidson, Christopher M. 22
Davies, Charles E. 11
decolonisation 2, 3, 35, 95–96, 105–106, 115–116, 122, 129, 131–136, 141, 146
Defence White Papers 40, 41, 42, 45
democracy 23
Deputy Rulers' meeting (October 1970) 106
Dinsmore, Lee 126
Dockrill, Saki 44, 48n.25, 62
Douglas-Home, Sir Alec 97, 98, 99, 109, 112
Dubai 22
  Abu Dhabi, secret agreement with 2, 96, 104, 108, 142
  Arab nationalism 21
  economic growth 78–79
  enclaves 18
  European and American community 92n.64
  independence 69, 96
  Iranian influence 69
  Japan, relationship with 72
  July negotiations (1971) 96–116
  leadership role 73
  Maritime Truce (21 May 1835) 9
  social instability 79
  UAE formation 115
  Dubai Agreement 76–83
  Dubai Radio 104

[160]

INDEX

Dumbrell, John 34
Dutch East India Company 8

East India Company *see* Dutch East India Company; English East India Company
'East of Suez' policy 29, 32, 34, 35–42, 46, 97, 141
 origin of term 35
economy 6, 7, 78–79, 130
EEC (European Economic Community) 59
Egypt, October War (1973) 127
 see also Organization of Arab Petroleum Exporting Countries
elites 22, 23, 81–82, 97, 132
empires 5, 29–30
 see also British Empire; Holy Roman Empire; Ottoman Empire; Persian Empire; Portuguese Empire
enclaves 18, 74
English East India Company 6, 8, 11
ENI (oil company) 113
European Economic Community *see* EEC
expatriates 21, 89n.2, 92n.64

F-111 aircraft 66n.64
Fabry, Mikulas 122
Fain, W. Taylor 86, 134
Faisal II, King of Saudi Arabia 71, 111, 112, 125
federation 23, 39, 40, 109
First World War 20
France 9, 72, 141
Friedheim, Daniel 135
Fujairah 18, 19, 22, 37, 69, 115, 123
 see also UAE

Gause, F. Gregory 59, 60, 135
Geyer, Martin H. 26n.57
Gordon Walker, Patrick 32
Gulf Squadron 10
Gulf States
 British influence 131–133, 134–136, 143
 constitutional power 104
 divisions 75–76
 formation 1
 government, post-British withdrawal 74–75
 political traditions 7
 populations 89n.2
 United States' influence 132–134
 see also Protected States; Trucial States

Halcrow, Sir William and Partners 20
Al-Hasa 10, 13
Healey, Denis 32, 35, 40, 48n.27, 54, 55, 61–62, 63, 99
Heard-Bey, Frauke 96
Heath, Edward 97–98
Hennell, Lieutenant Samuel 9
HMS *Achilles* 115
HMS *Eagle* 41
HMS *Hermes* 41
HMS *Intrepid* 115
Holy Roman Empire 5
Hong Kong 36
Hormuz 6

Imperial Airways 21
imperialism 121–122
 see also empires
independence 15, 20, 39, 67–68
 Abu Dhabi 69, 128–131
 Bahrain 87, 111, 112, 114, 116, 123, 142
 Dubai 69, 96
 Qatar 69, 111, 112, 116, 123, 128, 142
 Ra's al-Khaimah 123–124, 125–127, 135, 142
 UAE 2
India 9, 10, 15, 21
Indian Ocean 87
IPC *see* Iraq Petroleum Company
Iran
 Algiers Agreement (1975) 135
 Dubai Agreement 84–85, 88, 89, 101, 102
 influence 67, 74, 86
 Islamic Revolution (1978/9) 122–123
 L Day 124–125
 oil 43
 political ambitions 69
 Shatt al-Arab dispute 132

[161]

INDEX

Iran (cont.)
  threat from 56–57, 83, 86, 100, 114, 123–125, 132
  'twin pillars' policy 143
  UAE formation 110, 112
  United States, relationship with 71, 87, 133–134
  see also Organization of the Petroleum Exporting Countries
Iraq
  Algiers Agreement (1975) 135
  Shatt al-Arab dispute 132
  see also Organization of Arab Petroleum Exporting Countries; Organization of the Petroleum Exporting Countries
Iraq Petroleum Company (IPC) 131
irrigation 6, 19
Al-Ittihad (newspaper) 130

Japan 38, 71–72
Jenkins, Roy 52–54, 56, 58, 60–61, 62, 63
Johnson, President Lyndon B. 34, 70, 71, 133

Keene, Edward 12–13, 14, 23
Kelly, J.B. 9, 58, 59
Al Khalifa, Khalifa bin Salman, of Bahrain 85
Al Khalifa, Isa ('Isa) bin Sulman, of Bahrain 39, 40, 43, 57, 71, 80, 81, 83–84, 85, 87, 98, 111
Kipling, Rudyard 50n.92
Kishm 11
Kissinger, Henry 87, 134
Krasner, Stephen 129, 135
Kuwait
  British protection of 41
  British withdrawal from 57
  Dubai Agreement 85, 101
  independence 22, 34, 70
  social continuity 14
  see also Organization of Arab Petroleum Exporting Countries; Organization of the Petroleum Exporting Countries
Kuwait, Amir of 84

Labour government (1964–67) 29–47, 99
  Anglo-American relations 32–35
  currency crisis (1967) 45
  Defence and Overseas Policy (OPD) Official Committee 42–43, 44
  defence expenditure 51, 53, 56, 57, 59, 63
  devaluation 31, 45, 52, 56, 58
  'East of Suez' policy 29, 32, 34, 141
  economy 30, 31, 33–34
  social policies 58, 141
  South East Asia policy 43, 141
  split 60–61
Labour Party, general election (1970) 97
Lee, Kuan Yew 61
Libya 114
  see also Organization of Arab Petroleum Exporting Countries
Louis, Wm. Roger 20–21, 95–96, 100, 116, 122, 131
Luce, Sir William 33, 39, 40, 41, 51, 95, 98–99, 101, 124

McCourt, David M. 36, 40
Macris, Jeffrey 133, 134
Al Maktum, Rashid bin Sa'id, of Dubai 76, 88, 100, 102–103, 104–105, 106, 109, 110, 142
Malaysia 34, 42, 45, 61, 63
maps 140
Maritime Truces 9–10, 13
Masirah 22
Mattair, Thomas R. 130
Melamid, Alexander 130–131
Mendelson, M.H. 7, 14
Merrill Lynch 130
migration 79, 82–83, 85
MOD (Ministry of Defence) 113–114, 129
Mosaddeq, Mohammad 16
Muscat and Oman 16, 70, 79
  see also Oman
Muslims 8, 13, 68–69

Najd 13
Napoleonic Wars 9
National Democratic Front for the

[162]

INDEX

Liberation of Oman and the Arabian Gulf (NDFLOAG) 79–80
nationalism *see* Arab nationalism
Al Nahyan, Shakhbut bin Sultan, of Abu Dhabi 38–39
Al Nahyan, Zayid bin Sultan, of Abu Dhabi 2, 19, 39, 40, 56, 57, 73, 75, 76, 80, 100, 102–103, 104–105, 106, 108–109, 110, 114, 123, 130, 142
Newbury, Colin 105
Nixon, President Richard 87, 113
Nofal, Sayed 37, 55, 80
nomads 6
North Yemen 134

OAPEC *see* Organization of Arab Petroleum Exporting Countries
October War (6 October 1973) 127–128
oil 16–17, 22, 32–33, 72, 140
  Abu Dhabi 38
  American companies 71, 124, 126
  Central Treaty Organisation (CENTO) 43
  embargoes 128
  Iran 43
  price rises 45
  Ra's al-Khaimah 124
  revenues 75
  Soviet threat 55, 70–71
  UAE formation 113–114
'oil shock' 128, 142
'oil weapon' 128, 135, 142
Oman
  border disputes 69
  Buraimi Oasis dispute 17, 74, 130–131
  Dhufar rebellion 134
  Dubai Agreement 80
  enclaves 18
  social continuity 14
  tribes 6
  UAE formation 110
  see also Muscat and Oman; Organization of Arab Petroleum Exporting Countries
Onley, James 7, 10, 11, 114

Organization of Arab Petroleum Exporting Countries (OAPEC) 128
Organization of the Petroleum Exporting Countries (OPEC) 128
Ottoman Empire 5, 7, 10, 13

al-Pachachi, 'Adnan 103, 110
Parsons, Anthony 59, 80, 84
pearling industry 6, 9, 16, 38
Perpetual Maritime Truce (1853) 9–10
Persia 16
  see also Iran
Persian Empire 6–7, 13
  see also Safavids
Persian Gulf
  British presence 8
  British withdrawal 42–43, 44, 45, 46–47, 51–63, 67–89
  history 6
  United States policy 87–88
Petersen, Tore T. 34, 48n.25
Pham, Phuong 63
Pickering, Jeffrey 53
'pirates' 8–9, 11, 12, 23, 140
Political Residents 9, 13, 21, 101, 111, 114, 115, 116, 131–132
  see also Luce, Sir William; Parsons, Anthony
Popp, Roland 71
Portuguese Empire 6, 7
power balance 25n.48, 75
Protected States 14, 15, 16
  Arab League 21
  boundaries 18, 74, 140–141
  Britain's role 21, 45, 72, 82, 143–144
  Britain's withdrawal 145–146
  communication networks 75
  decolonisation 105–106
  Dubai Agreement 76–83, 88
  identity 68–69
  independence 39, 67–68
  Japan, relationship with 71–72
  leadership 73
  protection 40, 41
  social instability 80
  Soviet Union's influence 70
  status 33, 36, 140, 145

INDEX

Protected States (cont.)
  UAE formation 110
  Union of Nine 111–112, 116
  United States, relationship with 70
  water management 20

al-Qasimi, Khalid bin Muhammad, of Sharjah 37, 123
al-Qasimi, Khalid bin Saqr, of Ra's al-Khaimah 126–127
al-Qasimi, Saqr bin Muhammad, of Ra's al-Khaimah 108, 109, 110, 123–127, 132
al-Qasimi, Saqr bin Sultan, of Sharjah 37–38, 73, 79
al-Qasimi, Sultan Muhammad 11
Qatar 10, 13, 22
  Bahrain, relationship with 39
  currency unification 40–41
  Dubai Agreement 76, 77, 78
  independence 69, 111, 112, 116, 123, 128, 142
  leadership role 73
  oil 16, 135
  Saudi Arabian influence 69
  sovereignty 14, 127, 135, 143
  UAE formation 110, 112, 115
al-Qawasim 9, 11

RAF (Royal Air Force) 22, 113, 115
Ra's al-Khaimah 22
  disputes 74
  enclaves 18
  independence 123–124, 125–127, 135, 142
  Iranian claims 69
  L day 124–125
  riots 132
  road to Dubai 75
  UAE formation 110
religion 8
Roberts, Goronwy 45, 59
Robinson, Ronald 20–21, 116, 122, 131
Rousseau, Professor Charles 78
Royal Air Force *see* RAF
Royal Navy 115
Ruggie, John Gerard 88, 99
rulers
  British opinion of 72–73, 124
  and British withdrawal 96, 99
  and Dubai Agreement 77, 81, 83, 100–101
  and Trucial States Council meeting (July 1971) 102–103
Rusk, Dean 60, 70, 71
Russia, capture of Samarqand 10
  see also Soviet Union

Safavids 5
  see also Persian Empire
Salalah 22
Samarqand 10
Saqqaf, Omar 111
Saudi Arabia
  Buraimi Oasis dispute 74, 112, 130, 131
  Dubai Agreement 78
  influence 67
  oil 16
  political ambitions 17, 19, 69
  as a threat 57
  'twin pillars' policy 143
  and UAE 110, 111, 112, 113, 130–131, 142–143
  United States' relationship with 71, 87, 133–134
  see also Organization of Arab Petroleum Exporting Countries; Organization of the Petroleum Exporting Countries
Schlesinger, James 129
Second World War 15, 20
secret agreement, between Abu Dhabi and Dubai 2, 96, 104, 108, 142
self-determination 1, 122, 123–127, 142
Shah of Iran 36, 57, 71, 84–85, 112, 114
Sharjah 22
  airfield 21, 37
  coups 37–38, 132
  disputed lands 69, 74
  Dubai Agreement 115, 123
  enclaves 18
  RAF departure 113, 114
  see also UAE
Shatt al-Arab dispute 132
Sheridan, Robert 126
Singapore 35, 36, 42, 45, 46, 63, 141

INDEX

Sirri 69, 74, 85
Sisco, Joseph 126
Six-Day War (1967) 42, 43, 45
slavery 22
Slot, B.J. 14
Smith, Simon C. 96, 106, 125
social instability 79
South East Asia, British withdrawal 61
  see also Hong Kong; Malaysia; Singapore
sovereignty 5, 14, 15, 18, 23, 74, 76, 88–89, 127, 134, 135–136, 140, 143, 145–146
Soviet Union 22, 33, 55, 70, 84
sport 15
statehood 14–15
Stewart, Michael 32, 40, 55
Suez Canal 10, 21
Sultan bin Mohammed, Shaikh, of Sharjah 132
al-Suwaidi, Ahmad Khalifa 101, 103, 104, 105, 108, 110
Syria, October War (1973) 127

al-Tajir, Mahdi 103–104, 105, 106, 108, 110
Tapsell, Peter 57
telegraph lines 10
telephone system 75
territoriality 74, 141
Al Thani, Ahmad bin Ali, Ruler of Qatar 57, 100
Al Thani, Khalifa bin Hamad, of Qatar 39
Thant, U 86
Thomson, George 37–38
Times, The 23, 84
trade 5–6, 7, 8, 11
Treadwell, Charles James 103, 104, 105
treaties 13–14, 23
  General Treaty for the Cessation of Plunder and Piracy (1820) 9, 13, 25n.48
  philosophical foundation 12–13
  Treaty of Friendship 111, 114
  see also Maritime Truce (1835); Perpetual Maritime Truce (1853)
tribes 6, 11–12, 17, 79

tributes 7, 11–12
truces 9–10
Trucial Oman Scouts 22, 79, 114
Trucial States, use of term 14
Trucial States Council 21–22
  'majority of five' 106–107
  secret meeting (July 1971) 102–116
Trucial States Development Fund 37
TSR2 aircraft 41
Tunbs, Greater and Lesser 69, 74, 85–86, 114, 123–125, 132
  L Day 124–125

UAE
  border disputes 110
  Britain, diplomatic ties with 132–133
  Buraimi Oasis dispute 17
  capital 75
  constitution 104, 105, 106
  formation 76–77, 85, 88, 102, 103, 105, 106, 109, 114, 116, 142
  independence 2
  oil weapon 135
  presidency 123
  Saudi Arabia, rapprochement with 130–131, 142–143
  social continuity 14
  sovereignty 127, 130, 135, 143
  Supreme Council 123
  unity 23
  see also Organization of the Petroleum Exporting Countries
Umm al-Qaiwan 22, 37, 69, 71, 115, 123
  see also UAE
Union Oil Company 124, 126
United Arab Emirates see UAE
United Nations (UN) 20, 60, 106, 114, 127, 131
United States
  Anglo-American relations 21, 32–35, 42, 43–44, 129
  arms transfers 133–134
  army 126
  Asia policy 87
  British withdrawal from Gulf States 60, 67, 70, 71, 84
  Buraimi Oasis dispute 17
  Carter Doctrine 133

INDEX

United States (cont.)
  Dubai Agreement 101
  imperialism 20
  influence in Gulf 132
  Iran, relationship with 71
  Nixon Doctrine 87, 133
  Nixon Shock 113
  oil embargo 128
  'oil shock' 129
  Saudi Arabia, relationship with 71
  Shaikh Saqr's approach to 126
  'twin pillars' policy 133–134, 135, 143
  UAE formation 112, 113

'Voice of the Arabs' radio station 109

Al-Wahda (newspaper) 130
Wahhabi movement 13
Walker, Julian Fortay 17–18, 74, 101, 102, 103, 105, 106, 108, 109, 110, 123, 124–125, 132, 145
Walker, Patrick Gordon *see* Gordon Walker, Patrick
Washington Post, The 134
water 19–20
  see also irrigation
Watt, D.C. 50n.92
Wendt, Alexander 135
Wilson, Arnold T. 11
Wilson, Harold 29, 32–35, 34, 40, 41, 45, 48n.27, 51–52, 54, 55, 59, 61, 67, 83, 97, 99, 141
  see also Labour government (1964–67)
Winichakul, Tongchai 140
Winspeare-Guicciardi, Vittorio 86–87

Yemen *see* North Yemen

Zahlan, Rosemary Said 11

[166]